# Creating Alternative Discourses in the Education of Latinos and Latinas

# Studies in the
# Postmodern Theory of Education

Joe L. Kincheloe and Shirley R. Steinberg
*General Editors*

Vol. 253

PETER LANG
New York • Washington, D.C./Baltimore • Bern
Frankfurt am Main • Berlin • Brussels • Vienna • Oxford

# Creating Alternative Discourses in the Education of Latinos and Latinas

## A READER

Raul E. Ybarra & Nancy López,
### EDITORS

PETER LANG
New York • Washington, D.C./Baltimore • Bern
Frankfurt am Main • Berlin • Brussels • Vienna • Oxford

Library of Congress Cataloging-in-Publication Data

Creating alternative discourses in the education of Latinos and Latinas:
a reader / edited by Raul E. Ybarra & Nancy López.
p. cm. — (Counterpoints; v. 253)
Includes bibliographical references and index.
1. Hispanic Americans—Education. 2. Discrimination in education—
United States. I. Ybarra, Raul E. II. López, Nancy.
III. Counterpoints (New York, N.Y.); v. 253.
LC2669.C74    371.829′68073—dc22    2003019415
ISBN 0-8204-6801-0
ISSN 1058-1634


Bibliographic information published by **Die Deutsche Bibliothek**.
**Die Deutsche Bibliothek** lists this publication in the "Deutsche
Nationalbibliografie"; detailed bibliographic data is available
on the Internet at http://dnb.ddb.de/.

Cover design by Lisa Barfield
Cover art by Augustine Romero


The paper in this book meets the guidelines for permanence and durability
of the Committee on Production Guidelines for Book Longevity
of the Council of Library Resources.

# Table of Contents

Acknowledgments ............................................................................................... vii

Chapter 1:   Creating Alternative Discourses in the
             Education of Latinos and Latinas: Introduction
             *Raul E. Ybarra* ................................................................... 1

Chapter 2:   The Drift of Latino Students Through Public Higher
             Education: Testimonies on Slipping Through the
             Cracks of the Iron Cage
             *Ramona Hernández* and *Glenn Jacobs* ............................... 9

Chapter 3:   Rewriting Race and Gender High School Lessons:
             Second-Generation Dominicans in New York City
             *Nancy López* ...................................................................... 27

Chapter 4:   Jim Crow: A Phoenix Rising in Boston—
             The Trend Toward Separate and Unequal in the
             Boston Public Schools
             *Steve Fernandez* ................................................................. 45

Chapter 5:   Writing as a Hostile Act: A Reason for Latino Students'
             Resistance to Learning
             *Raul E. Ybarra* .................................................................. 89

Chapter 6:   Academic Success and the Latino Family
             *Roberto A. Ibarra* ............................................................ 113

Chapter 7:   Literacy for Change: Latina Adult Learners and Popular
             Education
             *Lorna Rivera* .................................................................... 133

Chapter 8:   The Effects of Family Background, Immigration Status,
             and Social Context on Latino Children's Educational
             Attainment
             *Gabriella C. Gonzalez* ...................................................... 157

Chapter 9:    Latino Parents Put Into Words: Immigrant Parents Share
              Their Beliefs on Education Through an After School
              Parents, Children, and Computers Project
              *Rosita M. A. Ramírez* ..........................................................................195

Chapter 10:   Latina and Latino Education: Rearticulating Discourses,
              Pedagogies, and Praxis,
              *Nancy López* .....................................................................................221

Notes..........................................................................................................233

List of Contributors..................................................................................239

Index ........................................................................................................241

# Acknowledgments

This book project would not have been possible if not for the encouragement and support of a number of people and organizations. This book project grew from numerous discussions with *colegas* at the University of Massachusetts, Boston. First, we are indebted to Ramona Hernández, Director of the Dominican Studies Institute at the City University of New York, for encouraging us to prepare a panel for the Latino Section at the 2001 Latin American Studies Association conference in Washington, DC, on the need for alternative discourse. Secondly, we would like to thank Donaldo Macedo for his support and encouraging us to develop our panel presentation into a book. The Gastón Institute for Latino Community Development and Public Policy has always served as a warm and loving *hogar de familia* for those who are committed to producing research that contributes to the development of the Latino community. *Gracias por todo su apoyo.* We would also like to extend our gratitude to the faculty, staff, and students in these departments: the Latino Studies Department in the College of Public and Community Service at the University of Massachusetts, Boston, and the Sociology Department at the University of New Mexico, Albuquerque. We are blessed with your support and nurturing. We would also like to thank the staff at Peter Lang Publishing, and Bernadette Shade in particular, for your professionalism and your support of our book projects. And finally, we would also like to express our love to our families and friends, who have always been supportive of our work. It is our hope that this book will help broaden the discourse and praxis on how we can improve the education of Latinas and Latinos in the United States.


*Raul E. Ybarra*

*Nancy López*

Chapter One

# Creating Alternative Discourses in the Education of Latinos and Latinas: Introduction

*Raul E. Ybarra*

While Latinos are the youngest and fastest growing U.S. minority group, they are also "the nation's poorest and least educated" (Rivera, Chapter 7). Thus, to help this population, and to help these students, a call for educational reform has been gone out across the nation. However, as every census indicator shows, Latinos are not improving economically or educationally. Why is this? As Steve Fernandez writes in Chapter 4, this call for educational reform has increasingly been and explicitly focuses on the political dimensions—the material/symbolic resources—such as the adoption of high stakes testing programs. On the other hand, as the schools systems across the country place a stronger emphasis on high stakes testing, broader areas of educational equity receive lesser attention. One area that has received less attention is the failure of elementary and secondary schools systems meeting the needs of Latino students.

When schools do focus on poor retention rates of Latinos, much of it is largely centered on the obstacles and barriers that influence Latinos to drop out. Lorna Rivera, in Chapter 7, found that while there are studies that have focused on education, the few studies that focus on Latinos' education in particular, look more at Latino immigrants in ESOL (English for Speakers of Other Languages), family literacy, or native–language literacy classes than they study native-born Latinos (Benmayor, 1991; Valdés, 1996; Young & Padilla, 1990). Another focal point is what Rosita Ramírez suggests in Chapter 9: many researchers still use "deficit model" framework to explain why many Latinos are not succeeding educationally, and Latino students are unable to place the same value on education as their mainstream white counterparts because education is not as important. As a result, much of the research and policy centers on changing the Latino students and their family structure in hopes of improving academic achievement. As Ramírez contends, many school institutions continue to wrestle with the challenges of educating students who come to school with different life and cultural experiences.

While part of the attention of each of the contributors in this collection is on the obstacles and barriers to the persistence of Latino students, each contributor is acutely aware that current educational theories and approaches for teaching Latinos are not working. What many of the contributors call attention to, and what is being ignored in much of the current research, is how to reverse the low retention rate of Latinos in both secondary and higher education. What is missing from this basic educational discourse is the demand to discuss a Latino education that explores and acknowledges the complex structural and cultural forces that play a major role in influencing Latino students to either stay in school or leave. Thus, as many of the contributors of this collection call attention to what is being ignored in much of the current research, they also address how to reverse the low retention rate of Latinos by looking beyond the hurdles and barriers that affect these students.

An argument that is explicit in each of the contributed chapters is that we must find different ways, different methods of teaching Latino students; methods that take into account advising, gender roles, immigration, age, family, culture, language, education, etc. Indeed, by taking many of these factors into account each contributor inevitably provides alternative methods to teaching Latino students—methods that will have a positive impact on Latino students—and by doing so, hopefully reduce the low retention rate of Latinos in our schools.

A major contribution of *Creating Alternative Discourses in the Education of Latinos and Latinas*, then, is providing alternatives to the traditional methods of education by challenging the mainstream education assumptions of Latinos. Moreover, as a collective document, this work proposes a framework that places the means to understanding and unraveling of the schooling trajectories of Latino youth on the understanding who these students are and where they come from, as well as on their lived experiences, and on their family influences. This collection is unique in that it pioneers a conceptual attempt to explore both different teaching methods and alternative discourses and engages in a debate with research that has traditionally examined the motivations and barriers to persistence of native-born Latinos in education. This collection further attempts to provide alternatives to the traditional methods of education by challenging the mainstream assumptions of the education of Latinos.

Additionally, each chapter in this work contributes heavily to the theory and practice of transformative, additive schooling and represents significant advancement in supporting the academic achievement of Latino students. Through its effort to redefine pedagogy, social organizations, and educational purpose for Latinos in ways that disrupt the reproductive tendencies of schooling, it strives to create a language and practice of possibility (Valenzuela, 1999; bell hooks, 1994; Giroux, 1992, and Bartholomae, 1988). This collection serves as an important foundation for the further research that seeks to counter the reproductive nature of traditional schools for Latino students.

In Chapter 2, *The Drift of Latino Students Through Public Higher Education: Testimonies on Slipping Through the Cracks of the Iron Cage*, Glenn Jacobs and Ramona Hernández report on findings of a qualitative pilot study of retention and persistence of Latino students at the University of Massachusetts, Boston, a 4–year state university urban campus. The pilot project was designed to draw a random sample of 60 students dispersed into subgroups consisting of (a) students of whose admissions were deferred, i.e., were encouraged to go to community college and then to reapply one year later, (b) students who were admitted and did not enroll, and (c) were enrolled one year later, i.e., retained. The objective was to interview subjects using a semi-structured protocol inquiring about the students' personal and family backgrounds, high school and secondary school experience, their initial and subsequent experiences on the campus with the faculty, administration, staff and fellow students, and finally, suggestions for change. This study was inspired by an earlier report issued by the university's Office of Institutional Research comparing retention and persistence rates among Anglo, Asian, African American, and Latino students.

Chapter 3, *Rewriting Race and Gender High School Lessons: Second-Generation Dominicans in New York City*, by Nancy López, examines the race-gender gap in education among the children of the largest new immigrant group in New York City: second-generation Caribbean young adults. While previous studies of the second-generation focus on assimilation, López places intersecting race and gender processes at the center of the analysis. López draws on life history interviews, focus groups, and participant observation and examines how the cumulative race-gender experiences of second-generation Dominicans, Haitians, and Anglophone West Indians influence their outlooks toward schooling. She finds that women maintained optimistic outlooks, while men expressed worries about their prospects for social mobility.

Steve Fernandez in Chapter 4, *Jim Crow: A Phoenix Rising in Boston—The Trend Toward Separate and Unequal in the Boston Public Schools*, finds throughout the United States that the call for education reform has increasingly been answered by the adoption of high–stakes testing programs. At the same time, Fernandez argues that though school systems across the country have been placing a stronger emphasis on high–stakes testing, broader areas of educational equity have received lesser attention. Many school systems have been abandoning affirmative action programs. Efforts toward desegregation and issues such as the achievement gap, when addressed, are often viewed exclusively in the context of student performance on high–stakes tests. Fernandez focuses on Boston because the push towards high stakes testing has been underway for a number of years there. Over the last two years several thousand students in the Boston Public Schools, BPS, have been retained in grade due to their inability to score above specified levels on standardized testing.

Chapter 5, *Writing as a Hostile Act: A Reason for Latino Students' Resistance to Learning,* Raul Ybarra moves from the macro-level issues regarding Latino student retention to the micro-level. He centers his chapter on the cultural schema of academic discourse of a writing classroom to show why academic writing is a difficult task for many minority students, in particular Latino students. He suggests that when we teach writing to Latino students, we are teaching more than just writing. We are asking them to change their cultural identity because we expect these students to change how they think. Students not part of the mainstream, particularly Latino students, not only see this pattern as confusing, but also as a hostile attempt to change who they are, causing epistemological violence to Latino students because of the marginalization and cultural implications that take place. He further proposes that teaching to this structural schema suggests a rationale for its own pervasiveness and functions in education, especially when teaching to minority (in particular, Latino) students. Understanding the model we use when we teach writing will give us insights into how this academic discourse contributes to the negative impressions Latino students have about writing and English courses.

In Chapter 6, *Academic Success and the Latino Family,* Roberto A. Ibarra's research objective was to identify which factors, if any, might indicate a potential for success for Latinos in graduate school. The study focuses on selected samples of Latino faculty, administrators, and graduate students working on master's or doctoral degrees. Ibarra interviewed non academic individuals with doctoral degrees who either left academe or never pursued an academic position. His primary goal in selecting participants was to sample populations by ethnicity and region. He selected the participants to reflect, as much as possible, a cross-section of ethnicity, national origin, gender, generation, region, and type of institution, academic discipline, and cohort groups—students, faculty, administrators, and non academics. The strategy was to investigate all social conditions, including characteristics associated with Latino families, communities, or other social systems, which could point to potentially significant influences. What follows from his study is the social profile of research participants and an analysis as to how Latino families shape cultural context among their offspring.

With Chapter 7, *Literacy for Change: Latina Adult Learners and Popular Education*, Lorna Rivera argues that Latino enrollments in adult literacy education have been steadily increasing over the past two decades. Yet the discourse in education often focuses on Latino children or youth, and few studies specifically examine the experiences of Latino adults who participate in adult literacy education programs. She examines the experiences of Latina adult learners who participated in a shelter-based popular education program. Popular education is a methodology of teaching and learning through dialogue that directly relates curriculum content to people's lived experiences. Rivera's article presents the voices of Latina adult learners who describe their motivations for returning to school, the poverty-related obstacles they face, and how they became inspired to take individual and collective action to change their life circumstances. This ethnographic research suggests that popular education addresses the women's personal, academic, and community goals. Moreover, Rivera argues that popular education challenges the mainstream discourse regarding what it means to be literate and the purposes of literacy.

Chapter 8, *The Effects of Family Background, Immigration Status, and Social Context on Latino Children's Educational Attainment* by Gabriella C. Gonzalez, fills the gaps in previous status attainment research of immigrants by examining how immigrant parents' differential experiences in the labor markets of their country of origin and in the United States affect their children's schooling experiences. Like the native-born population in the United States, the foreign-born population is a heterogeneous group. In addition to cultural and religious differences, there are great differences in the levels of social status (education level, occupation, and income) within the foreign-born population. As demonstrated in the previous chapter, the vast number of immigrants who have entered the United States since the Family Reunification Act of 1965 are either highly educated or have little to no formal schooling. Gonzalez investigates whether the children of immigrants with high levels of pre-arrival social status have similar levels of achievement in school as their peers of immigrants of lower pre–arrival social status.

Chapter 9, *Latino Parents Put Into Words: Immigrant Parents Share Their Beliefs on Education Through an After–School Parents, Children, and Computers Project,* Rosita M. A. Ramírez explores how certain social spaces provide participating Mexican parents an opportunity to communicate their own particular parenting beliefs and practices to show that Latino parents are in fact immersed and interested in the education of their children. The following questions helped her focus her study: In this setting, as parents' perceive different social pressures, what type of literate practices do parents employ in order to voice, write, or communicate to an audience (or each other) their roles as parents for their children? In communicating these parenting practice beliefs to an audience or each other, how do the parent's perceive to be applying these concepts to their own lives? In answering these questions, Ramírez's study gives further details about the practices of parents of Mexican descent to discredit the misconceptions about the lack of family involvement on the part of Latino parents in their children's education.

Nancy López, in her conclusion (Chapter 10) *Latina and Latino Education: Rearticulating Discourses, Pedagogies, and Praxis,* argues that the task before us is the "rearticulating of the problem"; as long as we continue to frame the problems of Latino education in terms of the hegemonic "common–sense" explanations, society will continue to blame Latino students and their families for their educational plight. As long as society continues to blame Latinos for their "own" problems—racism, segregation, inequitable distribution of resources—these problems will continue to plague the Latino community and will continue to remain unexamined.

The overall goal of authors in this collection is to expose some of these "common–sense" explanations for the educational crisis among Latino students, and in so doing pave a new road for finding radical solutions to the crisis. From this ideal we create different discourses that will lead to alternative solutions to improve the education of Latina and Latino students.

# Bibliography

Bartholomae, D. (1988). Inventing the University. In E. R. Kintgen, B. M. Kroll, & M. Rose (Eds.), *Perspectives on Literacy* (pp. 273–285). Carbondale, IL: Southern Illinois University .

Benmayor, R. (1991). Testimony, action research, and empowerment: Puerto Rican women and popular education. In Gluck and Patai (Eds.), *Women's words*. New York: Routledge Valdés (1996;)

Giroux, H. A. (1981). *Ideology, culture, and the process of schooling.* Philadelphia: Temple University.

hooks, b. (1994). *Teaching to transgress: Education as the practice of freedom.* New York: Routledge.

Valdes, G. (1996). *Con respeto: Bridging the distances between culturally diverse families and schools.* New York: Teachers College Press.

Valenzuela, A. (1999). *Subtractive schooling: U.S.–Mexican Youth and the Politics of Caring.* Albany: SUNY Press

Young, E., & Padilla, M. (1990). Mujeres Unidas en Accion: A popular education process. *Harvard Educational Review, 60*, No. 1, 1–17.

## Chapter Two

# The Drift of Latino Students Through Public Higher Education: Testimonies on Slipping Through the Cracks of the Iron Cage

*Ramona Hernández and Glenn Jacobs*

### Introduction

The abysmally low enrollments of Latinos in institutions of higher education and the linked phenomena of their astronomically high rates of non-retention and non-persistence through graduation have attained the dubious status of truisms. While it is no longer fashionable to refer to "dropping out" as a trait particular to Latino students, the equally dubious lacuna in campus multicultural awareness and appreciation of diversity is frequently cited as a key cause of the non-representation of Latinos in higher educational institutions, especially 4–year colleges. While the nostrums of inclusion, multicultural awareness, and appreciation should neither be gainsaid as sensitizing elements (or prerequisites) for developing recruitment strategies, nor as salves for atmospheric reconditioning, it is of key importance to first pinpoint the sources of structural discouragement keeping Latinos from attending, being retained, and persisting through to graduation.

Standard paradigmatic analyses of retention, such as Tinto's (1987) integration and assimilation model, now have an antediluvian slant due to the model's bias against minorities. The Tinto model is based upon the sociological notion of Emile Durkheim (1951), concerning the failure of the individual's integration into societal structures and groups as a cause of suicide, and Van Gennep's (1960) depiction of rites of passage (including the ritual sub stages of separation from the old, and the transition and incorporation into the new status) as mechanisms of status attainment and integration. Tinto suggests that attending college is an initiation with student retention tantamount to successful integration into the life of the academy and simultaneous dissociation from the student's community of origin. Thus, "to the degree individuals are integrated into the institution's fabric, the greater likelihood exists that the individual will not develop a sense of anomie, and will not commit 'suicide' by leaving the institution" (Tierney, 1992, p. 606).

This model has been criticized on the grounds that the application of Van Gennep's conception of rites of passage is inappropriate given "Van Gennep's anthropological model never assumed that a rite of passage was undertaken by individuals from one culture seeking initiation into a foreign culture" (p. 82). Moreover, rites of passage are always successful. In addition, the Tinto model "paints a disturbing portrait for students of color on predominantly white campuses" because the model actually prescribes a form of cultural suicide for them in breaking with the communities and cultures in which they were raised whilst integrating and assimilating "into the dominant culture of the colleges they attend" (p. 82).[1]

From a Latino-centered standpoint such schemes smack of "academic colonialism" or an extension of the internal colonialism which typifies practices and attitudes of the surrounding society. Moreover, these models perpetuate the "institutional practices that methodically exclude Hispanic participation" (Olivas, 1997, p. 480). Until rectification of such practices occur and result in institutional change, academic colonialism can best describe the extant practices and model of use in institutions of higher education evincing under-representation and the low retention and persistence of Latino students. As Olivas (1997) suggests, such a state of affairs requires the examination of structural barriers to Latino participation. What is called for is "an inquiry into organizational features" conducive toward high Latino attrition (p. 480).

The following is a report on the findings of a qualitative pilot study of retention and persistence of Latino students at the University of Massachusetts, Boston, a 4–year public university urban campus. The study was inspired by an earlier report issued by the university's Office of Institutional Research comparing retention and persistence rates among Anglo, Asian, African American, and Latino students, finding Latinos faring the worst of the four groups on all dimensions (Wilton, 1999). In addition, there exists a growing conviction among interested university faculty, staff, and students that despite the noticeable increase of Latinos in the Boston metropolitan area, the campus's Latino student population was neither increasing sufficiently nor adequately persisting through to graduation. In fact, a cursory perusal of enrollment figures confirmed a decrease in new enrollments over a 5–year period thus reflecting a national trend of, at best, fluctuating Latino higher education enrollments since the mid–1970s (Perez & de la Rosa–Salazar, 1997; de los Santos & Rigual, 1994).

A glance at Tables 1 and 2, both derived from a table giving yearly race/ethnicity statistics from the Census Current Population Survey (September, 1999) in the Appendices detail trends in enrollment rates in institutions of higher education, and reveal that there was no increase in enrollments for Latino high school graduates, or 18–24 year-olds, between 1975 (a peak year) and 1998.[2] Such stasis motivated the researchers to investigate the organizational sources of low representation and high attrition in their institution.

In the fall of 2000, the provost of the university granted the researchers seed money for a pilot project to explore these trends in view of designing a more comprehensive multi-method study, based on surveys and open-ended interviews. The pilot project was designed to draw a random sample of 60 students with subgroups consisting of (a) students whose admissions were deferred, i.e., were encouraged to go to community college and then reapply one year later, (b) students who were admitted and did not enroll, and (c) students were enrolled one year later, i.e., retained.

The objective was to interview subjects using a semi-structured protocol inquiring about (a) the students' personal and family backgrounds; (b) high school and secondary school experience; (c) their initial and subsequent experiences on the campus with the admissions office, advising, financial aid, other offices, staff, faculty, classes, and fellow students; and (d) suggestions for change. Herein we present findings from section (b): experiences on the university campus.

## Sample and Method

The authors developed a protocol, or interviewer's guide, consisting of a number of questions and focal concerns in the aforementioned categories. While the protocol was quite detailed, time permitting, interviewers were instructed to employ their conversational skills to acquire the information from their informants in the most comfortable and effective manner they could and to probe where it might be deemed useful to do so. A group of bilingual student-interviewers were trained in doing open-ended interviewing on the assumption that they would be closer in age and experience to the subjects and so could more easily establish rapport.

As mentioned above, the study was designed to draw a randomly selected sample of 60 students in the aforementioned categories. Using categorized lists provided by the admissions office of the university, we attempted to randomly sample the above–mentioned categories of students. The interviewers were provided with these lists, containing names and telephone numbers, and proceeded to call subjects to arrange for interviews. However, we found the lists to be extensively flawed in terms of providing accurate information regarding residence and telephone access, as well as flaws regarding current status. In addition, it was discovered that many of the potential interview subjects were reluctant to be interviewed. Some were actually hostile to the university and underscored their disinclination to cooperate with a study that was to benefit from it. These were often individuals who were not accepted or deferred. Several expressed anger and resentment at not having been accepted or for being deferred. Significantly, one individual's parent told the interviewer on the phone that she was angered by the university's treatment of her child. In either case, whether information error or refusal, when a name was not viable, another name immediately below the selected one was chosen. However, so numerous were the errors on the lists and so frequent the refusals to be interviewed that the integrity of the random sample was nearly compromised resulting in considerably fewer than the target goal of 60. The process of contacting interviewees had been time-consuming, and while we have not totally abandoned the goal of random choice, we have had to reconcile ourselves to a slowing down of the selection process. At this point, we are still in the midst of securing the rest of our targeted sample.

Accordingly, the report herein is based upon 21 completed and transcribed interviews each taking between 30 and 90 minutes. The material gathered so far is significant in terms of what it suggests of institutional research concerning Latinos and other groups, and, substantively of public higher education practice and policy toward Latinos.

## Findings

### Admissions and Advising:
### A Weak Link Depleting the Ranks of Latino Students

The most fruitful findings in this research concern the students' experiences and perceptions of the campus atmosphere as it has either retarded or facilitated their motivation to continue their education. The students who did not persist (i.e., dropped out), chose not to attend after acceptance, or chose to transfer characterized the campus as a non user–friendly institution for a number of reasons. For many the size, impersonality, and maze-like layout of the campus (which consists of five massive brick housing project-like buildings connected by enclosed catwalks on a lonely spit of land jutting out into Boston Harbor) invoke loneliness, confusion, and frustration. One student who enrolled in U. Mass–Boston as her second choice after U. Mass–Amherst reports that she stopped attending after a month and a half:

> I was basically alone there and then there's a lot of old people [i.e., adult and older students]. I felt...I hated it. Another thing was parking. When I saw there wasn't any parking and they tried to send me to Bayside Expo center [about a quarter mile away], I would go around the rotary and go back home. I hated that. [I]t didn't seem like the typical college environment.

This student concluded that U. Mass–Boston "just seemed like high school all over again, with old people...and bad parking. I don't think I ever knew where the cafeteria was." Poor, inadequate, or unavailable advising exacerbated the loneliness and confusion the physical plant induces. Thus, the above student stated that

> I didn't feel I could go anywhere. I mean I was scared that I'm a mess-up.... But advising, they don't care. I never heard from nobody. I went there [advising office] once to see a guy, and he wasn't there. I left him a note and I never got a phone call.

While this student only attended this campus as her second choice, perhaps more effective advising would have encouraged her to stay.

The admissions office represents an important, although not exclusive, university interface with the outside community. By definition, the admissions office serves as the frontline stanchion supporting the university's permeable membrane. In an urban university it is a critical gatekeeper, or selective boundary maintenance organizational unit, used to interface with diverse populations. It is also a critical information dispenser to new students. Advising serves as the delegated student navigating facility of the university imparting counseling and critical information on course selection, prerequisites, degree and major requirements, and so on. For Latino students, as for others, admissions, advising, the registrar, and financial aid offices most clearly stand for the university administration and the official posture presented to them. At U. Mass–Boston, this complex is anathema to Latino students. As one woman, recently graduated, characterizes it, her chief difficulties with the university are "[o]nly with administration.... They're always messing everything up, paper work. You have to be on top of them or they don't fix the mistakes they made." These constitute misplacing copies of student documents brought into the office, posting incorrect figures for loans and grants, consequently delaying her registration, and causing her to lose a course she wished to take. When faced with their errors no apologies were made. This student could only conclude that

> They are not interested in making it easier for the student. They know that the students are there to get an education and to succeed, but if the student cannot do that because of their fault[s], they do not care. They don't try to do their best to make it easier for the student.... They just make it hard.

Advising appears to be the most significant factor in discouraging students from initially attending or remaining at U. Mass–Boston. One student who dropped out reports that attending this particular school is virtually her only option since she lives with her parents and is financially dependent. She feels that she could not get what she was looking for at U. Mass–Boston because at registration time she never had an advisor counsel her on what she should, could, or could not take. Consequently, she made poor choices with the result that her grade point average was low and is now too fearful to return. Her goal was to study management at the university but after several semesters of poor grades she found that "that was a dream that looked more impossible every day."

For students who applied and decided not to attend, a similar set of circumstances applied, chiefly with respect to being given proper guidance and information on how to navigate through the institution at the admissions and entrance phase of the student career. One student, who knew other people who were attending, maintains that she initially chose U. Mass–Boston because of its convenience, then finally decided not to attend because "I got paranoid and very nervous, and I said, 'Well, I'm not ready to come to this campus.'" She decided on a smaller community college. Questioned further on the decision, she maintains that

> You know this campus is beautiful.... [E]ven though it is not very convenient I decided that I would travel by bus and train. But...I had such a hard time, like to walk through the pathway [i.e., the catwalk] through the hallways and they told me that to go to the CPCS program you go to one side. I went there [and] the lady wasn't supposed to leave till three, and ten minutes before three she told me that I had to come the week after, and I was like, I was not ready to deal with all of that. And I went to North Shore [Community College] and I found it so different, the atmosphere, the people, the way...they, you know, tell you where to go.

Similarly, a student who has transferred to anther community college says in retrospect of U. Mass–Boston, "I really think it wasn't what I was looking for in...[a] school. Since the campus was so big and I really didn't connect with anybody."

Thus, for students who have left or decided not to go to U. Mass–Boston, an important factor appears to be their sense of being unable to find anchorage and to navigate through a place that is architecturally confusing, emotionally impersonal, and bereft of consistent guidance and reliable information. However, among those who do not drop out, there is a split among those who report experiences similar to those like the above and those who have made an adjustment and have succeeded in adapting to the environment.

## Advising: The Weak Link for Those Who Remain

Even for those who remain, the atmosphere at U. Mass–Boston is daunting. One male indicates that having come from a high school where he received support from teachers and counselors, and who applied because many friends did, felt intimidated by the crowded urban campus. He felt lost at orientation and now feels isolated, craving peers, staff, and faculty who are Spanish-speaking. He reports that he works on his own and only sees his advisor when he has specific questions. When asked if he has been given sufficient, accurate, and detailed information in order to navigate through the institution, he replies, "Enough to get by. I check the UMB website a lot, but I don't like to ask many questions. I don't know many places here at UMB." A married student reports that she received little understanding and help from an advisor. She notes "that lady that was supposed to be helping me didn't really do much for me.... [E]very time I went to meet with her she wasn't there and I would have to leave her a note." In addition, she did not get accurate information from her advisor: "Like she advises me to take classes that I really don't need and I think that's a waste of time." She relied upon other students for information and now is considering transferring out. The graduated senior, quoted earlier, remarks that advisors gave her the run around, directing her to speak to someone else other than someone she was familiar with because that individual was purportedly busy, insisting that it was not necessary for her to speak to one whom she preferred. This is a frequent occurrence and results in confusion, especially when students are prevailed upon to wait interminably and leave disgusted and confused. The aforementioned student surmises that the administrative/advising staff is often "confused...so they're frustrated [and] sometimes take it out on students." A sophomore describes her earliest experiences, commencing with a Latino admissions

counselor as, "Awful! Awful!" She says the counselor, endeavoring to make
certain that she was not merely going to enter capriciously, grilled her until "I
was almost at the point of crying; I wanted to walk out of the interview....I
guess I stuck through it, and I was like 'You know what? I don't care what you
say, but I know what I want, I'm not a 15 year-old making this decision.'"
Pushing on to the advisor's office this student comments: "The first day I
came... it wasn't too helpful. Everybody was rushing in the door; they didn't
really have time to stick with anybody and talk with them."

The above experiences point to serious problems with the admissions and
advising process. These problems clearly have an adverse effect on prospective,
entering, and continuing Latino students, but while they may have more serious
consequences for them than for other groups, these problems represent
institutional, as opposed to individual or attitudinal, racism (e.g., by the above
anecdote involving a Latino admissions officer). This is also revealed by
testimonies such as the perceptive commentary of a female student who, when
asked if she felt welcome or unwelcome, replied: "A little bit of both.... Well, in
the administration office I felt lost, but once I went to the financial aid office
and other departments I felt a little bit awkward." Replying to the interviewer's
question as to whether this was due to an attitude on the part of the staff, she
explains how poor institutional advising logistics contribute toward
disorientation, lending a sense of non-reality to the advising process:

> I wouldn't say to me personally. Individuals have different personalities and it is hard to
> accommodate some of them.... I would say their personalities do not fit their job
> descriptions, which...do not say what they are [actually] doing. It made me feel not
> necessarily rejected, but...like I didn't belong there.

A small number of students actually manage to get along better on their own
without resorting to campus advising. As one sophomore puts it, "I haven't had
time to associate with the advisor or anything." He states that when "I need to
know something...I'll just go and find a book or something. Because all the
pamphlets they offer you in school...really help you deciding what classes you
need to take."

The above testimonies provide a clue to the significance of the loneliness
that so many of these students report. It is a loneliness stemming from being
overwhelmed by a place that is architecturally confusing, and is augmented by
an uncaring bureaucratic maze that supplies them with few tools and no social
networks to help navigate through the university system. Inadequate orientation

and information, limited support services, and personal, cultural alienation are often-cited barriers to Latino student participation (Ramirez, 1987).

We see how ritualistic bureaucratic red tape combined with insensitivity has an especially deleterious effect on Latinos. The campus in question is chronically underfunded by a hostile state legislature and has no viable constituency supporting it. Higher education is a commodity in Massachusetts, which contains one of, if not the highest, densities of private colleges and universities in the nation. Thus, even in times of bountiful state revenue and notably low unemployment, the university essentially is level funded and has insufficient funds to adequately train and staff its advising center. On the other hand, better planning could alleviate much of the logistical tangle evidenced here.

## The Need for On-Campus Support

The experiences reported here suggest that surviving the obstacle course of admissions and advising requires compensating experiences with other programs, welcoming and helpful contact with teachers, fellow students, or backup from home and friends outside of school. Thus, one woman recounts that, as a result of receiving a scholarship awarded to minorities from a local newspaper she had to enroll in a compulsory class of recipients at the university which was assigned a special advisor. She benefited from the support of her group, which helped her to adjust to university life by sharing information, engaged in group educational activities, and assisted each other with assignments. Some members have remained friends and continue to take classes, study together, share and compare notes, etc.

For Latino students, a potential source of great support is the Gastón Institute for Latino Public Policy. A recently graduated woman participated in this institute's Latino Leadership Opportunity Program (LLOP). She reports that "We went to Washington, DC, and presented our research papers. There we met a lot of highly influential people…, especially Latinos." She notes that through the program's activities she also met Latinos from other parts of the country. Currently, she works for the Gastón Institute on the university campus and testifies to the fact that having graduated from the program, "I felt the need to help other students" and so has participated in leadership development and the institute's other community outreach efforts. Clearly, such experiences are invaluable from the standpoint of support, and particularly for their building and widening of perspective networks.

Other students find refuge in the Latino student organization on campus. Thus, one young woman living at home with her parents says in response to a question concerning the ease of making friends on campus:

> [S]ince U. Mass–Boston is a commuting school, I find that there's more people older than me who already have a family and are…really don't want to have a friend of a girl that hasn't even graduated from college…. They have other things to do, so they go to their classes. It's difficult, especially for freshmen, but once you go to clubs, like, for instance Casa Latina, I guess that's where I started to make friends because…if it wasn't for that I would have just had a few [friends] like a studying partner.

The clear majority of Latino students interviewed do not participate in the Latino student organization. This student organization has limited value to a diversified Latino population for a number of reasons, including the fact that it is an organization more devoted to leisure activity than to scholastic or political concerns. In addition, the adult, married, working, or single–parent students alluded to in the above quote, which constitute more than a third of Latino students, do not have the time to participate in this organization.

## Support and Identity: Bilingual University Publications, Latino Faculty and Staff

Concerning the issue of Spanish–language signage, information bulletins, and university publications, responses are split along the lines of linguistic ability. For those who are Spanish–dominant, many respond in the spirit of the following second–year student: "I would love to [see more Spanish bulletins, signs, university publications]. Spanish is my first language and I still have to struggle with the English language." On the other hand, another says, "I don't care. I can understand both languages. It would be necessary for other students who do not understand English." Another says that "I don't think the Spanish [i.e., Latino] students want to read in Spanish." For those desiring more bilingual or Spanish– language materials, this preference points to the larger issue, which, according to one student, consists of "trying to relate to our cultural meaning." Or it, along with providing more Latino staff and faculty, concerns the matter of isolation and establishing a comfortable atmosphere, which boils down to the issue of support. Thus, responding at the end of an interview to the question, "What do you see as being the biggest problem concerning Latino/a students on campus?" one woman states:

I think the lack of support…the language barrier, because some of the Latino students
that go into college if they don't find the support that they need cultural, if they don't find
people of their culture at the schools, if they don't find people that they can identify with
of their own culture, they feel isolated and that comes from not having literature in
Spanish, not having information in Spanish…in the financial aid office. If they have stuff
in Spanish that they can read, I think that the students would feel more comfortable.

The issue of Spanish–language publications actually is a subset of a much
larger question concerning university outreach to Latinos. At present there is no
targeted outreach. This is so egregious as to be shameful. The university exists
in a metropolitan region that has recently witnessed a spurt in the population
growth of Latinos. But this is no excuse, for Latinos have been present in
sufficient numbers for more than a decade to merit such outreach. Historically,
Boston's business institutions have been dominated by Yankees (a
Protestant/Brahmin upper class), and Boston politics, its civil service and other
public institutions, have been dominated by the Irish. The state legislature has
less than a handful of Latino representatives. William Bulger, former chair of
the state senate, now serves as the president of the Massachusetts state
university system. The administration of this university system is largely white.
All of this is to offer an all-too-cursory explanation of the relative late
responsiveness of the university to a Latino constituency. It also is a partial
explanation of the lack of sensitivity from the admissions and advising offices
to Latino student needs. Perhaps on these grounds alone publications and
targeted outreach to Latinos are warranted.

In general, opinions seem to be split on the narrower question concerning the
desirability of hiring more bilingual staff. Similar to the case of Spanish–
language publications, some maintain, as this second–year student does, that "I
never look for the bilingual person because I am able to communicate with
them in English." On the other hand, another second–year student states,
"There isn't enough [bilingual personnel]. I think we should have more…
Students who see minorities working at a higher level, they're encouraged to do
better like them or even go beyond." Thus, bilingual here means definitively
Latino, in the sense of the aforementioned discussion of the desirability of
hiring Latino faculty who are *simpatico*.

Latino faculty and staff can succeed the students' families, friends, and home
communities in supplying support. In fact, a recently hired dynamic and energetic
full-time faculty member in a recently installed Latino Studies Program is
reported by several students to have made a difference for them in untangling
the maze of university rules and requirements and in reinforcing students'

self-confidence in their abilities not only to make it through but to achieve in an exemplary fashion.

Concerning the interviewees' opinions regarding the hiring of Latino faculty and staff, there is virtual unanimity in support for this measure. However, some of this support for such hiring, albeit a minority, presents a double-edged issue reflecting identification with meritocratic values. Thus, one student suggests hiring more Latino faculty on the heels of stating "If Latino students aren't good enough to be in college, they shouldn't just enroll. I think that the people that are going to come to college should be prepared." He concludes, "and for the faculty and all that stuff, of course I would like to see more Latino faculty and more Latino teachers." However, most interviewees, when asked whether they would like to see more Latino faculty and staff hired, replied affirmatively, largely echoing sentiments concerning the practical issues of navigating through the institution and the closely related theme of support, stressing the efficacy of faculty and staff with common experiences and perceptions. As one Puerto Rican second–year student comments, "I definitely would like to have more classes taught by Latinos. The race doesn't matter, but I'm more comfortable with Latino teachers." Asked why this is so, she replies, "I don't know. I think we can talk about Puerto Rico and what is going on." One interviewee would like to see "more advisors that you know actually go through the things that you went through when they were in college." Similarly, as one sophomore puts it,

> The advising office, I think, needs some Spanish people, just to encourage you to keep you going, give you motivation if you really don't get it from others. To have someone who has your background who really knows how hard it is to keep going and get a higher education. You need [someone], you know, to guide you with a mentor.

Some students have had the good fortune to come into contact with some of the very few energetic, available, and helpful Latino faculty members and most indicate that they would like to see more Latino faculty hired, who, as one sophomore (in terms echoing the above quote on hiring more advisors) puts it, "actually understand what you're going through." Thus, the most important aspect of having more Latino faculty is that they are a bulwark against an uncaring and unsupportive environment. One student, asked if non-Latino professors are helpful, answered:

> They help you, but they're not as interested in seeing you succeed as a Latino professor, because they want to see Latino students succeed and get an education. I am not saying that the others don't, but if you get a good grade in their class, fine, and, if not, that is

fine too.... [T]he Latino professors that I had are on top of you until you do what you need to do to succeed and get the grades that you deserve.

## Conclusion

Support appears to be a theme summarizing this research. In terms of the crippling effects of advising and information dispersal, certainly reform of the current system as it stands, short of substantially increasing the number of Latino staff and faculty, would have some value, but even such reform will be limited in its effects, since an understaffed and insensitive advising corps can only be reconstituted just so much in order to rectify the institutional and attitudinal racism lurking in its interstices. The coldness and indifference reported by our interviewees may indeed be exacerbated by work overload, but some of it clearly stems from cultural and subcultural antipathies. Currently, two Latinas are working in advising. More Latinos are needed. Likewise, there are few Latinos working in admissions and financial aid.

Having a sufficient contingent of Latino faculty and staff to serve the needs of Latino students may at first seem to be a daunting prerequisite for a public university to fulfill. Nonetheless, it is a necessary condition to assure admissions and continued enrollment, that is, as a dropout prevention measure. Faculty, in particular, serves as both successors to family, community, and other pre-collegiate role models representing *cariño* to Latino students. This is a difficult notion to translate into English, but such loving care roughly equates into what Anglos refer to as the maintenance of an optimum "comfort level."

In sociological terms such figures play important roles as societal surrogates both legitimatizing wider moral imperatives, such as the value of education and its function as a conduit to occupational participation and success in U.S. society. At the same time these surrogates can uphold the validity of an emerging and evolving pan-Latino identity, actually an "ethnoid segment" constituted of what in reality is a highly diverse spectrum of nationalities, ethnic groups, and cultures. Thus, the identity question contains two dimensions: the emergent identity of Latinos as a differentiated population segment working toward establishing common social, political, and economic ground and the particular ethnic and national identities contained under the rubric "Latino." The tensions existing between the former and the latter continue to be debated and played out through university politics vis-à-vis the development of Latino Studies programs. In a sense, these are counterparts to the conflicts and tensions to the political and social struggles occurring among Latinos' major areas of diverse settlement. For our purposes here, and for what we perceive as the general benefit accruing to all, we opt for the common identity theme. We see this unifying theme operating in our data. Clearly the interviewees' attitudes and opinions embody it. In hiring more Latino faculty and staff, it is likely the case that the university, as other institutions (most proximately national and some aspects of municipal politics, for example) can play an important role in solidifying pan-Latino identity and simultaneously enlarging its constituency. Ultimately, this will redound to its benefit since it can play an important part solidifying what is now a weak and fragmented body of support in the state legislature. The presence of a viable contingent of faculty and staff is instrumental to increasing Latino retention, which, in turn is indispensable to an agenda of enlarging support for the university among the fastest–growing population segment in the Boston metropolitan area.

# APPENDIX 1

### Table 1:
**Enrollment rates of 18–24 year-olds as a percent of high school graduates in institutions of higher education by race/ethnicity, 1975–1998.**

| Year | Total | White, non-Hispanic | Black, non-Hispanic | Hispanic origin |
|------|-------|---------------------|---------------------|-----------------|
| 1975 | 31.4 | 31.3 | 30.1 | 33.0 |
| 1980 | 30.5 | 31.0 | 26.0 | 27.6 |
| 1985 | 32.5 | 33.9 | 24.5 | 25.0 |
| 1990 | 37.7 | 39.2 | 30.4 | 26.8 |
| 1995 | 42.3 | 44.0 | 35.4 | 35.2 |
| 1998 | 45.2 | 46.9 | 40.0 | 33.9 |

Source: U.S. Department of Commerce, Bureau of the Census, Current Population Survey Table of Yearly Statistics (September 1999).

# APPENDIX 2

## Table 2
### Enrollment rates as a percent of 18–24-year-olds in institutions of higher education, by race/ethnicity, 1975–1998.

| Year | Total | White, non-Hispanic | Black, non-Hispanic | Hispanic origin |
|------|-------|---------------------|---------------------|-----------------|
| 1975 | 26.3  | 27.4                | 20.4                | 20.4            |
| 1980 | 25.7  | 27.3                | 19.4                | 16.1            |
| 1985 | 27.8  | 30.0                | 19.6                | 16.9            |
| 1990 | 32.1  | 35.2                | 25.3                | 16.2            |
| 1995 | 34.3  | 37.9                | 27.5                | 20.7            |
| 1998 | 36.5  | 40.6                | 29.8                | 20.4            |

Source: U.S. Department of Commerce, Bureau of the Census, Current Population Survey Table of Yearly Statistics (September 1999).

# Bibliography

Durkheim, E. (1951). *Suicide*. New York: The Free Press.

Olivas, M. A. (1997). Research on Latino college students: A theoretical framework and inquiry. In A. Darder, R. D. Torres, & H. Gutíerrez (Eds.), *Latinos and education: A critical reader* (pp. 468–486). New York: Routledge.

Pérez, S. M. & de la Rosa-Salazar, D. (1997). Economic, labor force, and social implications of Latino educational and population trends. In A. Darder, R. D. Torres, & H. Gutíerrez (Eds.), *Latinos and education: A critical reader* (pp. 45–79). New York: Routledge.

Ramirez, G. M. (1987). *Retention of the Latino university student* (Student paper, unpublished). The annual meeting of the National Association for Bilingual Education. (30 March–3 April). Denver, CO: Affirmative Action at CSULB.

de los Santos, A. Jr. & Rigual, A. (1994). Progress of Hispanics in American higher education. In M. J. Justiz, R. Wilson, & L. G. Bjork (Eds.), *Minorities in higher education* (pp. 172–194). Phoenix, AZ: Oryx.

Tierney, W. G. (1999). Models of minority college-going and retention: Cultural integrity versus cultural suicide. *Journal of Negro Education, 68*, 80–91.

Tierney, W. G. (1992). An anthropological analysis of student participation in college. *Journal of Higher Education, 63*, 603–618.

Tinto, V. (1987). *Leaving college: Rethinking the causes and cures of student attrition*. Chicago: University of Chicago Press.

U.S. Department of Commerce, Bureau of the Census, (1999. Current Population Survey Table of Yearly Statistics.

Van Gennep, A. (1960). *The rites of passage*. Chicago: University of Chicago Press.

Wilton, J. (1999). *Retention and persistence of the undergraduate entering cohorts 1984 to 1986* (Report). Boston: University of Massachusetts, Boston, Office of Institutional Research.

Chapter Three

# Rewriting Race and Gender High School Lessons: Second-Generation Dominicans in New York City[1]

*Nancy López*

## Introduction

At high school graduation ceremonies across the country, a curious fact has emerged: more women graduate than men, particularly in Latino and black communities. It is predicted that by 2007 the gender gap will reach 2.3 million, with 9.2 million women enrolled in college, compared with 6.9 million men (Lewin, 1998). It is significant that although the gender gap occurs across all racial and ethnic groups, it is most pronounced in Latino and black communities (Dunn, 1988). In the Boston public high school graduating class of 1998, it was estimated there were 100 black and Hispanic males for every 180 black and Hispanic males attending a 4-year college (Sum, Kroshko, Fogg, & Palma, 2000). In New York City public high schools, where the majority of the student population is nonwhite (86%), more women graduate than men (New York Board of Education, 2000). Even at the City University of New York (CUNY) women also comprise the majority of enrolled black and Latino undergraduates and make up to 70% of graduate programs.

Despite the social, cultural, and political significance of this trend, there is little research on the race-gender gap in education (Kleinfeld, 1998; López, 2003; Sum, Kroshko, Fogg, & Palma, 2000; Washington & Newman, 1991). This trend begs several questions: Why do more women graduate than men? How do formal and informal institutional practices within high schools "race" and "gender" students? How do racialize(ing) and gender(ing) processes intersect in the classroom setting? Finally, how can teachers work toward dismantling race, gender, and class oppression in their classrooms? A guiding premise of the study is that race and gender are socially constructed processes that are overlapping, intertwined, and inseparable.[2] This understanding of race differs in fundamental ways from the essentialist perspective, which assumes that race is an innate and static biological essence (Omi & Winant, 1994).

To understand why women attain higher levels of education than men, I investigated race(ing) and gender(ing) processes in the high school setting. High school is a crucial site for exploring the origins of the gender gap because it is in this institution where it begins to become most pronounced. I therefore focus on how ordinary day-to-day school practices and classroom dynamics are racial(ized) and gender(ed), and in turn shape men's and women's views about the role of education in their lives. My primary data comes from 5 months of participant observation at Urban High School, a New York City public high school that is 90% Latino; most of the students are second-generation Dominicans who were born in the United States or had most of their schooling there.

During the spring of 1998, for 3 days a week, I regularly observed four mainstream classes in the social studies department: two economics classes for seniors, one American history class for juniors, and one global studies class for sophomores. The two economics courses were taught by Mr. Green, a self-described biracial man in his early 20s who could "pass" for white in terms of phenotype. Ms. Gutierrez, a Latina teacher in her early 20s, who was from South America but could not "pass" for white, taught the American history course. And Mr. Hunter, a white man in his mid 20s, taught the global studies class for sophomores. Each of these classes had between 25 and 30 students. Only Mr. Green's classes had unequal gender proportions. In his first class less than a third of the students were female. Conversely, in the second class only a third of the class was male. This skewed gender balance in the classroom proved quite useful for examining how race and gender intersect in the school setting.

Reactions to my presence in the field were varied. Depending on my attire, despite the fact that I was in my late 20s, students and teachers alike often mistook me for an older high school student. One morning a white, middle-aged teacher came to Mr. Hunter's class to conduct a teacher evaluation. Because I was wearing a pair of jeans and a T-shirt, he assumed that I was a student and asked me if he could see yesterday's class notes. Students, on the other hand, saw me as a fellow Dominican; they usually approached me in Spanish, sometimes inquiring about what part of the "DR" my family was from. Sometimes, if I were dressed in more professional clothing, students whom I would meet in the hallways and lunchroom asked me in Spanish if I was a psychologist reporting on students who were "bad." Other students simply saw me as a college student and asked me about getting into college.

Before beginning my analysis of how race and gender processes intersect in the classroom setting, I describe the neighborhood and institutional context in which Urban High School is embedded. Next, I bring into focus some of the invisible race(ing) and gender(ing) processes that transpire in high school classrooms as well as through school policies. And, finally, I outline some of the ways in which teachers and school administrators can interrupt the cycle of race, class, and gender oppression of racially stigmatized and language minority students.

## Backdrop for Urban High School

Urban High School is emblematic of what Anyon (1997) refers to as "ghetto schooling"—the grossly inferior education available to racially stigmatized low-income immigrant youth. Scaffolding enveloped the entire four story building which was built circa 1900. Sections of the roof regularly collapsed and pigeons could be found flying around in the auditorium and hallways, sometimes making their nests in the stairwells. Both inside and out, the building appeared to be falling apart and bursting at the seams (New York Immigration Coalition, 1999).

Originally intended to accommodate approximately 2,500 students, in the late 1990s Urban High School had a student population of about 3,000. To accommodate the overflow of students, 28 makeshift orange trailer classrooms have been squeezed onto the disused baseball field located behind the main school building. Ironically, despite the trailer classrooms having only one toilet for about 40 students, their facilities appeared more hygienic than those in the main building. Even the bathrooms for faculty and staff located in the main building were missing doors, did not flush, and lacked toilet paper and working faucets. During the course of my study, I always brought a water bottle with me because I could not locate a single working water fountain in the entire building. When queried about the possibility of moving to a habitable school building, Mr. Perez, the middle-aged Latino school principal lamented, "There is no public willing to build new schools."

As a de facto hyper-segregated school, Urban High School is representative of the schools attended by most racially stigmatized groups, such a Latinos and African Americans. It is located in a neighborhood that experienced intensive Dominican immigration from the 1970s through the 1990s. Most of the students who attend Urban High School have been zoned to attend this school.

Although most of teachers are white, the student population is overwhelmingly Latino (90%), mostly from the Dominican Republic. The remaining student population, which is categorized as black, includes second-generation youth from Haiti, the Anglophone West Indies, and Africa. The enrollment of Asian and white students is negligible (1%). Because the majority of students were from low-income families, three fourths were eligible for free school lunch. Only a quarter of students graduate within the traditional 4 year time frame, and about a quarter drop out, with the rest of the students remaining beyond the traditional 4 years of high school. Over half of 9th and 10th graders were older than is designated for their grade, and 7% of the students were classified as special education. In the hallways and in the lunchrooms I often overheard students, particularly young men, remarking that they had been at Urban High School for more than 5 or 6 years but had not been able to graduate. Ironically, then, in part because more women graduate than men, it was men who were more likely to remain enrolled beyond the 4th year, making Urban High Schools' enrollment slightly more male than female (55%).

At our first meeting, Mr. Perez, the school principal, expressed enthusiasm about my research project, because during his 8 year tenure as principal he had been observing the race-gender gap and was curious to learn what I would find. Mr. Perez introduced me to Ms. Rivera, who was an assistant principal and the chair of the social studies department. Both Mr. Perez and Ms. Rivera were pleased that I was a Dominican graduate student born and raised in the United States, because they hoped that I could serve as a role model for their student body.

Ms. Rivera, a veteran teacher of 20 years, promptly took me under her wing, introducing me to the different department faculty in the school. While giving me a whirlwind tour of the school, Ms. Rivera tried to reassure me that Urban High School was not as dangerous as everyone thought it was. Indeed, media representations of the Urban High School neighborhood included very negative images of drug wars, gang fights, and criminality. However, far from the depictions of Urban High School as a violent school, I noted that students were quite cordial toward each other. While exchanging classes and the latest gossip, student conversations peppered the hallway in a mixture of English and Spanish. Young men walking in the hallways usually greeted each other in Spanish by touching, not shaking hands, and young women embraced and kissed each other on the cheek.

As we walked down the hallways, Ms. Rivera greeted students in both Spanish and English. Although I chatted freely with Ms. Rivera in both Spanish and English, at a daylong teacher workshop I attended, several teachers openly expressed their belief that students should only speak English while they were in school. In another instance, a white middle-aged teacher overheard one of her students speaking Spanish in the hallway and stopped him to say, "Pedro, I know you know how to speak English. Speak English!" The entire time, Pedro, understandably dejected about the prohibition of his native language in the school setting, just stared down at the floor while he was being scolded. During the course of my fieldwork, like Pedro, I received a number of frowns and disapproving glances from some white teachers because I was speaking in Spanish with other students and teachers.

As Ms. Rivera and I made our way to the department office, I queried her about why there were classrooms filled with students, but no teachers. Ms. Rivera lamented that at the beginning of every semester there was always a shortage of teachers (Calderone & Buettner, 1999). Urban High School has a high teacher turnover rate, with close to half of the teachers leaving after 2 years. Some of the veteran teachers remarked that in the fall of 1997, the figure was closer to 70%. Close to one third of the social studies teachers that spring were new recruits. Indeed, Ms. Rivera later admitted that she had only recently joined the staff after teaching for more than 20 years in another high school. The need for teachers was so great that during the middle of the semester, Ms. Rivera tried to entice me to consider teaching at Urban High School even though I had no prior experience with high school students and was not certified.

Despite being an assistant principal and the head of social studies department, Ms. Rivera's office, due to lack of office space, had been transformed into the headquarters for the 24 teachers she supervised. During their free periods these teachers huddled elbow-to-elbow, cramped into a space designed to comfortably accommodate perhaps two to four people. Without access to a computer, they bubbled in attendance sheets, planned lessons, organized school trips, graded tests, advised students and, in the few minutes that remained, tried to eat their lunches. Teachers often sat in each other's classes, just so they could have a space in which to prepare their next lesson.

Every time I entered the makeshift social studies headquarters I was struck by how dedicated the teachers were, despite not being treated—or

compensated—as professionals. I marveled over how they were able to perform their duties when they were lacking even the most basic supplies, such as books, chalk, or even a desk. Working under such dreadful conditions, even the most student-centered teachers received the message that their job was not important.

Likewise, even the most school-oriented students invariably learned that the education of low-income, Latino, immigrant students was not important, as they were not expected to amount to much.

## On the Intersection of Overcrowding, Policing, Race(ing) and Gender(ing)

Beyond the decrepit conditions of the school building, one of the most striking aspects of Urban High School was the ubiquitous security presence. All students had to enter the main building through a smaller side door because the main entrance was boarded up. Upon entering, students had to present their picture identification cards and pass through state-of-the-art full-body metal detectors, filmed by video cameras that were staffed by half a dozen security personnel that included guards, peace officers, and armed New York City police officers. I queried the head of security about why they had begun using metal detectors and why they had requested a police officer on campus years before it became a city-wide policy. Mr. Castellanos explained that it was not because Urban High School was among the most violent in the system, but rather because it was among the most overcrowded in the city. Seemingly, crowd control was one of the major functions of the security personnel. During the 5 minutes that students were given to change between their 40 minute classes, security guards with bullhorns were positioned at the corners of the hallways yelling, "Move it!" Long after students were quietly seated in their classrooms, teachers often had to compete with the noise emanating from security guards' walkie-talkies as they patrolled the corridors and stairwells.

When asked about the interactions between young men and women, security guards, most of whom were Latino and black men, admitted that they seldom dealt with altercations involving young women. They even joked that male security guards were not allowed to make physical contact with female students who had been involved in fights. According to school policy, only female security guards were allowed to do that. However, only two of the more than two dozen security personnel were women. In contrast, male security guards were allowed to chase, manhandle, and apprehend male students. Therefore, although officially security guards were supposed to protect and supervise all students, in practice they were only patrolling the young men. In due course, the problematic student was profiled as a male.

Security measures in the trailer classrooms were even more extreme. 9th graders, all of whom were housed in the trailers, were required to wear school uniforms—a blue shirt and beige pants—or face penalties, including having their identification card confiscated and losing their lunchroom privileges. Only students with swipeable identification cards were permitted access. Not surprisingly school administrators, students, and teachers colloquially referred to the trailer park as Riker's Island, after the prison located in the Bronx.

The racialization of black and Latino youth as a stigmatized group that was prone to crime manifested during 1990s controversy spearheaded by New York City Mayor Rudolph Giuliani (Van Gelder, 1997). The mayor insisted that crime could be reduced in the city if police officers had access to high school yearbooks in an effort to apprehend wanted criminals. Given that the New York City public school system is predominantly Latino and black, this demand can be interpreted as what Omi and Winant (1994) describe as a racial project.[3] Regardless of intention, this discourse links dark-skinned male bodies to crime and simultaneously attempts to reallocate resources based on that definition. To be sure, in September of 1998, police officers finally gained complete control of the security personnel at all New York City public schools.

Overcrowding, and the subsequent increased security, is turning many public high schools, which are supposed to be institutions of learning, into spaces where urban Latino and black youth (particularly young men) are humiliated and criminalized through searches and other demeaning encounters (Pastor, McCormick, & Fine, 1996; Rosenbaum & Binder, 1997). While doing field work at Urban High School, I did witness violence directed toward young men. In one such instance, Ms. Rivera asked a security guard to chase a young man who ignored her request to remove his hat. School rules stipulate that no student could wear a hat on the school premises. This rule was never enforced with young women, but was often a source of problems for young men.

Another worrisome institutional practice was the forging of a pipeline between low-income, racially stigmatized schools and prisons. When I was a New York City public high school student in the 1980s, students who had been engaged in scuffles were sent to the Dean's office. I was alarmed to see that at Urban High School such students were quickly whisked away in handcuffs by the white police officer permanently assigned to the school. The prevailing assumption that low-income and working-class Latino and black youth (especially young men) are prone to aggression has resulted in the normalization of physical violence against them in urban schools nationwide (Stanton-Salazar, 1997).

One morning while sitting in Mr. Green's class I heard a commotion in the hallway. Immediately after class I went to the security office and learned that the fight involved young men in the special education program. Although there had been no weapons used and no one had been seriously injured, the school's police officer arrested the young men involved in the fight. The Latino security guards who were involved in stopping the incident spoke angrily about pressing charges against the students. Again, although no weapons were involved, these young men were arrested and processed into the prison system. Given the growing link between urban, low-income, overcrowded, and racially stigmatized public schools and the prison industrial complex, it is not surprisingly that black and Latino men continue to be disproportionately arrested and convicted (Davis, 1997).

## Unearthing Race-Gender Lessons in the Classroom

Regrettably, classrooms are not impervious to the social narratives that frame Latino and black students (particularly young men) as "problems" (Fine, 1991). The following analysis of Mr. Green's third- and fourth-period economics classes for seniors provides a window to the invisible ways in which race(ing) and gender(ing) transpire in many high school classrooms across the United States. Mr. Green was a well-intentioned and hardworking teacher I often saw during my morning commute. To compensate for the lack of books in his classroom, Mr. Green used his own money to purchase newspapers and make photocopies. In an effort to prepare his class for the statewide Regents examinations, Mr. Green assigned journal writing at the beginning of each class. Because he did not have a space in which to leave his students' work, at the end of every semester, Mr. Green could be seen lugging a green duffel bag filled with student journals. Mr. Green was emblematic of the hardworking teachers that sacrifice for our students. However, despite his good intentions (Fine, 1991), Mr. Green, like other dedicated teachers across the country, was unaware of the ways in which his pedagogical style and demeanor inadvertently contributed to the growing race-gender gap in education.

One morning, Mr. Green, who always wore a shirt and tie to class, locked the door shut after the bell rang and announced, "You will have exactly 7 minutes to complete this quiz. Please take off your hats." Because the doors were locked shut from the inside, all latecomers had to knock to be let in, and they were required to sign a late book. While students were completing the quiz,

Mr. Green inched his way down the crowded aisles checking for homework, often walking over desks to get to the next row. Disappointed at the number of students who did not hand in their homework, Mr. Green remarked, "Students, this is unacceptable; only a handful of you have submitted your homework. Many of you will lose points for not handing in homework."

One young man in the class called out, "How come you didn't used to give us homework last year?" Mr. Green retorted, "You guys quiet down! Do you want to be here? I suggest that you follow the rules," pointing to the blackboard. A large piece of cardboard above over the blackboard listed "Mr. Green's Rules for Success."

1. Be present every day.
2. Be in your seat when the bell rings.
3. Homework is due at the beginning of class.
4. Do not wear hats, Walkmans, or beepers.
5. Be quiet and attentive when some one is speaking.
6. Do not bring food or drinks to the classroom.
7. Raise your hand and wait to be recognized before speaking.
8. Be prepared for school.
9. Treat faculty and other students with respect.

Another informal rule in Mr. Green's class was "English only." Sometimes during classroom discussions students who replied in Spanish were completely ignored.

Exactly 6 minutes after the quiz began, Mr. Green warned, "Okay students, you have 1 minute," and seconds later, "Okay students, time is up. Put your pens down. Put your names and pass them forward. If I see you writing I will take points off." Mr. Green's classroom often felt like a very controlled environment that had a definite inviolable time schedule.

During classroom discussions, Mr. Green inadvertently framed Latino young men as potential drug and crime statistics (Fine, 1991). Another morning, Mr. Green began class by asking students to talk about the problems that existed in contemporary society. Students called out: crime, drugs, pollution. Mr. Green continued, "Is crime directly or indirectly caused by poverty?" Leo, a male student replied, "Drugs are a way to escape from reality; therefore we have a drug problem. But poverty doesn't necessarily cause crime. People come from New Jersey, buy their drugs and what kind of life do they lead?" Leo argued that white suburban youth come to Latino neighborhoods in New York City to purchase drugs, but they are not low-income. Likewise, Jose chided, "I read about a study in the newspaper that states that 40% of 'weedheads' are in the 'inner city,' but 60% are from the suburbs!" The rest of the young men clapped, made remarks in Spanish, and cheered Leo's and Jose's social critique of the racialization of low-income black and Latino communities as the only space where criminal activity takes place. Noticeably upset, Mr. Green responded, "Students, I don't need the heckles. You need to raise your hands."

Due in part to the fact that Mr. Green had to cover a given amount of material within the 40 minute time-block, substantive dialogue was constrained. Mr. Green responded in textbook fashion, "In an indirect way poverty can lead to drugs." Flustered by the symbolic taint that was cast upon his community, one young man muttered under his breath, "Just because you're poor doesn't mean that you use drugs." Given that the majority of the students at Urban High School are from low-income and working-class Dominican families, and that the media has stigmatized Latino and black men as drug lords, the young men in Mr. Green's class were understandably upset by his comments.

In an effort to contribute to the classroom discussion, Jose continued the debate saying. "Many of the people who engage in crime do not have drugs." Again the rest of the class applauded and made remarks in Spanish. Oblivious to his students' social critique, Mr. Green continued to press them to agree with his prescriptions: "What is the broad social goal of the minimum wage? Come up with alternative methods." After a deafening silence, which can be interpreted as form of resistance to the racialization processes that had taken place in the class thus far, Mr. Green offered another textbook solution: "Tax breaks to employers who create jobs." After another pause, Viscaino, a young man, offered, "train people for higher skilled jobs." Other students clapped, and from his seat Viscaino took a bow and smiled at his friends. But, Jose chided, "What good is job training if the jobs are not there?" Mr. Green reproached, "There is a demand for skilled workers, such as actuaries. They make over a hundred thousand dollars a year." Lionel rejoined, "You have to understand that there are people out there who have an education but who still sell drugs because the jobs are already taken by people out there who have experience."

Time and again Mr. Green's laudable attempts to encourage classroom discussion were undermined by his pedagogy. Although Mr. Green was a hardworking teacher his pedagogical style was quite authoritarian and alienating. Mr. Green appeared to promote participation only if students agreed with the "official" responses. The young men in Mr. Green's economics class were participating in classroom discussion by making biting references to job ceilings, racism, and police brutality, but their social critique was often muffled by the oppressive pedagogy fixated on maintaining order and producing "correct" answers. More importantly, once again young men who wanted to participate in a classroom dialogue were defined as disruptive and as problems.

The gender balance of the class had a visible effect on Mr. Green's social interactions with students. While Mr. Green was always on guard for his third-period class, which consisted mostly of men, his demeanor changed almost instantaneously during his fourth-period class, in which the majority of the students were women. Mr. Green described these two classes as being like night and day.

One morning, just as Mr. Green began to take attendance in his fourth-period class, Juan, who arrived a few minutes late, knocked on the door to be let in. While Juan was signing the late book, Mr. Green demanded that he remove his hat. Juan refused and asked why Mr. Green had not asked the women in the class to remove their hats. (Indeed four women were wearing hats.) At Urban High School, school rules stated that no student could wear a hat inside the school building. However, although this rule was strictly enforced for young men, it was never enforced for young women. Angrily, Mr. Green replied, "Ladies can wear it because it's fashion!" Unscathed by Mr. Green's insistence, Juan who was dressed in designer sportswear rejoined, "I'm fashion, too, Mr. Green." At that point, Mr. Green was noticeably irate and threatened to send Juan to the principal's office, but Juan would not budge. After an uncomfortable silence, Mr. Green glanced at me, then back at Juan, and reluctantly asked the women to remove their hats. Juan then finally obliged. Before the end of the class, however, the "ladies" (but not Juan) had their hats back on without a word from Mr. Green. Shortly thereafter, Juan stopped coming to class. Later that month, I found Juan in the office. When asked why he had stopped attending class, Juan said he left because he had "problems" with Mr. Green.

The next month in the same fourth-period class, Ani, another class clown who, like Juan, sometimes came in late wearing a baseball cap, joked about Mr. Green's resemblance to television personality Pee Wee Herman. In part because of Mr. Green's likeness to the comedian, of course, the entire class burst out laughing, including Mr. Green. In disbelief, a young man turned to another young man sitting behind him and whispered, "Imagine if we had said that, he would have kicked us out of the class!"

While I did note that young women misbehaved less often than men and teachers, regardless of gender and race, were generally more lenient with young women who transgressed school rules partly because some teachers did not feel physically threatened by female students. They tended to be more understanding of young women who were absent from class, came in late, or did not hand in homework. Moreover, in many overcrowded urban schools, so-called feminine traits, such as silence and passivity, are valued and rewarded. Therefore, the "good" student is profiled as a "young lady," whereas the "bad" student is constructed as a male troublemaker.

## Rewriting Race-Gender High School Lessons

How can we erase the race-gender gap in education? How can we begin rewriting some of the race and gender lessons students learn in high schools about who they are and who they can be? There is ample evidence that large public institutions can be successfully recreated into alternative spaces in which students that were previously defined as "at-risk" are turned into scholars, citizens, and activists (Fine & Sommerville, 1998; Fine, Weis, & Powell, 1997; Hartocollis, 1999; Meier, 1995).

Ms. Gutierrez was emblematic of the transformative teacher who nurtured social critique and critical consciousness among her students (Aronowitz & Giroux, 1993). In her American history class, Ms. Gutierrez created a safe space for student social critique, empowerment, and social change. A key aspect of Ms. Gutierrez's success was due in large part to her willingness to be innovative and take risks with pedagogical strategies (hooks, 1994). Instead of employing traditional pedagogical practices, which constitute students as empty receptacles that should be ready for the educational "deposits" made by an authoritative teacher, Ms. Gutierrez worked toward teaching students how to transgress the illusion that all teachers are omniscient (Freire, 1985; hooks, 1995). As explained by Freire (1985), banking education, where a student records, memorizes, and repeats information without perceiving issues of relative power and contradictions, serves as an instrument of oppression. Her classes were often physically structured as semicircles and students worked on small-group and multiple-group projects. Students co-taught lessons, wrote and performed plays depicting historical events, and conducted research on their immigrant neighborhood and family experiences. During one of Ms. Gutierrez's classes, the Industrial Revolution was brought to life as students simulated a nineteenth century, lower Manhattan sweatshop.

In terms of content, Ms. Gutierrez tried to make sure that topics that were not deemed important for inclusion in the standardized statewide Regents exams, such as the history of the United States intervention in Latin America and the Caribbean, were covered in her class. In a deviation from the official curriculum, Ms. Gutierrez took her juniors on a class trip to the Native American Museum. "Although you will not be tested on this in the Regents, I still think this history is important for you to know." Of course, because Urban High School had limited funding for extracurricular activities, Ms. Gutierrez paid for the lunch of the 60 students who attended. As a chaperone for this trip, I accompanied the group to a special lecture and film presented by one of the museum's staff members. Here, students linked the decimation of the Tainos, the indigenous peoples of the Dominican Republic and Haiti, with the current experiences of the indigenous peoples of South America. By weaving her students' experiences, histories, and cultures into her course on American history, Ms. Gutierrez successfully inspired students to become lifelong learners.

Ms. Gutierrez's success with students stemmed from her efforts to make their culture and language an integral part of the class; students did not have to leave their culture outside the classroom door (Delgado, 1992; López, 1997; Nieto, 1992, 1999; Stanton-Salazar, 1997; Ybarra, 2000). Unlike teachers who often viewed the use of any language other than English as a deficit and an impediment to "real" learning, Ms. Gutierrez welcomed the use of different languages in the classroom, including languages she did not know—such as Haitian Creole. Moreover, Ms. Gutierrez was not fixated on maintaining an artificial order in the classroom. With exception of the day that state inspectors were visiting the school, she generally allowed men to wear their hats in class. Young men felt accepted and welcomed in her classroom and therefore were not experienced as "problems." In turn, young men volunteered to come rearrange desks, decorate the classroom, erase the chalkboard, and clean up the classroom. Young men felt that they were genuinely appreciated for who they were in her classroom.

In turn, both young men and women respected and admired Ms. Gutierrez, and she truly admired and respected her students. Although she was South American, Ms. Gutierrez practiced a sense of solidarity with her predominantly Caribbean Latino students. Of course, part of the reason Ms. Gutierrez was successful with her students was that she was a second-generation Latina herself, who spoke Spanish fluently. However, it was pedagogical praxis and genuine respect for her students that made her successful with both males and females.

My experience with some Latino teachers as a student in a New York public school throughout the 1970s and 1980s was completely different from what I witnessed in Ms. Gutierrez's classroom. A couple of my Latina teachers held disdain for Dominican culture and ridiculed Dominican Spanish. To be sure, some of the teachers who early on took an interest in me and proclaimed that I was "college material" were Jewish, Italian, and African American teachers who did not speak a word of Spanish. These teachers practiced a politic of caring, and genuinely respected my language and cultural heritage (Valenzuela, 1999). In short, because a teacher's racial and ethnic background is different from that of her students should not necessarily pose an impediment to creating a classroom environment where her students' cultural backgrounds and experiences are validated and affirmed. In an environment where the culture and history of students are an integral part of the learning process, the race-gender gap in education will be eradicated.

## Conclusion

In examining the race-gender gap in educational attainment among Dominicans, I found that both institutional practices and classroom pedagogy are important spaces in which to work toward its reversal. At Urban High School, like at other low-income public urban schools, young men from racially stigmatized groups are viewed as threatening and potential problem students, whereas young women are treated in a more sympathetic fashion. In effect, although males and females attend the same high schools and come from the same socioeconomic backgrounds, they have fundamentally different cumulative experiences with the intersection of race and gender processes in the school setting. In turn, these experiences shape both men's and women's views about the role of education in their lives in fundamentally different ways (López, 2002). Given the race(ed) and gender(ed) ways in which school rules and policies are implemented at many urban schools, it is not a surprise that Latino and black men comprise a disproportionate number of students who drop out, are discharged, expelled, and tracked into low-level curriculum tracks, including special education.

What would a school that seeks to eliminate the race-gender gap in education look like? There are many changes, both institutional and pedagogical, that can be made in an effort to dismantle the race-gender gap in education. At the institutional level, principals and other school administrators must pay close attention to the ways in which overcrowding translates into increased authoritarian practices informally directed toward young men, particularly those from racially stigmatized groups. Are security guards only patrolling young men?

Are school rules applied in an excessive fashion toward young men? Is there a bridge between low-income public schools and the prison industrial complex? Zero tolerance regulations in school and the presence of metal detectors and armed police officers in the schools may be creating an inhospitable school environment for racially stigmatized young men, especially Latinos and blacks.

As the heads of their school, principals can work toward ending race, gender, and class oppression by actively seeking to create a climate that provides a space for the democratic discussion of racial, class, and gender inequality (Aronowitz & Giroux, 1993; Ayvazian, 1995; Cummins, 1993; Freire, 1993). Instead of ignoring issues of race, class, and gender oppression, principals can counteract power relations between Latino students and the dominant society by opening a dialogue on these issues. In this environment, issues of diversity are not relegated to particular "ethnic" days, months, or festivals but rather are constitutive of the curriculum, institutional practices, and the relationship between the school and the surrounding community.

At the classroom level, teachers can be more attentive to they ways in which they are interacting with students. Are authoritarian pedagogical practices undermining the education of Latinos? Are young men perceived as disruptive and punished disproportionately when compared with their female counterparts? Is the history and experience of students reflected in the curriculum? The omission and repression of Latino students' culture, language, and experience is a form of academic violence, which seriously undermines their learning, as well as their democratic right to express themselves in any language.

If our goal is to eliminate the race-gender gap in education, it is extremely important that we examine the processes through which students are racialized and gendered through school policies and through classroom pedagogy. Once we become aware of the invisible ways in which gender(ing) and race(ing) processes take place at both the macro and micro levels in schools, we can then begin to rewrite the race and gender lessons integral to so many students, particularly black and Latino students. It is only then we can change the way black and Latino students learn about who they are and who they can be (Meier, 1995). It is my hope that being attentive to the race(ing) and gender(ing) in the classroom, and with school policies, we will be on our way to eradicating the race-gender gap in education.

# Bibliography

Anyon, J. (1997). *Ghetto schooling: A political economy of urban educational reform.* New York: Teachers College.

Aronowitz, S., & Giroux, H. (1993). *Education still under siege.* Westport, CT: Bergin and Garvey.

Ayvazian, A. (1995, Jan./Feb.). Interrupting the cycle of oppression: The role of allies as agents of social change. *Fellowship,* 138–141.

Calderone, J., & Buettner, R. (1999, Nov. 8). Vicious cycle of failing schools: Uncertified teachers flood poor nabes. *Daily News,* p. A1.

Crenshaw, K., Gotanda, N., Peller, G., & Thomas, K., (1996). *Critical race theory: The key writings that formed the movement.* New York: New Press.

Cummins, J. (1993). Empowering minority students: A framework for intervention. In L. Weis, & M. Fine (Eds.), *Silenced voices: Class, race and gender in United States schools.* Albany: SUNY.

Davis, A. (1997). Race and criminalization: Black Americans and the punishment industry. In W. Lubiano (Ed.), *The house that race built.* (pp. 264–279). New York: Vintage.

Delgado, C. (1992). School matters in Mexican-American homes: Socializing to education. *American Educational Research Journal, 29,* No. 3, 495–513.

Delgado, R., (Ed.). (1995). *Critical race theory: The cutting edge.* Philadelphia: Temple University.

Dunn, J. (1998). The shortage of black male students in the college classroom: Consequences and causes. *The Western Journal of Black Studies,12* No.2, 73–76.

Fine, M. (1991). *Framing dropouts: Notes on the politics of an urban public high school.* Albany: SUNY.

Fine, M., & Sommerville, J. (1998). *Small schools, big imagination: A creative look at urban public schools.* Chicago: Cross City Campaign for Urban School Reform.

Fine, M., Weis, L., & Powell, L. (1997). Communities of difference: A critical look at desegregated spaces created for and by youth. *Harvard Educational Review, 67,* No. 2, 247–284.

Freire, P. (1993). *Pedagogy of the oppressed.* New York: Continuum.

Freire, P. (1985). *The politics of education: Culture and power and liberation.* New York: Bergin and Garvey.

Gramsci, A. (1971). *Selections from the prison notebooks.* Q. Hoare & N. Smith (Eds.). New York: International Publishers.

Hartocollis, A. (1999, Jan. 28). Crew plans charter schools, his way. *New York Times,* p. B1.

Hill-Collins, P. (1990). *Black feminist thought: Knowledge, consciousness, and the politics of empowerment.* Boston: Unwin Hyman

hooks, b. (1994). *Teaching to transgress: Education as the practice of freedom.* New York: Routledge.

Hurtado, A. (1996.) *The color of privilege: Three blasphemies on race and feminism.* Ann Arbor: University of Michigan.

Kleinfeld, J. (1998). *The myth that schools shortchange girls.* Washington, DC: Women's Freedom Network.

Lewin, T. (1998, Dec. 6). American colleges begin to ask: Where have all the men gone? *New York Times,* p. A1.

López, N. (2003). *Hopeful girls, troubled boys: Race and gender disparity in urban education.* New York: Routledge.

López, N. (1997). Bilingual or bilingüe? In P. Alexander, I. Estrada, B. Heller, & P. T. Reid (Eds.), *Before the class: A handbook for the novice college instructor,*(pp. 147–149). New York: CUNY Graduate

School and University Center.

Meier, D. (1995). *The power of their ideas: Lessons for America from a small school in Harlem*. Boston: Beacon Press.

New York Board of Education. (2000). *Class of 1999 four year longitudinal report and 1998–1999 event dropout rates*. (Report.) New York: New York Board of Education.

New York Immigration Coalition. (1999). *Immigrant and refugee students: How the New York City school system fails them and how to make it work*. (Report.) New York: New York City Coalition for Immigrant Rights.

Nieto, S. (1999). *The light in their eyes: Creating multicultural learning communities*. New York: Teachers College.

Nieto, S. (1992). *Affirming diversity: The sociopolitical context of multicultural education*. New York: Longman.

Omi, M., & Winant, H. (1994). *Racial formation in the United States: From 1960s to 1990s*. New York: Routledge.

Pastor, J., McCormick, J., & Fine, M. (1996). Making homes: An urban girl thing. In B. Leadbetter, & N. Way (Eds.), *Urban Girls: resisting stereotypes, creating identities* (pp. 15–34). New York: New York University.

Rosenbaum, J., & Binder, A. (1997). Do employers really need more educated youth? *Sociology of Education, 70,* 68–85.

Stanton-Salazar, R. (1997). A Social capital framework for understanding the socialization of racial minority children and youths. *Harvard Educational Review, 67,* No. 1, 1–40.

Sum, A., Kroshko, J., Fogg, N., & Palma, S. (2000). *The college enrollment and employment outcomes for the class of 1998 Boston public high school graduates: Key findings of the 1999 follow-up surveys*. Boston: Northeastern University Center for Labor Market Studies.

Valenzuela, A. (1999). *Subtractive schooling: The politics of schooling in a U.S.-Mexican high school*. Albany: SUNY.

Van Gelder, L. (1997, Mar. 28). Police use of yearbooks draws protest from schools. *New York Times,* p. B7.

Washington, V., & Newman, J.. (1991). Setting our own agenda: Exploring the meaning of gender disparities among blacks in higher education. *Journal of Negro Education, 60,* No. 1, 19–35.

Ybarra, R. (2000). Latino students and Anglo-mainstream instructors: A study of classroom communities. *Journal of College Student Retention Research, Theory & Practice, 2,* No. 2, 161–171.

Chapter Four

# Jim Crow:
# A Phoenix Rising in Boston—
# The Trend Toward Separate and
# Unequal in the Boston Public Schools

*Steve Fernandez*

The members of the Boston school committee have, "knowingly carried out a systematic program of segregation affecting all of the city's students, teachers, and school facilities and have intentionally brought about and maintained a dual school system."

(Lukas, 1985, p. 238)

## Introduction

In their 1954 ruling on *Brown v. Board of Education*, the U.S. Supreme Court determined segregation in public schools to be unconstitutional. This historic ruling had a profound impact upon school districts throughout the United States. Following *Brown v. Board of Education*, as well as subsequent lower court rulings regarding segregation, programs designed to promote integration were implemented in many school districts around the country. Such was the case in Boston where, in 1974, Federal Judge Wendell Arthur Garrity found that the leadership of the Boston public schools had intentionally maintained a segregated school system. To remedy this segregation, Judge Garrity devised a desegregation program for Boston's public schools.

In Boston, as well as a number of other school districts that adopted desegregation programs, the initiation of these programs did not go smoothly. Following Judge Garrity's ruling, Boston saw protests, pickets, and incidents of violence. As the bellicose public outcry began to subside, many school districts that implemented desegregation programs, including Boston, experienced the phenomena of "white flight" and an increased embrace of conservative ideology toward public education.

For many decades prominent conservatives, such as economist Milton Friedman, had been advocating for a "market-based" approach to education.

Proponents of this approach to education asserted that school reform should be driven by "free market" dynamics. Initiatives proposed by advocates of the "market-based" approach to education reform included vouchers, charter schools, standardized testing, and an end to desegregation and affirmative action programs. By the 1990s, as voucher and charter school programs were adopted in several states throughout the nation, many school districts also began to implement high–stakes testing programs. High–stakes testing programs generally establish a policy by which student promotion is contingent upon students scoring at or above minimum levels on one or more standardized test. According to a study by the American Federation of Teachers, by the year 2000, 17 states had promotion policies at the elementary or middle school level tied to meeting standards, and 27 states linked graduation eligibility to standards based high school exit exams (American Federation of Teachers, 2001, p. 5).

President Bush's signing of the No Child Left Behind Act (2001) represented a quantum leap in the high–stakes testing movement. Also known as the Elementary and Secondary Education Act (ESEA), this law mandates that in return for federal education funds, all states must develop accountability systems to determine whether students are meeting standards. Local and statewide departments of education have generally equated standards and accountability systems with standardized tests and high–stakes testing.

Conspicuously absent from the high–stakes testing education reform movement has been a focus on broader areas of educational equity. Thus, while school districts across the country have been placing a stronger emphasis on high–stakes testing, little attention has been paid to addressing the disparities between white students and students of color in various measures of educational success, often referred to as the achievement gap. To the extent that it is addressed, the achievement gap is often dealt with exclusively in the context of student performance on high–stakes tests. In the meantime, many of the affirmative action and desegregation programs established in the 1970s have begun to be dismantled.

While the trends toward high–stakes testing and away from broader areas of educational equity has taken place nationwide, this chapter focuses exclusively on the Boston public school system (BPS). Beyond what can be learned about issues of education reform and educational equity in Boston, the BPS serves as a model for the impact of the high–stakes testing education reform movement on equity in public schools. The BPS is an example of a school system that has both embraced the notion of high–stakes testing and been praised as a national model of successful education reform. On April 30, 2003, the Broad Foundation announced, for the second consecutive year, that the Boston public school district had been selected as a national finalist for the Broad Award. This was for its success in improving student educational achievement and closing the achievement gap. In November 2003, the national organization, Education Trust, announced that the Boston public school district was one of 20 schools and school districts nationwide to be honored with its "Dispelling the Myth" award for improving student achievement and reducing gaps between groups of students. Yet, while school department officials point to higher daily attendance rates and increasing test scores as evidence of improvement, critics point to consistently poor academic achievement of black, Hispanic, limited English proficient, and low-income students as evidence of shortcomings in the Boston public school system.

In this chapter, several areas of educational achievement are analyzed with particular focus on the disparities of performance for black and Hispanic students in comparison to white and Asian students. The goals and objectives that BPS administration has set regarding the achievement gap are presented and reviewed with respect to how well the BPS has done in meeting these goals. In addition, disparities in areas that are not the focus of the BPS administration are also reviewed. Disparities between the educational outcomes of students are found to begin at the elementary school level, continue through middle and high school, and ultimately manifest themselves in what students decide to do after high school graduation.

## Sources of Data

The information in this chapter is based largely upon data produced by Boston's public school system. In some cases, data used in this chapter comes from public reports, and in other cases data was obtained from tally sheets. Other sources of data used in this chapter include the Boston Redevelopment Authority, the Boston Private Industry Council, and the Gastón Institute at the University of Massachusetts, Boston, the Massachusetts Department of Education, Northeastern University, and the Steppingstone Foundation. The author has attempted to present the most recent data possible; however, in some cases the most recent data has not been made public.

## Demographics of the Boston Public Schools

The Boston public school system is a moderately sized urban school district consisting of 136 schools. This number includes 6 early learning centers, 70 elementary schools (grades K–5), 9 elementary/middle schools (grades K–8), 20 middle schools (grades 6–8), 1 middle/high school (grades 6–12), 19 regular high schools (grades 9–12), 3 exam schools (grades 7–12), 3 special education schools (grades K–12), and 5 non-diploma granting special programs. Of the approximately 82,300 school–age children in Boston, about 75% (62,400 students) attend a Boston public school (Boston Public Schools, 2002n). The remaining 25% of school–age students in Boston attend private/parochial, public charter, private special education, or public schools in other cities through the METCO program. Of those students enrolled in the Boston public schools, 62% are eligible for free lunch and another 9% are eligible for reduced–price lunch (Boston Public Schools, 2002n).

Like many other urban school districts in the United States, many of the students in the Boston public schools are students of color. The racial/ethnic makeup of Boston's youth and students attending the Boston public schools are shown below in Table 1.

**Table 1**
**Racial/Ethnic Makeup of Boston's Youth and BPS Students**

| Race/Ethnicity | Boston's Youth Population | Students Attending the Boston Public Schools |
|---|---|---|
| BLACK | 37% | 48% |
| HISPANIC | 24% | 28% |
| ASIAN | 7% | 9% |
| WHITE | 25% | 15% |
| OTHER | 6% | <1% |

Sources:
1. Liu et al., 2001, p. 3.
2. Boston Public Schools, 2002c.

## Who Runs the Boston Public Schools?

While both the population of the city's youth and the students in the BPS are predominately children of color, this racial and ethnic makeup is not reflected among BPS teachers nor is it reflected among those who direct the schools. As shown in Table 2, BPS teachers and administrators are predominantly white.

Table 2

Racial/Ethnic Makeup of Students, Teachers, and Administrators in the BPS

| Race/Ethnicity | Students | Teachers | Administrators |
|---|---|---|---|
| BLACK | 48% | 26% | 28% |
| HISPANIC | 28% | 9% | 7% |
| ASIAN | 9% | 4% | 2% |
| WHITE | 15% | 61% | 62% |

Source: Boston Public Schools, 2002n.

Among those who set general policy and direct the running of the school system overall (the BPS administration), the racial and ethnic makeup is even less representative of the student population. The superintendent of the Boston public schools, the majority of the superintendent's senior leadership team, and the majority of the entire BPS leadership team—including the chief operating officer, the chief of staff, the director of curriculum development, the director of the budget, the director of special education, the director of integrated student services, the director of human resources, and the director of facilities—are all white. In addition, the BPS ombudsperson, the education advisor, and the mayor, who appoints all school committee members, also are all white. Of the seven members of the Boston school committee, three are black, one is Hispanic, and three are white.

At the school level, parents have limited input into decision making through School Site Councils. However, while School Site Councils provide a means for parental input into decision making at individual schools, these bodies have no role in system wide decision making. The public is permitted to make brief statements (1 to 3 minutes) at the beginning of school committee meetings. However, there is no formal structure that allows for parents, students, teachers, school administrators, and community members to participate in centralized decision making on a regular basis.

## "Education Reform" in the Boston Public Schools

### The Move Toward High–Stakes Testing

In Boston, a significant move toward adoption of conservative education policy took in the early 1990s with the replacement of the elected school committee by an appointed body. While characteristic of conservative political ideology, this change took place under a Democrat, Mayor Raymond Flynn. The trend toward conservative education policy continued under another Democrat, Mayor Thomas Menino (who campaigned as the "Education Mayor") and his newly appointed superintendent of public schools, Thomas Payzant.

Shortly after he was appointed superintendent, Payzant began articulating a new paradigm for education reform. Payzant and the top administrators of the BPS implemented a program of standardized testing as a means of evaluating the success of education reform in Boston. Starting in May 1996, the BPS began testing students in grades 3, 5–7, 9, and 11 using the standardized Stanford 9 Assessment tests in Reading and Math. In August 1996, when the Boston school committee released its education reform program *Focus on Children*, standardized tests were described as a form of assessment in the interim. Rather than promoting high–stakes testing, *Focus on Children* stated: "Over time the Boston Public Schools assessment system will incorporate multiple measures of academic assessment with an increased emphasis on using performance assessments" (Boston Public Schools, 1996, p. 19).

In the initial stages of Boston's education reform program, standardized testing did not take on a high–stakes nature. However, as a national movement began to build around the paradigm of high–stakes testing, Boston's schools began moving in this direction. In 1997, the state mandated the use of the *Massachusetts Comprehensive Assessment System* (MCAS) test with the high–stakes requirement that students pass both the 10th grade English and Math sections in order to be eligible to receive a high school diploma. The next year, without any public involvement or debate, the BPS administration abandoned the goal of instituting multiple assessments of student performance and adopted a new promotion policy in which standardized tests took on a high–stakes nature for students in grades 2, 3, 5–9, and 12. According to this policy, students failing to pass specified course or testing requirements face grade retention, or the need to attend a summer transition program. Since the year 2000, several thousand students in the BPS have been retained (not promoted) due to their inability to score above specified levels on standardized tests.

Boston's new promotion policy mandated, beginning with the class of 2003, that students in grade 12 are required to have passed both the English Language Arts and Math sections of the 10th grade MCAS test in order to be eligible to receive a high school diploma. Students who fail the test in the 10th grade have three opportunities to retake the MCAS tests before their graduation deadline. In addition to these promotion requirements, the school committee put into practice an attendance requirement according to which, students who have three or more unexcused absences a term or 12 or more unexcused absences a year, cannot be promoted. In June 2003, hundreds of students who had passed all other graduation requirements were prohibited from receiving a high school diploma because they had failed to pass both the English Language Arts and Math sections of the MCAS test.

While the MCAS graduation requirement was established by the state, Boston's superintendent of public schools has given strong public support to the use of the MCAS. Given the influence Boston has in state politics and the fact that the BPS is the largest school district in the state, the support Boston's superintendent has given to this graduation requirement has been influential in ensuring the successful implementation of the MCAS graduation requirement.

A further step in the Boston public school system's move toward the high–stakes testing paradigm of education reform was the adoption of *Focus on Children 2* in April 2001. As opposed to the 1996 *Focus on Children,* which identified standardized tests as a means of assessment in the interim, *Focus on Children 2* emphasizes "high standards" as aligned with the high–stakes MCAS test.

## The Elimination of Affirmative Action/Desegregation Programs

During the same period that the top administration of the Boston public schools was developing its education reform program based on a high–stakes testing paradigm, the school committee voted to end several policies designed to eliminate segregation and promote diversity and equity. These policies resulted from the June 21, 1974 findings by Federal Judge Wendell Arthur Garrity when he decreed that the Boston public schools were unconstitutionally segregated. To remedy this segregation, Judge Garrity imposed student assignment guidelines designed to desegregate the schools, including a provision to ensure diversity in the enrollment of students at the city's elementary, middle, and comprehensive high schools, and a provision to ensure that 35% of the invitations to the city's exam schools be awarded to qualified black and Hispanic applicants.

The first policy to be changed by the school committee was the exam school admissions policy. Boston has three elite exam schools. These schools are the most academically rigorous in the city. Enrollment in these schools is by invitation only. Students must apply for admission to these schools and are chosen based upon their grades and their performance on a standardized entrance examination. Following Judge Garrity's 1974 ruling, 35% of the invitations to Boston's exam schools were awarded to qualified black and Hispanic applicants. On August 11, 1995, a lawsuit was filed on behalf of Julia McLaughlin against the Boston school committee alleging that as a result of the city's exam school admissions policy she, a white student, was unjustly denied admission to Boston Latin School. After convening a task force to study exam school admissions, on December 18, 1996, the Boston school committee adopted a two–tier admissions policy. According to this policy, for one half of the available seats, students would be invited solely based on their rank. The rank was determined by a combination of the student's score on the school's entrance exam and the student's 6th grade GPA. For the second half of the available seats, students from the various racial or ethnic groups (black, Hispanic, white, Asian, and Native American) were invited according to the proportion of applicants from the particular racial or ethnic group scoring in the top 50th percentile on the exam school entrance examination. The school committee also voted to invite to the 9th grade at Boston Latin School (BLS) and Boston Latin Academy (BLA) approximately 300 white and Asian students who had not been invited for the 1995–96 and 1996–97 school years, but would have been if the admissions policy were based solely on rank.

As a result of the changes to exam school admissions policy the McLaughlin suit was ruled mute. However, on August 25, 1997, a second lawsuit was filed against the Boston school committee on behalf of Sarah Wessman. This new lawsuit alleged that Sarah Wessman was unjustly denied admission to Boston Latin School as result of the school system's policy in which race was used as a factor in the admissions of 50% of the students invited to exam schools. In May, 1998, Federal District Court Judge Tauro ruled against Wessman. On November 19, 1998, the First Circuit Court of Appeals held that the exam school admissions policy was unconstitutional. On December 10, 1998, the school committee voted to invite students to exam schools solely based on their rank. A number of recommendations were presented to the school committee during public hearings, including recommendations that income or enrollment in public school be used as a factor in determining rank for exam school admissions and the recommendation that native–language examinations be given to students for whom English is not the first language. Nonetheless, on November 10, 1999, the school committee adopted an exam school admissions policy based solely on GPA (based on grades from the 6th grade and the latter-half of the 5th grade) and student scores on the standardized Independent Secondary Entrance Examination (ISEE) test.

As can be seen in Graphs 1 and 2, for each of the exam schools, the percentages of black and Hispanic students invited were less than the percentages of students in the population of public school students the previous school year (the year which race was a determinate for exam school admissions). The greatest disparity between the percentage of black and Hispanic invitees and the percentages of students in the public school population was for the Boston Latin School, Boston's top elite exam school. The BPS administration presently has not set any goals regarding increasing the percentages of black and Hispanic students invited to exam schools.

**Graph 1**

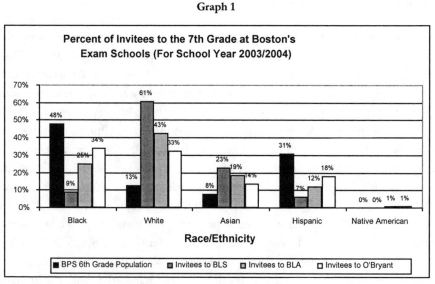

Sources: Boston Public Schools, 2002c, 2003e.

**Graph 2**

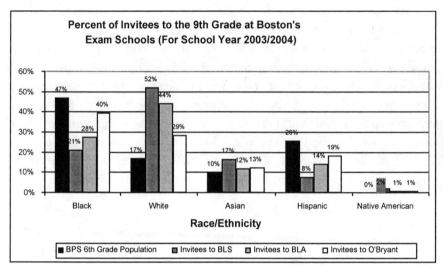

Percent of Invitees to the 9th Grade at Boston's
Exam Schools (For School Year 2003/2004)

Sources: Boston Public Schools, 2002c, 2003e.

The second policy to be changed by the school committee was the admissions policy for Advanced Work Classes. The Advanced Work Class (AWC) program was designed for students in the 4th through 6th grades, who were deemed academically talented. AWC curriculum was designed to be more rigorous than the regular education program, and class sizes have been kept significantly smaller than in the regular education program. Prior to February 3, 1999, all students scoring at levels 3 or 4 on the Stanford 9 test were deemed to be qualified for admissions to AWC. Invitations were awarded to 1,000 students in the qualified applicant pool based on guidelines for maintaining racial and ethnic diversity. Although no specific lawsuit was pending against the BPS, on February 3, 1999, the school committee voted to invite to AWC the top–scoring 1,000 students, of every grade level, in order of their Stanford 9 scores. As a result of the change in AWC admissions policy, a number of black and Hispanic students who scored at level 3 on the Stanford 9 and might have previously been invited to AWC were denied admission. By the present AWC admissions policy, it is possible that even students who score at level 4 on the Stanford 9 test could be denied admissions to AWC if 1,000 students had higher test scores. Prior to and during the February 3, 1999 school committee meeting, several community members suggested alternative AWC admissions policies and some advocated for expanding the AWC program to all students scoring at levels 3 and 4 on the Stanford 9. The superintendent and school committee rejected all alternative proposals. AWC was available for students enrolled in the Spanish bilingual education programs; these students were given equivalent standardized tests in Spanish. However, with the fall 2002 passage of the *Unz Initiative*, bilingual education programs—including AWC classes offered in Spanish—are slated to be eliminated by school year 2003–04.

Graph 3 shows that in recent years the percentages of black and Hispanic students invited to Advanced Work Classes (AWC) with respect to their overall populations in grades 3, 4, and 5 have been at their lowest points. The BPS administration presently has not set any goals regarding increasing the percentages of black and Hispanic students invited to the AWC.

**Graph 3**

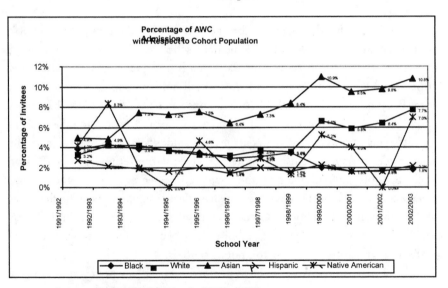

Sources: Boston Public Schools, 2002b, 2002h.

The third policy changed by the school committee was the assignment process for elementary, middle, and non-exam high schools. In 1987, the First Circuit Court of Appeals vacated Judge Garrity's order regarding the school assignment process. Mayor Flynn hired Charles Willie and Michael Alves of Harvard University to work with BPS administrators in developing a new school assignment process. On February 27, 1988, following public hearings, the school committee adopted this "Controlled Choice" assignment policy. By this policy, parents would submit their top choices for schools to the school department. The particular school to which a student was assigned was dependent upon a number of factors including the parent's top choices, where the child lives (the neighborhood and corresponding school zone), whether the student has siblings in that school, and the school's racial and ethnic mix. In June 1999, a group called Boston's Children First sued the BPS on the grounds that the school assignment process was unfair toward white students. On November 10, 1999, before the Childrens First suit had been litigated in court, the school committee voted to remove all considerations of race from school assignment decisions. In addition, the new school assignment plan instituted a policy by which 50% of seats available in a particular school would be set aside for students who choose schools within a region defined as their "walk zone." Students who do not live in the walk zone of any school are given priority for remaining seats.

A study of the demographic breakdown in the Boston public schools reveals that in 37% of Boston's elementary schools, 37.5% of Boston's K–8 schools, and 43% of Boston's middle schools the percentage of black and Hispanic students (with respect to the overall student population) is 90% or more (Boston Public Schools, 2002i). Moreover, in 63% of Boston's elementary schools, 75% of Boston's K–8 schools, and 62% of Boston's middle schools the difference between the percentages of students at the school and the system-wide average is 20% or more for at least one ethnic group (Boston Public Schools, 2002i). Despite the increased re-segregation of the Boston public schools, Mayor Thomas Menino has given public support to the drive for "neighborhood" schools. Given the degree of segregation in Boston's neighborhoods, such a change to admissions policy would likely lead to even greater re-segregation in the Boston public schools.

School department officials have justified their recent policy shifts on the ground that ending desegregation programs was necessitated by several lawsuits filled in the middle to late 1990s on behalf of white litigants against the Boston school committee. However, the courts ruled against a particular component BPS policy in only one such lawsuit, *Wessman vs. Boston School Committee.* The new policies adopted by the school committee lack any provisions specifically targeting the promotion of equity among traditionally under-performing students and were not mandated by the courts. Furthermore, the BPS policy program for 2001–2006 *Focus on Children 2* provides a very clear example of the shift on the part of the school district's leadership toward emphasizing high–stakes testing and moving away from broader areas of educational equity. The document, an articulation of the framework for education reform in the BPS, identifies the "Unifying Goal of the BPS" to "[a]ccelerate the continuous improvement of teaching and learning to enable all students to meet high standards" (Boston Public Schools, 2001a, p. 6). The document goes on to define these "high standards" in terms of performance on high–stakes standardized tests. Throughout the entire 23–page document there are only two references to closing the achievement gap. What is clear from the list of accomplishments and the goal that has been identified in *Focus on Children 2* is the focus on standardized test scores and high–stakes testing; what is lacking is any reference of progress toward eliminating disparities in the educational outcomes of black and Hispanic students in comparison to white students, and disparities in the educational outcomes of students identified as limited English proficient and low income.

## How Has the BPS Addressed the Achievement Gap?

Over the last several decades, researchers have undertaken numerous studies to characterize, quantify, and analyze the disparity between the performance of black and Hispanic students in comparison to white students on standardized tests. The poor performance of students from low-income families on standardized tests has also been well researched. While the initial articulation of Boston's new education reform program, Focus on Children, stated that the primary goal of the BPS was to "[i]mprove teaching and learning to enable all students to achieve high standards of performance," the achievement gap was not directly addressed (Boston Public School, 2001a, p. 15). In 1998, around the time that the BPS administration was adopting a high–stakes testing program and changing the exam school admissions policy, the superintendent issued a system–wide goal to close the achievement gap by school year 2002–03 to ensure that every racial group is within 5 percentage points of the highest-scoring racial group in standardized tests (Boston Public Schools, 1998a).

After the articulation of his goal for closing the achievement gap, the superintendent began identifying specific goals for the percentages of students passing standardized tests. These goals appear in a document that has been produced yearly, titled "Superintendent's Goals and Objectives." Since fall 1998, goals for 2003, as well as yearly objectives for the percentages of students passing standardized tests, have been included in this document. For the first several years following the articulation of the 2003 goal for closing the achievement gap, the superintendent's objectives have included the following (Boston Public Schools, 2000c, p. 55):

1.  By school year 2002–03, the achievement gap will be reduced so that 99% of students in every racial group (Asian, black, Hispanic, white) who have been in the Boston Public Schools for a minimum of 3 consecutive years will achieve at levels 2–4 on the Stanford 9 Multiple Choice Achievement tests;

2.  By school year 2002–03, the achievement gap will be reduced so that 99% of the students in every racial group (Asian, black, Hispanic, white) who have been in the Boston Public Schools for a minimum of 3 consecutive years will achieve at levels 2–4 on the Massachusetts Comprehensive Assessment System (MCAS).

Another goal for eliminating disparities in student performance on standardized tests was presented in the report by the BPS Office of Research, Assessment, and Evaluation, titled *Reducing the Racial/Ethnic Gap—Analysis of Performance on the MCAS by Racial/Ethnic Group, May 1998 to May 1999.* This report stated the goal of increasing the percentages of students who score at levels 3–4 on the MCAS to 60% of the students in each racial/ethnic group by school year 2002–03 as another of the superintendent's goals (Boston Public Schools, 2000d, p.  ).

Following the articulation of the superintendent's goal to close the achievement gap by school year 2002–03, Tim Knowles, deputy superintendent, presented an "Action Plan for Closing the Achievement Gap in the Boston Public Schools" (Boston Public Schools, 2000b). This memorandum presented various measures that would be taken in the BPS in order to accomplish the superintendent's goals for eliminating the achievement gap. The plan includes measures addressing policy, data analysis, academic support and acceleration, unified students services, professional development for school leaders, professional development for teachers and paraprofessionals, and parent and community engagement.[1] While the plan presented by Deputy Superintendent Knowles is comprehensive, the program contains very broad measures that are not particularly focused upon eliminating disparities in educational achievement. The only direct references to closing the achievement gap are in the section on data and in the section on professional development for school leaders. However, these references are only in regard to student achievement on the Stanford 9 and MCAS tests. Even if the action plan for closing the achievement gap were to be fully implemented, it is not clear that the BPS would achieve the limited goals that the superintendent set forth.

As Boston's education reform program has grown to take on a more high–stakes nature, and as programs to promote diversity and equity have been dismantled, the manner in which school department officials have addressed the achievement gap has also changed. In *Focus on Children 2*, which elucidates education reform in the BPS for 2001 through 2006, the achievement gap is only referred to twice in the entire 23 page document. In the first reference, it is mentioned that "[t]he instructional focus on literacy and mathematics is intended to improve student achievement across the board and help close the achievement gap" (Boston Public Schools, 2001a, p. 10). The second reference states:

> Boston will take a more active role in encouraging the sharing of best practices within and between schools. The district will identify Effective Practice Schools based on both qualitative data (gathered from school visits) and quantitative data (Stanford 9 and MCAS results, especially progress in closing the achievement gap). (Boston Public Schools, 2001a, p. 15)

While identifying effective practice schools is a step in the right direction, there is no specific articulation of a framework to provide guidelines or any timeline by which to eliminate disparities in students' educational achievement.

Since the articulation of the goal to close the achievement gap by 2003, school department officials have directly addressed the achievement gap through two series of public forums. The first forum was held in 1999. While community concerns were aired, no policy regarding the achievement gap came out of this forum. Two school committee members sponsored another series of forums on the achievement gap during the 2002–03 academic school year. During this set of forums, presentations by school department officials focused on data on student performance on standardized tests. As a result of this second forum series, the school committee members who sponsored the forum series produced a document titled "Report on Boston School Committee Community Forum Series: Closing the Achievement Gap." With respect to how the BPS could address the achievement gap, the report listed three priorities: professional staff development, academic support for failing students, and extra supports beyond the classroom. Five other items were also listed as priorities for consideration and action including identification of *pro bono* resources to aid communication between the schools and families, installment of a parent outreach staff position at each school, connecting staff performance assessment with student academic results, development and use of a protocol for assessing school climate, collection and use of data regarding the achievement gap.

While the report represents an initiative on the part of a few members of the school committee, it has several shortcomings. In the first place, there is a prevailing notion among many in the schools that the achievement gap only refers to differences in standardized test scores. While a more encompassing definition of the achievement gap can be implied from the document, the report does not directly articulate a definition of achievement gap. Second, none of these suggestions in the report call for any changes in BPS policy regarding student assignment to schools or special programs. Finally, the report sets neither goals nor a timeline for closing the achievement gap. By the end of the 2002–03 academic school year, the report was presented to the school committee but had not been adopted as official policy.

A more dramatic change to the goals for closing the achievement gap took place as the date that the superintendent set for closing the achievement gap arrived. While previously setting the target pass rate at 99% for all students, the *Superintendent's Goals and Objectives* now sets the target pass rate for black and Hispanic seniors at 80% to 90% for the English MCAS tests and 70% to 80% for the Math MCAS, while the target scores for the percentages of white and Asian seniors passing the English and Math MCAS tests are 95% to 100% (Boston Public Schools, 2002m). Furthermore, the BPS administration has completely abandoned the goal of closing the achievement gap so that every racial group is within 5 percentage points of the highest scoring racial group on standardized tests by the year 2003.

Several observations can be made regarding the efforts of the BPS administration for eliminating disparities in educational achievement. In the first place, the goals that have been articulated focus exclusively on the performance of students from various racial/ethnic groups on the Stanford 9 multiple–choice tests and the MCAS tests. No goals have been set for the elimination of disparities in educational achievement in any other areas. In the second place, there is a greater focus upon ensuring that students do not fail these tests, as opposed to ensuring that students excel on these tests. In the third place, the BPS administration has no concrete plan of action for eliminating disparities in educational achievement, and they have established no accountability system to ensure that the system–wide goals and objectives regarding the elimination of disparities in educational achievement are met. The fact that when the date that the superintendent set for closing the achievement gap arrived (June 2003) the BPS administration abandoned the goal, calls into question the commitment of the BPS administration toward the elimination of disparities in educational achievement.

### Differing Views on Student Performance on Standardized Tests

#### How Does the School Department Present Student Performance on Standardized Tests?

Given the fact that the top administration of the Boston public schools has adopted "Standards–Based Reform" and pointed to student performance on standardized tests as one of the key indicators of educational success, it begs the question: "How have students in the BPS been performing on standardized tests?" In their public comments, school department officials have generally focused upon the favorable trends in student test scores. These favorable reports are also prominent in Focus on Children 2 where the school department notes that (Boston Public Schools, 2001a, p. 5):

- From 1997 to 2000, the percentage of students scoring in the upper three performance levels of the Stanford 9 test has increased steadily—in reading from 75% to 81%, and in mathematics from 52% to 63%. The percentage of students in the lowest scoring level has decreased in every grade;
- Since 1998, Boston's MCAS results have improved across all grades and subject areas. BPS gains exceeded statewide gains in every grade and subject, except grade 8 in reading and science, where Boston and state gains are equal.

Following the release of the results of the December 2002 retest of the MCAS test, the March 12, 2003 *BPS in the News* contained the following glowing commentary regarding student performance on standardized tests (Boston Public Schools, 2003d, p. 1):

- In high schools throughout the city, Boston's strategies to set and reach high standards are proving successful;
- Results demonstrate that the district's targeted strategies—including intensive focus on literacy and mathematics and additional academic support programs for students at greatest risk of failure—have been successful and should be accelerated;
- BPS made progress in closing the racial achievement gap, with black and Latino students making gains at a greater rate than in previous years.

## Disparate Performance on Stanford 9 and MCAS Tests

While the BPS administration has tended to present the improvement in Stanford 9 and MCAS scores, further inspection of student performance on these tests reveals that while student scores have improved, it is still the case that at every grade level, on both the Stanford 9 and MCAS tests, black and Hispanic students continue to perform worse than white and Asian students. In particular, blacks and Hispanics have greater percentages who fail and smaller percentages whose scores are proficient enough to advance. Tables 3 through 6 below show the percentages of students who failed the Stanford 9 multiple choice and MCAS tests given during the spring of 2001.

Table 3

**Percentage of Students Failing the Reading Section of the Stanford 9 Multiple–Choice Tests (Spring 2001)**

| GRADE | WHITE | ASIAN | BLACK | HISPANIC |
|-------|-------|-------|-------|----------|
| 3 | 14 | 8 | 27 | 26 |
| 5 | 9 | 10 | 26 | 27 |
| 6 | 12 | 13 | 29 | 28 |
| 7 | 10 | 14 | 26 | 33 |
| 8 | 6 | 7 | 22 | 27 |
| 9 | 13 | 17 | 33 | 34 |
| 11 | 15 | 31 | 48 | 53 |

Source: Boston Public Schools, 2001c, p. 11.

Table 4

**Percentage of Students Failing the Math Section of the Stanford 9 Multiple–Choice Tests (Spring 2001)**

| GRADE | WHITE | ASIAN | BLACK | HISPANIC |
|-------|-------|-------|-------|----------|
| 3 | 13 | 2 | 28 | 22 |
| 5 | 21 | 9 | 44 | 40 |
| 6 | 27 | 11 | 55 | 51 |
| 7 | 23 | 15 | 58 | 59 |
| 8 | 18 | 8 | 53 | 52 |
| 9 | 20 | 11 | 50 | 47 |
| 11 | 37 | 37 | 86 | 86 |

Source: Boston Public Schools, 2001c, p. 13.

### Table 5
### Percentage of Students Failing the English Language Arts Section of the MCAS Tests (Spring 2001)

| GRADE | WHITE | ASIAN | BLACK | HISPANIC |
|-------|-------|-------|-------|----------|
| 3 | 10 | 7 | 21 | 24 |
| 4 | 16 | 14 | 31 | 37 |
| 7 | 14 | 11 | 32 | 21 |
| 8 | 9 | 6 | 25 | 24 |
| 10 | 17 | 21 | 50 | 50 |

Source: Boston Public Schools, 2001b, pp. 13–15.

### Table 6
### Percentage of Students Failing the Math Section of the MCAS Test (Spring 2001)

| GRADE | WHITE | ASIAN | BLACK | HISPANIC |
|-------|-------|-------|-------|----------|
| 4 | 20 | 13 | 48 | 45 |
| 6 | 40 | 20 | 72 | 67 |
| 8 | 27 | 16 | 66 | 60 |
| 10 | 19 | 8 | 59 | 57 |

Source: Boston Public Schools, 2001b, pp. 13–15.

As can be seen in Tables 3 through 6, in most cases students performed more poorly on the Math section of the tests than on the Reading/English Language Arts section. At every grade level, for both the Reading/English Language Arts and Math sections, the percentages of black and Hispanic students failing the Stanford 9 tests was much greater than the percentages of white and Asian students failing the tests.

During the first year that students were required meet the MCAS graduation requirement, Boston public school officials released data regarding the percentages of students passing the MCAS retest offered in December, 2003. This was the last opportunity for students from the class of 2003 to pass the MCAS test in time to be eligible to graduate with the rest of their class in June. In their statements to the public, school department officials pointed to the high pass rate (78%) as a measure of the success of Boston's education reform program. However, the pass rates determined by the school department were calculated based on the number of students from the class of 2003 who were still enrolled as seniors in the BPS in the fall of 2002. Such statistics ignore students who have dropped out of school or who were retained in grade. MCAS pass rates are much smaller when based upon the 9th grade enrollment of the class of 2003. Table 7 shows the MCAS pass rates for class of 2003 as reported by the school department and Table 8 shows the MCAS passing rates calculated using the 9th grade enrollment for the class of 2003.

Table 7
MCAS Pass Rate for the Class of 2003

| Race/Ethnicity | Pass Rate as Reported by the BPS | Pass Rated as Determined from 9th Grade Enrollment |
|---|---|---|
| BLACK | 76% | 51% |
| WHITE | 86% | 58% |
| ASIAN | 94% | 84% |
| HISPANIC | 71% | 42% |

Source: Boston Public Schools, 2003b, pp. 3–5.

Table 8
MCAS Pass Rate for the Class of 2003

| Race/ Ethnicity | Seniors who Passed MCAS | Early Grad- uates | Moved or Transfer- red to Other Schools | Seniors Who Failed MCAS | Students Retained in Grade | Drop- outs | Other |
|---|---|---|---|---|---|---|---|
| BLACK | 38.2% | 1.2% | 11.9% | 9.2% | 13.8% | 23.8% | 1.9% |
| WHITE | 53.5% | 1.1% | 14.4% | 4.8% | 6.3% | 19.0% | 0.8% |
| ASIAN | 68.3% | 0.0% | 12.1% | 3.2% | 6.9% | 8.6% | 0.9% |
| HISPANIC | 34.2% | 1.0% | 19.7% | 9.4% | 10.0% | 24.8% | 0.9% |

Source: Boston Public Schools, 2003c.

The data presented in Table 8 shows that the MCAS passing rate for the class of 2003 was less than 70% for all racial and ethnic groups. The MCAS passing rates for black and Hispanic students (38.2% and 34.2%, respectively) were significantly less than those of white and Asian students.

Tables 9 through 12 show the percentages of students scoring proficient to advance on the Stanford 9 multiple–choice and MCAS tests given during the spring of 2001. According to BPS policy, students must score at these levels on the Stanford 9 tests in order to be eligible for special academic programs such as Advanced Work Classes and exam school preparation programs such as the "Best You Can Be" program.

**Table 9**

**Percentage of Students Scoring Proficient to Advanced on the Reading Section of the Stanford 9 Multiple–Choice Tests (Spring 2001)**

| GRADE | WHITE | ASIAN | BLACK | HISPANIC |
|-------|-------|-------|-------|----------|
| 3 | 59 | 58 | 29 | 30 |
| 5 | 48 | 48 | 21 | 19 |
| 6 | 44 | 44 | 19 | 17 |
| 7 | 61 | 45 | 21 | 16 |
| 8 | 69 | 50 | 28 | 23 |
| 9 | 60 | 47 | 22 | 21 |
| 11 | 61 | 33 | 15 | 15 |

Source: Boston Public Schools, 2001c, p. 11.

**Table 10**

**Percent of Students Scoring Proficient to Advanced on the Math Section of the Stanford 9 Multiple–Choice Tests (Spring 2001)**

| GRADE | WHITE | ASIAN | BLACK | HISPANIC |
|-------|-------|-------|-------|----------|
| 3 | 54 | 72 | 26 | 30 |
| 5 | 48 | 67 | 19 | 19 |
| 6 | 43 | 70 | 15 | 18 |
| 7 | 46 | 60 | 12 | 11 |
| 8 | 56 | 69 | 14 | 14 |
| 9 | 49 | 61 | 11 | 16 |
| 11 | 38 | 34 | 4 | 7 |

Source: Boston Public Schools, 2001c, p. 13.

**Table 11**

**Percent of Students Scoring Proficient to Advanced on the English Language Arts Section of the MCAS Tests (Spring 2001)**

| GRADE | WHITE | ASIAN | BLACK | HISPANIC |
|-------|-------|-------|-------|----------|
| 3 | 52 | 44 | 26 | 24 |
| 4 | 43 | 49 | 17 | 18 |
| 7 | 59 | 54 | 24 | 23 |
| 8 | 69 | 69 | 31 | 32 |
| 10 | 63 | 48 | 19 | 16 |

Source: Boston Public Schools, 2001b, pp. 13–15.

Table 12

Percent of Students Scoring Proficient to Advanced on the Math Section of the MCAS
Tests (Spring 2001)

| GRADE | WHITE | ASIAN | BLACK | HISPANIC |
|---|---|---|---|---|
| 4 | 34 | 44 | 8 | 9 |
| 6 | 30 | 51 | 6 | 9 |
| 8 | 47 | 59 | 8 | 9 |
| 10 | 61 | 70 | 14 | 12 |

Source: Boston Public Schools, 2001b, pp. 13–15.

As can be seen in the data shown in Tables 9 through 12, in most cases lower percentages of students performed proficient to advanced on the Math section of the tests than on the Reading/English Language Arts section. In addition, at every grade level, for both the Reading/English Language Arts and Math sections of the tests, the percentages of black and Hispanic students scoring proficient to advanced was much greater than the percentages of white and Asian students scoring proficient to advanced.

## How Has the BPS Performed in Meeting Its Yearly Goals for Closing the Achievement Gap?

For the last several years, the school department has made public the superintendent's goals for closing the achievement gap. As mentioned above, these goals refer only to the percentages of students passing the Stanford 9 and MCAS tests. In school department presentations of these goals, the percentages of students passing the test the previous year are presented alongside the goals for the present year. From this form of presentation, it is not possible to gauge whether or not the superintendent's goals have been met. In addition, since the 2000–01 school year, the BPS administration has not made public much data on Stanford 9 test results. Table 13 below shows the progress made meeting the superintendents yearly goals for percentages of students passing the MCAS tests. In order to determine whether or not the superintendent's yearly goals were met, the 2000–01 goals for students passing the MCAS tests were compared to actual results for the MCAS.

Table 13

**Progress in Meeting Yearly Superintendent's Yearly Goals Regarding Percentages of Students Passing MCAS Tests (Spring 2001)**

| | | ELA | | | Math | | |
|---|---|---|---|---|---|---|---|
| Grade Level | Race/ Ethnicity | Goal | Actual | Difference | Goal | Actual | Difference |
| ELEMENTARY | | | | | | | |
| | BLACK | 74% | 69% | -5% | 64% | 52% | -12% |
| | WHITE | 86% | 84% | -2% | 82% | 84% | 2% |
| | ASIAN | 92% | 86% | -6% | 94% | 86% | -8% |
| | HISPANIC | 73% | 63% | -10% | 66% | 63% | -3% |
| | | | | | | | |
| MIDDLE | | | | | | | |
| | BLACK | 80% | 75% | -5% | 48% | 34% | -14% |
| | WHITE | 89% | 91% | 2% | 74% | 73% | -1% |
| | ASIAN | 90% | 94% | 4% | 82% | 84% | 2% |
| | HISPANIC | 77% | 76% | -1% | 49% | 40% | -9% |
| | | | | | | | |
| HIGH | | | | | | | |
| | BLACK | 56% | 50% | -6% | 46% | 41% | -5% |
| | WHITE | 79% | 83% | 4% | 74% | 81% | 7% |
| | ASIAN | 76% | 79% | 3% | 83% | 92% | 9% |
| | HISPANIC | 55% | 50% | -5% | 48% | 43% | -5% |

Sources: Boston Public Schools, 2001b, 2001d.

Table 13 shows that the superintendent's yearly goals for the percentages of white and Asian students passing the MCAS tests were exceeded. For all grade levels, for both the ELA and Math sections of the tests, the superintendent's goals for the percentages of black and Hispanic students passing the Stanford 9 and MCAS tests were not met.

Linear regression analysis was performed on the data for the percentages of students, at each grade level, failing the Stanford 9 and MCAS tests over the last several years. For this analysis Stanford 9 data from spring 1997 to spring 2000 and MCAS data from spring 1998 to spring 2001 was used. Tables 14 and 15 show the rate of increase in the percentages of students passing the Stanford 9 and MCAS tests and the expected year by which 99% of students can be expected to pass these tests.

Table 14

Year by which 99% of Students Can Be Expected to Pass the Stanford 9 Tests

| | | Reading | | Math | |
|---|---|---|---|---|---|
| Grade Level | Race/ Ethnicity | Increase in Percent of Students Passing per Year | Expected Year by which 99% of Students Pass Stanford 9 | Increase in Percent of Students Passing per Year | Expected Year by which 99% of Students Pass Stanford 9 |
| **GRADE 5** | | | | | |
| | BLACK | 0.29 | 2060 | 2.86 | 2012 |
| | WHITE | 0.44 | 2013 | 1.56 | 2009 |
| | ASIAN | -0.19 | Failures Increase | 1.11 | 2004 |
| | HISPANIC | 0.59 | 2030 | 3.09 | 2010 |
| | | | | | |
| **GRADE 6** | | | | | |
| | BLACK | -0.49 | Failures Increase | 2.72 | 2017 |
| | WHITE | -0.18 | Failures Increase | 2.01 | 2011 |
| | ASIAN | 0.7 | 2014 | 2.56 | 2002 |
| | HISPANIC | 1.51 | 2016 | 4.29 | 2010 |
| | | | | | |
| **GRADE 7** | | | | | |
| | BLACK | -0.29 | Failures Increase | 3 | 2018 |
| | WHITE | 0.37 | 2010 | 1.34 | 2015 |
| | ASIAN | 3.54 | 2002 | 2.01 | 2004 |
| | HISPANIC | 0.9 | 2027 | 2.96 | 2018 |
| | | | | | |
| **GRADE 8** | | | | | |
| | BLACK | 1.75 | 2009 | 5.74 | 2008 |
| | WHITE | 1.03 | 2002 | 3.35 | 2005 |
| | ASIAN | 4.13 | 2002 | 4.83 | 2001 |
| | HISPANIC | 3.2 | 2006 | 5.63 | 2008 |

*Continues on next page*

| | | Reading | | Math | |
|---|---|---|---|---|---|
| Grade Level | Race/ Ethnicity | Increase in Percent of Students Passing per Year | Expected Year by which 99% of Students Pass Stanford 9 | Increase in Percent of Students Passing per Year | Expected Year by which 99% of Students Pass Stanford 9 |
| **GRADE 9** | | | | | |
| | BLACK | 2.98 | 2008 | 8.35 | 2005 |
| | WHITE | 1.92 | 2003 | 5.31 | 2003 |
| | ASIAN | 3.71 | 2004 | 5.88 | 2001 |
| | HISPANIC | 4.17 | 2006 | 9.81 | 2004 |
| **GRADE 11** | | | | | |
| | BLACKBlack | 0.71 | 2062 | 2.57 | 2032 |
| | WHITEWhite | 0.18 | 2071 | 4.45 | 2009 |
| | ASIANAsian | 4.01 | 2007 | 5.5 | 2007 |
| | HISPANICHispanic | 1.87 | 2025 | 2.25 | 2037 |

Table 14—*continued*

Sources:
Boston Public Schools, 1997.
Boston Public Schools, 1998.
Boston Public Schools, 1999.
Boston Public Schools, 2000.

## Table 15

Year by which 99% of Students Can Be Expected to Pass the MCAS Tests

| | | ELA | | Math | |
|---|---|---|---|---|---|
| Grade Level | Race/ Ethnicity | Increase in Percent of Students Passing per Year | Expected Year by which 99% of Students Pass MCAS | Increase in Percent of Students Passing per Year | Expected Year by which 99% of Students Pass MCAS |
| **GRADE 4** | | | | | |
| | BLACK | 3.4 | 2011 | 4.43 | 2013 |
| | WHITE | 3.04 | 2007 | 5.83 | 2005 |
| | ASIAN | 2.94 | 2006 | 3.53 | 2004 |
| | HISPANIC | 1.78 | 2022 | 4.18 | 2013 |

*Continued on next page*

Table 15—*continued*

| GRADE 8 | | | | | |
|---|---|---|---|---|---|
| | BLACK | 2.63 | 2012 | 4.05 | 2019 |
| | WHITE | 3.06 | 2005 | 4.75 | 2008 |
| | ASIAN | 4.57 | 2003 | 4.92 | 2005 |
| | HISPANIC | 6.04 | 2006 | 6.75 | 2011 |
| GRADE 10 | | | | | |
| | BLACK | 4.26 | 2015 | 8.16 | 2010 |
| | WHITE | 4.93 | 2006 | 9.63 | 2004 |
| | ASIAN | 5.09 | 2007 | 11.53 | 2003 |
| | HISPANIC | 4.69 | 2014 | 9.76 | 2008 |

Sources:
Boston Public Schools, 2000d, 2001b.
Massachusetts Department of Education, 2001.

A few positive signs can be seen in Tables 14 and 15. In most cases, from 1997 through 2000, there has been an increasing trend in the percentages of students passing the Stanford 9 tests. In all cases, for all grade levels, and all racial and ethnic groups from 1998 through 2001, there has been an increasing trend in the percentages of students passing the MCAS tests. However, significant disparities are present in the performance of students from various racial and ethnic groups on these tests. Only in the case of Asian students on the grade 8 English Language Arts section of the MCAS and on the grade 10 Math section of the MCAS is the BPS expected to meet the superintendent's goals of increasing the percentages of students passing to 99% by school year 2002–03. On both the English Language Arts and Math sections of the MCAS, the date by which the 99% of white and Asian students pass the test is expected to be significantly earlier than for black and Hispanic students. For black and Hispanic students in the 10th grade, 99% of students are not expected to pass the English Language Arts section of the MCAS until 2014 for Hispanic students and 2015 for black students.

Linear regression analysis was performed on the data for the percentages of students, at each grade level, scoring at the top two levels on the Stanford 9 (1997–2000) and MCAS tests (1998 through spring 2001). Tables 16 and 17 show the rate of increase in the percentages of students scoring at the top two levels and the expected year by which 60% of students can be expected to score at these levels.

Table 16
Year by which 60% of Students Can Be Expected to Score at the Top Two Levels of the
Stanford 9 Tests

| Grade Level | Race/ Ethnicity | Reading | | Math | |
|---|---|---|---|---|---|
| | | Increase in Percent of Students Scoring at Top Two Levels per Year | Expected Year by which 60% of Students Score at Top Two Levels | Increase in Percent of Students Scoring at Top Two Levels per Year | Expected Year by which 60% of Students Score at Top Two Levels |
| **GRADE 5** | | | | | |
| | BLACK | -0.04 | Proficiency Declines | 1.76 | 2021 |
| | WHITE | 0.58 | 2016 | 1.72 | 2007 |
| | ASIAN | 0.69 | 2016 | 5 | Achieved |
| | HISPANIC | 1.71 | 2020 | 2.53 | 2013 |
| | | | | | |
| **GRADE 6** | | | | | |
| | BLACK | 0.55 | 2064 | 2.2 | 2019 |
| | WHITE | -0.28 | Proficiency Declines | 1.17 | 2015 |
| | ASIAN | -0.55 | Proficiency Declines | 2.98 | Achieved |
| | HISPANIC | 0.5 | 2077 | 2.64 | 2015 |
| | | | | | |
| **GRADE 7** | | | | | |
| | BLACK | 0.36 | 2095 | 1.46 | 2032 |
| | WHITE | 0.97 | Achieved | 1.65 | 2005 |
| | ASIAN | 3.97 | 2001 | 3.85 | Achieved |
| | HISPANIC | 1.03 | 2035 | 0.39 | 2120 |
| | | | | | |
| **GRADE 8** | | | | | |
| | BLACK | 1.86 | 2015 | 2.48 | 2017 |
| | WHITE | 2.41 | Achieved | 4.94 | Achieved |
| | ASIAN | 4.22 | 2002 | 7.77 | Achieved |
| | HISPANIC | 0.61 | 2060 | 2.74 | 2015 |

*continued next page*

Table 16—*continued*

| GRADE 9 | | | | | |
|---|---|---|---|---|---|
| | BLACK | 2.17 | 2015 | 4 | 2011 |
| | WHITE | 3.4 | Achieved | 8.6113 | Achieved |
| | ASIAN | 3.87 | 2004 | 11.31 | Achieved |
| | HISPANIC | 2.71 | 2014 | 4.66 | 2009 |
| | | | | | |
| GRADE 11 | | | | | |
| | BLACK | -0.97 | Proficiency Declines | NA | NA |
| | WHITE | 1.4 | Achieved | 1.39 | 2040 |
| | ASIAN | 0.22 | 2123 | 4.95 | 2005 |
| | HISPANIC | 0.72 | 2064 | 6.87 | 2003 |

Sources:

Boston Public Schools, 1997.
Boston Public Schools, 1998.
Boston Public Schools, 1999.
Boston Public Schools, 2000.

**Table 17**

**Year by which 60% of Students Are Expected to Score at the Top Two Levels of the MCAS Tests**

| | | ELA | | Math | |
|---|---|---|---|---|---|
| Grade Level | Race/ Ethnicity | Increase in Percent of Students Scoring at Top Two Levels per Year | Expected Year by which 60% of Students Score Levels 3–4 | Increase in Percent of Students Scoring at Top Two Levels per Year | Expected Year by which 60% of Students Score Levels 3–4 |
| GRADE 4 | | | | | |
| | BLACK | 0.45 | 2127 | 1.55 | 2035 |
| | WHITE | 3.8 | 2012 | 5.25 | 2006 |
| | ASIAN | 1.95 | 2023 | 6.1 | 2003 |
| | HISPANIC | 0.2 | 2290 | 1.75 | 2030 |

*Continued on next page*

Table 17—*continued*

| GRADE 8 | | | | | |
|---------|---|---|---|---|---|
| | BLACK | 2 | 2017 | 0.25 | 2216 |
| | WHITE | 4.1 | Achieved | 3.1 | 2007 |
| | ASIAN | 6.55 | 2001 | 3.6 | 2004 |
| | HISPANIC | 3.2 | 2012 | 0.55 | 2098 |
| | | | | | |
| GRADE 10 | | | | | |
| | BLACK | 0.9 | 2055 | 2.4 | 2022 |
| | WHITE | 0.3 | 2047 | 8.75 | 2002 |
| | ASIAN | 3.65 | 2007 | 12.95 | 2001 |
| | HISPANIC | 0.95 | 2053 | 1.55 | 2035 |

Sources:
Boston Public Schools, 1997.
Boston Public Schools, 1998.
Boston Public Schools, 1999.
Boston Public Schools, 2000.

Again, signs of progress similar to those in the case of student passing rates can be seen in Tables 16 and 17. In most cases, from 1997 through 2000, there has been an increasing trend in the percentages of students scoring at the top two levels of the Stanford 9 tests. In all cases (for all grade levels and all racial and ethnic groups), from 1998 through 2001, there has been an increasing trend in the percentages of students scoring at the top two levels of the MCAS tests. However, significant disparities in the performance of students from various racial and ethnic groups still persist. In most cases the increase in the percentages of white and Asian students scoring at the top two levels on the Reading/ELA and Math sections of the Stanford 9 and MCAS tests has been greater than the increase in the percentages of black and Hispanic students scoring at the top two levels of the tests. In most cases, on both the Reading and Math sections of the Stanford 9 tests, the date by which the 60% of white and Asian students score at the top two levels of the tests is expected to be significantly earlier than for black and Hispanic students. At all grade levels, on both the ELA and Math sections of the MCAS, the date by which the 60% of white and Asian students score at the top two levels of the tests is expected to be significantly earlier than for black and Hispanic students.

**What Support Has the BPS Given Students to Help Them Improve Their Performance on Standardized Tests?**

To provide more support to students who may be in danger of not meeting the requirements of the new BPS promotion policy and as part of their program to address the achievement gap, the BPS administration instituted after school programs in literacy and math. While these programs may provide students with much needed support, the BPS has failed to develop a means to assess the number of students who are in need of the extra support provided by the after school programs. In response to a request for such data, the after schools program coordinator, Dishon Mills, replied:

> Currently there are up to five After School Programs operating simultaneously in any one school building on any given day, and in most cases completely independently of the other programs. This climate makes it very difficult if not impossible, to collect accurate data on who is, or is not, being served by these programs as compared with students that have been assessed as in need of these services. (Boston Public Schools, 2002j)

Analysis of these programs performed in the year 2000 showed that the number of students who received after school academic support during the 1999–2000 school year was significantly less than the number of students in need of academic support. In a memorandum presented at the April 20, 2000 meeting of the Boston school committee, deputy superintendent Tim Knowles presented, as part of an outline to close the achievement gap, after school tutoring programs in math and literacy to be implemented in all schools. While there are 136 schools in the BPS, only 76 (59% of the total number of schools) offered such programs during the 1999–2000 school year (K. Caldwell, BPS Chief of Staff, personal communication, August 2, 2000). For the 1999–2000 school year, 6,207 BPS students were targeted to receive transition services by their schools (Boston Public Schools, 2000a). However, only 2,150 students participated in the BPS after school literacy or math programs for grades 3, 6, and 9 (K. Caldwell, BPS Chief of Staff, personal communication, August 2, 2000). Thus, of those students targeted, only 37% of those received support.

In addition to after school tutoring offered directly by the BPS, students in the BPS were offered tutoring through the Mayor's 2–6 Initiative. In the 1999–2000 academic school year, the initiative operated in 57 middle and elementary schools. Since the BPS claims 99 elementary and middle schools, the initiative served only 58%. According to the BPS Chief of Staff, Ken Caldwell, for school year 1999–2000 approximately 2,750 students were served by the Mayor's 2–6

Initiative (K. Caldwell, BPS chief of staff, personal communication, August 2, 2000). During that same school year, there were 40,071 students in BPS elementary and middle schools (Boston Public Schools, 2002h), and the initiative only served 6.9% of these students. In the report "Schools Are Not Enough," The Mayor's task force on after school time noted the following:

> Several studies have found that children, particularly those from lower socioeconomic levels who attend high quality programs have better peer relations, emotional adjustment, grades, and conduct in school compared to their peers who are not in programs. (Mayor's Task Force on After School Time, 2000, p. 8)

This same report cites research by the consulting firm Bain & Company and the opinion research firm Harrison & Goldberg which found that while approximately 16,000 elementary and middle school children were in after school programs, there are an additional 16,000 children whose parents would like them to be in after school programs but are not primarily due to the high cost and low availability.

## Gauging the Success of BPS Transition Programs

Faced with large numbers of students failing to pass standardized testing requirements for grade promotion, the BPS administration has developed a "transition program" to support students identified as academically at risk. The BPS Transition Program, which began in school year 1999–2000, was designed to provide students with extra support in both English language arts and math. A team from Harvard and Northeastern Universities released an evaluation of the BPS transition program in December of 2001. They found that of the 8,371 students who participated in the program during school year 2000–01, the percentage of students promoted to the next grade was 52.7%; 47.3% were not promoted (Pierce & Portz, 2001).

In addition to identifying students as in need of Transition Program support during the school year, the school department required students failing to meet benchmarks set by the promotion policy to attend summer school. Since the summer of 2000, about one third of students in grades 2, 3, and 5–11 have been required to attend summer school. Of the 13,970 students who completed summer school in 2002, 57% were promoted, 12% were assigned to transition programs, and 31% were retained in their grades (Pierce & Portz, 2002).

## Disparities in Educational Outcomes at the
## Elementary/Middle School Level

### Participation in ISEE Preparation Programs

Boston's three exam schools are recognized as being among the best schools in the city. Students compete for the limited spaces at these schools by taking the Independent Secondary Entrance Examination (ISEE) test in 6th or 8th grade. Students are then admitted to the exam schools based on their ISEE score and their grades the previous year and the first two marking periods of their current grade. For the last several years, the BPS has been providing programs specifically designed to prepare students to take the ISEE test. The ISEE preparation programs offered in the summers are titled the "Summer of Learning" program. For the summers of 1997 and 1998, all 5th graders were invited to attend this summer program. In the years following, the summer programs have only been open to those students who scored at levels 3 or 4 on the Stanford 9 tests. Graph 4 shows the percentages of BPS students enrolled in the 5th grade (rising 6th graders) along with the percentages of students invited to attend the BPS Summer 2002 ISEE prep program. The percentages of black and Hispanic students invited to attend the ISEE program is significantly less than the percentages of black and Hispanic students who are rising 6th graders.

**Graph 4**

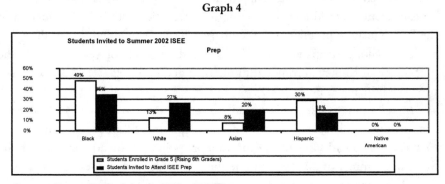

Sources: Boston Public Schools, 2002a, 2002k.

Graphs 5 and 6 shows the percentages rising among 6th and 9th graders who participated in ISEE preparation programs in the fall of 2001.

**Graph 5**

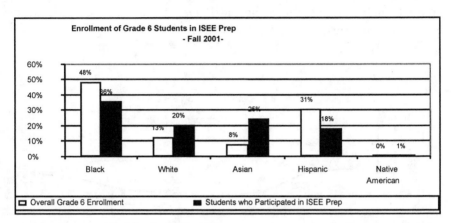

Sources: Boston Public Schools, 2002h, 2002l.

**Graph 6**

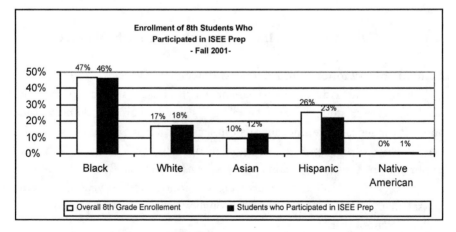

Sources: Boston Public Schools, 2002h, 2002l.

As can be seen in Graphs 5 and 6, the percentages of black and Hispanic students who participated in the fall ISEE preparation programs, for 6th and 8th graders, was less than the overall percentages of black and Hispanic students in the respective grades. Black and Hispanic students were underrepresented to a greater degree in the 6th grade ISEE preparation programs.

## Middle School Dropout Rates

In general, students drop out during high school. Dropout rates are usually very small for students in middle schools. Graph 7 shows that, after an initial decrease in the middle school dropout rate in the early 1990s, the middle school dropout rate has increased since the mid-1990s. The rise in the dropout rate has been particularly sharp among black students.

**Graph 7**

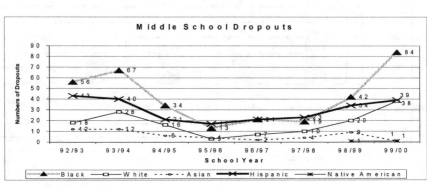

Source: Wheelock, 2003.

## More Educational Inequities at the High School Level

### Enrollment in Honors and Advanced Placement Classes

Honors and Advanced Placement (AP) classes are the highest level academic classes students can take in high school. The curriculum in Honors and AP classes is more rigorous than in standard High School classes and the classes serve as an impressive component of a student's record, which can be important in the college admissions process. Graphs 8 and 9 show the percentages of BPS students who were in Honors and Advanced Placement classes in the various high schools throughout the city of Boston during the 2002–03 school year.

## Graph 8

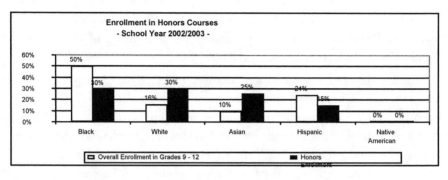

Sources: Boston Public Schools, 2003a, 2003g.

## Graph 9

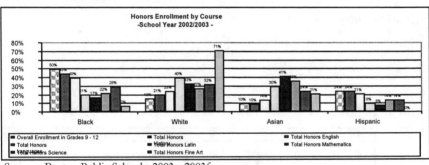

Sources: Boston Public Schools, 2003a, 2003f.

## Graph 10

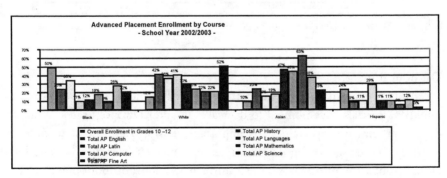

Sources: Boston Public Schools, 2003a, 2003g.

As shown in Graphs 8 and 9, the percentages of black and Hispanic students in both Honors and AP classes are significantly less than the overall population of black and Hispanic students. The percentages of black and Hispanic students in Advanced Placement classes, in particular, are less than half of the overall population of black and Hispanic students.

Among those students who were enrolled in AP classes during the 2002–03 academic school year, there was also a disparity between the type of classes taken by students of various racial and ethnic groups. Graphs 10 and 11 show the enrollment of students in the various Honors and AP classes offered during school year 2002–03. With respect to Honors classes, the greatest under-representation of black and Hispanic students occurred in Language, Latin, and Fine Arts courses. With respect to Advanced Placement classes, the greatest underrepresentation of black students occurred in Language, Latin, and Computer Science courses, while the greatest underrepresentation of Hispanics students occurred in Computer Science and Fine Arts classes.

**Graph 11**

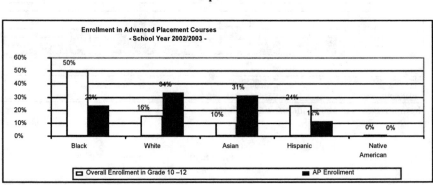

Sources: Boston Public Schools, 2003a, 2003f.

## Dropout Rates

An important measure of the performance of a school system is its dropout rate. BPS officials have pointed to decreases in annual dropout rates. While the decline in annual dropout rates is important, it is also important to note the disparity that exists among dropout rates for students from various racial and ethnic groups. Graph 12 shows the 9 through 12 cohort dropout rate from BPS students from the 1979–1983 cohort through the 1996–2000 cohort. In determining the cohort dropout rate, school department officials included those students who entered in the 9th grade, were not retained, and dropped out of a BPS school. School department officials do not include those students who entered the BPS after the 9th grade nor do they include students who reported transferring from BPS.

**Graph 12**

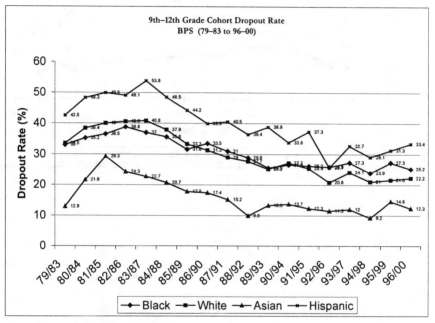

Source: Boston Pubic Schools, 2002g.

Graph 12 shows that, while the cohort dropout rate was highest during the mid-1980s, since the mid-1990s the cohort dropout rate has increased. It can also be seen that the cohort dropout rate has been highest for Hispanic students while the cohort dropout rate has been slightly higher for black students than for white students.

### Postsecondary Plans

Graphs 13 and 14 show the data collected by the Private Industry Council and school department officials on the postsecondary plans of students graduating from the BPS. These figures indicate that even for those students who remain in and graduate from the BPS, there is a significant disparity in the postsecondary plans of students from the various racial and ethnic groups.

**Graph 13**

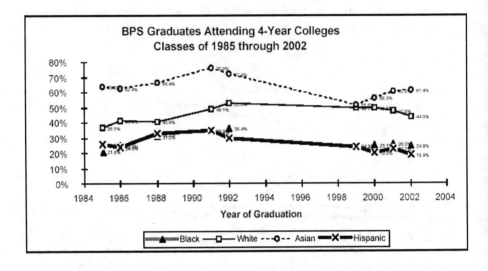

**Graph 14**

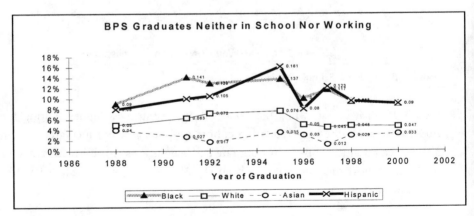

Sources:

Boston Private Industry Council Inc, Undated-a, Undated-b, Undated-c.

Anonymous, 1997.

Sum et al., 1999a.

Sum et al., 1999b.

Boston Public Schools, 1999a, 2002d, 2002e, 2002f.

The BPS has been praised for the high percentages of graduates who attend post-secondary education. Graphs 13 and 14 indicate that the percentages of students attending 4–year postsecondary institutions, attending some form of postsecondary institution, and neither in school nor working has remained relatively constant since the mid-1980s. Graphs 13 and 14 also show significant disparities in the post-secondary plans of black and Hispanic students in comparison to white and Asian students. Since 1988, the percentage of black and Hispanic graduates from the BPS attending 4–year public or private colleges or universities has always been lower than the percentages of white and Asian students attending 4–year public or private colleges or universities. For BPS students graduating in 1999, Hispanic students had the smallest percentages of students seeking some form of post-secondary education. Since 1988, the percentage of black and Hispanic graduates from the BPS, neither planning to seek postsecondary education nor working, has always been higher than the percentages of white and Asian students neither planning to seek post-secondary education nor working.

## Maintaining a Dual–Track/Jim Crow Educational System

Washing one's hands of the conflict between the powerful and the powerless means to side with the powerful, not to be neutral.

—Paulo Freire, 1985, p. 102

Starting in the mid-1990s, the Boston public school administration began to adopt key initiatives of the "market–based" approach toward education reform, including high–stakes standardized testing. An analysis of student educational outcomes in the BPS reveals that 5 years after the administration adopted a promotion policy featuring high–stakes testing standardized testing student attendance as well as overall student performance on the Stanford 9 and MCAS tests has improved. However, despite these overall improvements, the scores of black and Hispanic students on these tests continue to be significantly lower than the scores of white and Asian students. Significant disparities persist between the percentages of black and Hispanic students failing the Stanford 9 and MCAS tests and the percentages of white and Asian students failing these tests. Similar disparities also exist between students scoring at the highest levels of these tests. Yet despite these persistent disparities, the BPS administration abandoned several goals they established regarding closing the achievement gap.

Furthermore, many of the students the BPS has identified as in need of support have not received any after school tutoring. With the MCAS graduation requirement, the percentages of black and Hispanic from the class of 2003 who have not received high school diplomas is even higher than percentages of blacks and Hispanics who did not received high school diplomas during the mid-1980s, when the dropout rate was the highest.

At the same time that the BPS administration has made student performance on standardized tests a major focus of education reform, other areas of student performance have received less attention. In particular, the BPS administration has not developed any policy or programs to address the disparities in the educational outcomes of black and Hispanic students in comparison to white students as measured by enrollment in AWC, ISEE prep programs, Honors, and Advanced Placement enrollments, dropout rates, and postsecondary planning. In the meantime, the city's elementary and middle schools are growing increasingly more segregated.

The BPS is a school system that provides huge disparities in educational offerings to its students. There are pockets of excellence, but it is almost exclusively the more affluent parents who ensure that their children get into these programs. A few others may be lucky enough to get into excellent programs, but the majority faces inadequate educational experiences. As a consequence, the BPS provides distinct educational experiences, and lower educational outcomes, for black and Hispanic students in comparison to white and Asian students. Now, almost 50 years since the U.S. Supreme Court ruled segregation in schools unconstitutional and 30 years since Federal Judge Wendell Arthur Garrity imposed a desegregation program, the Boston public school system is, once again, a dual educational system.

# Bibliography

American Federation of Teachers. (2001). *Making standards matter, 2001*. Washington, DC.

Anonymous. (1997, July). *The schooling and employment status of class of 1995 Boston public high school graduates: Key findings of the 1996 follow-up surveys*. Prepared for the Boston Private Industry Council. Boston, MA: Northeastern University, Center for Labor Market Studies.

Boston Private Industry Council Inc. (1992, Jan.). *The class of 1991, a follow-up survey*. Boston, MA.

Boston Private Industry Council Inc. (1989, Jan.). *The class of 1988, a follow-up survey*. Boston, MA.

Boston Private Industry Council Inc. (1985, Nov.). *The class of 1985,a follow-up study*. Boston, MA.

Boston Private Industry Council Inc. (Undated-a). *The class of 1986, a follow-up survey*. Boston, MA.

Boston Private Industry Council Inc. (Undated-b). *The class of 1992, a follow-up survey*. Boston, MA.

Boston Private Industry Council Inc. (Undated-c). *Activity of 1996 Boston public high school graduates at the time of the survey*. Boston, MA.

Boston Public Schools. (1996). *Focus on Children*. Adopted by the Boston School Committee in 1996. Boston, MA.

Boston Public Schools. (1997, Spring). *Stanford 9 achievement test: Report–Part I, Spring 1997*. Prepared by the Boston Public Schools Office of Research, Assessment, and Evaluation. Boston, MA.

Boston Public Schools. (1998a, Oct. 28). *Proceedings of Meetings*. Prepared by the Secretary of the Boston School Committee. Boston, MA.

Boston Public Schools. (1998b, Spring). *Stanford 9 achievement test: Report–Part I, Spring 1998*. Boston Public Schools Office of Research, Assessment, and Evaluation. Boston, MA.

Boston Public Schools. (1999a). *Plans for the class of 1999*. Prepared by the Office of Student Support Services. Boston, MA.

Boston Public Schools. (1999b, Spring). *Stanford 9 achievement test: Report–Part I, Spring 1999*. Boston Public Schools Office of Research, Assessment, and Evaluation. Boston, MA.

Boston Public Schools. (2000a, Apr.). *Boston pubic schools transition services interim report of student progress*. Prepared by the Boston Public Schools Office of Research, Assessment, and Evaluation and the Office of Teaching and Learning Support Services. Boston, MA.

Boston Public Schools. (2000b, Apr. 20). *Closing the achievement gap*. (Memorandum). To Superintendent Thomas Payzant Presented at School Committee Meeting by Timothy Knowles, Deputy Superintendent of Teaching and Learning. Boston, MA.

Boston Public Schools. (2000c, Nov. 17). *Goals and objectives*. [Online]. Available: <http://www.boston.k12.ma.us/supt/obj.asp>.

Boston Public Schools. (2000d, Apr.). *Reducing the racial/ethnic gap: Analysis of performance on the MCAS by racial/ethnic group May 1998–May 1999*. Boston Public Schools Office of Research, Assessment, and Evaluation. Boston, MA.

Boston Public Schools. (2000e, Spring). *Stanford 9 achievement test: Report–Part I, Spring 2000*. Boston Public Schools Office of Research, Assessment, and Evaluation. Boston, MA.

Boston Public Schools. (2001a, Apr. 25). *Focus on Children 2. Boston's education reform plan: 2001–2006*. Adopted by the Boston School Committee. 25 April 2001. Boston, MA.

Boston Public Schools. (2001b, Oct. 21). *Massachusetts comprehensive assessment system*. Results: May, 2001. Boston Public Schools Office of Research, Evaluation, and Assessment. Boston, MA.

Boston Public Schools. (2001c, Spring). *Stanford 9 achievement test: Report–Part I, Spring 2001.* Boston Public Schools Office of Research, Assessment, and Evaluation. Boston, MA.

Boston Public Schools. (2001d, Feb. 22). *Superintendent's goals and objectives for calendar year 2001.* (Memorandum). Presented by Superintendent Payzant to the Boston School Committee. Boston, MA.

Boston Public Schools. (2002a, Jan. 24). *Analysis of students by race by grade–assigned enrollment 01/24/02.* Boston, MA.

Boston Public Schools. (2002b, Jul. 23). *AWC admissions tally by grade and specified categories.* Boston Public Schools Office of Research, Evaluation, and Assessment. Boston, MA.

Boston Public Schools. (2002c, Mar.). *Boston public schools enrollment as of 10-10-2001.* Online]. Available: <http://www.boston.k12.ma.us/bps/enrollment.asp>.

Boston Public Schools. (2002d, Oct. 1). *Student Data Report. 2001–2002. Chapter 188–individual school, table 14–plans of high school graduates.* Prepared by the Boston Public Schools Office of Student Support Services. Boston, MA.

Boston Public Schools. (2002e, Jul. 23). *Distribution of graduates–class of 2000.* Prepared by Boston Public Schools Office of Student Support Services. Boston, MA.

Boston Public Schools. (2002f, Jul. 23). *Distribution of graduates–class of 2001.* Prepared by the Boston Public Schools Office of Student Support Services. Boston, MA.

Boston Public Schools. (2002g, Jan.). *Dropout by racial/ethnic group for 9th grade cohorts: 1979–83 through 1996–2000.* Prepared by the Boston Public Schools Office of Research, Assessment and Evaluation. Boston, MA.

Boston Public Schools. (2002h, Jul. 23). *Enrollment data tally by grade and specified categories.* Prepared by the Boston Public Schools Office of Research, Evaluation, and Assessment. Boston, MA.

Boston Public Schools. (2002i, Jul. 23). *Enrollment data tally by school and race.* Prepared by the Boston Public Schools Office of Research, Evaluation, and Assessment. Boston, MA.

Boston Public Schools. (2002j, May 3). *Dishon Mills, after school program coordinator to Karen Hall Redcross, office of research, assessment, and evaluation in compliance with public record request from Jim Crow.* (Letter). Boston, MA.

Boston Public Schools. (2002k, Jul. 17). *Karen Richardson to Maryellen Donahue, director of research, assessment, and evaluation in response in compliance with a request for data by Jim Crow.* (Letter). Boston, MA.

Boston Public Schools. (2002l, Apr.). *Results of the "Best We Can Be" exam school prep program.* Prepared by Karen Richardson, Director of the Boston Public Schools Exam School Initiative. Boston, MA.

Boston Public Schools. (2002m). *Superintendent's goals and objectives–calendar year 2002–2003.* Boston Public Schools. [Online]. Available: <http://www.boston.k12.m1.us/supt/obj.asp>.

Boston Public Schools. (2002n, Sept.). *The Boston public schools at a glance.* [Online]. Available: <http://www.boston.k12.ma.us/bps/bpsglance.asp>.

Boston Public Schools. (2003a, May). *Analysis of students by race by grade.* All Assigned. 05/01/2003. Prepared by Boston Public Schools Office of Information Services. Boston, MA.

Boston Public Schools. (2003b, Mar.). *Class of 2003: In-depth analyses–MCAS performance: Update with December 2002 re-test.* Boston Public Schools Office of Research, Assessment, and Evaluation. Boston, MA.

Boston Public Schools. (2003c, Jul.). Data prepared for Boston Globe journalists Bill Dedman and Michele Kurtz for the 1 June 2003 "Faithful Attendance Seen as an MCAS Key" and provided to Jim Crow in compliance with Massachusetts Public Records Act (M.G.L. c. 66, sec. 10). Boston, MA.

Boston Public Schools. (2003d, Mar. 12). *MCAS retest results show unprecedented improvement in Boston.* BPS in the News. Boston, MA.

Boston Public Schools. (2003e, Mar.). *Tally of invitees and acceptances to exam schools for SY 2003/2004.* Prepared by Shirley Burke, Department of Implementation. Boston, MA.

Boston Public Schools. (2003f, Feb. 12). *2002–2003 Advanced Placement course enrollment as of 02/12/2003.* Prepared by Boston Public Schools Office of Research, Assessment, and Evaluation. Boston, MA.

Boston Public Schools. (2003g, Feb. 12). *2002–2003 honors course enrollment as of 02/12/2003.* Prepared by the Boston Public Schools Office of Research, Assessment, and Evaluation. Boston, MA.

Freire, P. (1985). *The politics of education: Culture, power, and liberation.* Westport, CT: Bergin and Garvey.

Liu, L., et al. (2001, Mar.). *Boston's Population–2000. The youth and adult population in Boston and in Boston's neighborhoods for the year 2000.* (Report #542). Boston Redevelopment Authority. Boston, MA.

Lukas, A. J. (1985). *Common ground: A turbulent decade in the lives of three American families.* New York.: Vintage Books.

Massachusetts Department of Education. (2001, Jul.). *Report of 2000 Massachusetts and local school district MCAS results by race/ethnicity.* Malden, MA.

Mayor's Task Force on After School Time. (2000, May). *Schools alone are not enough–why out of school time is crucial to the success of out children.* Convened by Thomas M. Menino, Mayor of Boston, MA.

Pierce, G., & Portz, J. (2001, Dec. 14). *Evaluation of Boston public schools school year 2000–2001 transition services program. Part I–student profile, program description and student achievement based upon BPS transition program data.* Boston: Northeastern/Harvard Transition Services Evaluation Team.

Pierce, G., & Portz, J. (2002, Sep. 23). *Transitional services program–summer 2002. Tables on attendance, promotion status and benchmark achievement.* Boston: MA: Northeastern/Harvard Transition Services Evaluation Team.

Sum, A., et al. (1999a, Nov.). *The schooling and employment outcomes for class of 1998 Boston public high school graduates: Key findings of the 1999 follow-up surveys.* (Report.) Prepared for the Boston Private Industry Council. Boston, MA: Northeastern University Center for Labor Market Studies

Sum, A., et al. (1999b, Feb.). *The schooling and employment status of class of 1997 Boston public high school graduates: Key findings of the 1998 follow-up surveys.* Prepared for the Boston Private Industry Council. Boston, MA: Northeastern University, Center for Labor Market Studies.

Wheelock, Anne. (2003, Apr.). *Dropout crisis developing in Boston middle schools.* [Online]. Available: <http://www.massrefusal.org/papers/dropouts.html>.

Chapter Five

# Writing as a Hostile Act: A Reason for Latino Students' Resistance to Learning

*Raul E. Ybarra*

## Introduction

I have been studying the teaching of writing and the effect it has on Latino students for over 10 years. This interest began while teaching writing courses at California State University, Fresno, in 1985. While teaching there, I noticed significant cultural differences in the various composition courses. The majority of students in Basic Writing classes, for instance, were black and Asian, but a large portion was Latino, while in the Introduction to Composition courses the students were mostly white. I wanted to know why. I wanted to know: Why did many Latinos fail to acquire the writing level expected of them even after 12 years of schooling? Why is writing so difficult for Latino students?

Understanding why Latinos do poorly in school is becoming more important because Latinos are the fastest–growing group in the United States. As Lorna Rivera (Chapter 7) explains, "according to the 2000 U.S. Census, the Latino population increased by more than 50% since 1990 and Latinos now make up 13.2% of the total U.S. population." With the increasing Latino population one would assume a corresponding increase in the Latino college completion rate, but sadly, the opposite is true. Indeed, current census data shows not only is the retention rate for Latinos at all levels of schooling worsening, but the prediction is this trend will to continue because "Latinos are also the fastest-growing, and youngest, United States ethnic group" (Rivera, Chapter 7).

I argue here that writing is one important factor bearing on this phenomenon. I suggest that when we teach writing to Latino students, we are teaching more than just grammar and style. We are asking them to change their cultural identity because we essentially expect these students to change how they think. Students who are not part of the mainstream, particularly Latinos, see this pattern as confusing, and also as a hostile attempt to change who they are. This pattern of teaching does epistemological violence to Latinos students because of the marginalization and cultural implications that take place. This further suggests a rationale for the pervasiveness (and function) of this structure in education, especially when teaching to minorities—and in particular, Latino students. In this chapter, I show how learning to master academic writing is not a smooth transition over the course of the semester, but rather a hostile course of action. This style of pedagogy contributes to what I term cultural dissonance. It highlights issues of cultural differences and dominance in the context of English and writing courses in higher education. In this argument I expose the larger hidden curriculum of assimilation (Ybarra, 2001, p. 46).

## The Study

In the following pages I describe and analyze the language of a specific writing classroom. I show how this language is specific to a particular cultural group; namely academe: the dominant mainstream culture in higher education. Teaching in this schema then suggests a rationale for the pervasiveness and function of its structure in education, especially when teaching writing to Latino students. The teaching of academic writing is a hostile and invasive course of action which ultimately leaves a negative impression on Latino students.

### Overview of the Study

This paper is based on a much larger ethnographic study.[1] The purpose of this study was to assess whether pedagogical assumptions and practices, together with the communication patterns of Basic Writing instructors toward their Latino students, affected writing performance. Since student placement statistics reveal that a disproportionate number of students assigned to Basic Writing courses are Latino, these classrooms were chosen as the sites for the study. For the purposes of this argument, and to illustrate the cultural complexities involved in the seemingly higher ratio of failure among Latino students than other ethnic groups, I shall focus on one particular course.

## Overview of Basic Writing Course

The purpose of Basic Writing at the University of Illinois, Chicago (UIC), as stated by Downs et al. (1991) in the Content Guidelines for the teaching of Basic Writing, is not so much "to teach students how to write, but to help students understand how writing works in the world, especially the world of the university":

> Remember that the goal is not to turn students into expert critics, but rather to give them a sense of confidence by helping them realize that each piece of writing is produced by a human being for some purpose in the real world, a world of which they are a part. (p. 5)

Thus, the focus of Basic Writing, though still a preparatory course, is not on skills, but rather on understanding the writing process as a whole, from the beginning stages of ideas to the final product. Instructors of Basic Writing at UIC are encouraged to assign their students a significant amount of reading and writing, drafting and revising (both the in-class essays and out-of-class essays), and conferencing with students (Downs et al., 1991, pp. 4–9). By steering students through a series of revisions, the students will not only create their own models of writing, but will learn academic discourse through using it (Downs et al., 1991, p. 32; Farr & Daniels, 1986, p. 81).

## Background of Instructor

The instructor, whom I shall call Pat, came to this course with the requisite background in composition teaching. Pat was a white female graduate student between 45–50 years of age, a single mother with an 18 year-old daughter in college at another university.

She had taught–college level writing courses at two other urban institutions (De Paul and Loyola Universities), and was entering her second year teaching Basic Writing at UIC. She also held the reputation of being considered one of the better instructors in the program due to her energetic style of teaching and her propensity for encouraging lively discussions among her students. I thus predicted that I would witness a positive impact of her pedagogical practices and interaction with her Latino students on their written performance.

## The Students

To help in the identification of Latinos I relied on Marin and Marin's (1991) definition: any student who referred to himself or herself as a person of "Mexican, Puerto Rican, Cuban, Central or South American or other Spanish culture or origin, regardless of race…," I included as belonging to the general group Latino (p. 23). In this particular class, three students (of the 14) self-reported their identities as Latino.[2]

Connie, an entering freshman and 18 years-old, categorized herself ethnically as half Ecuadorian and half Argentinean, though neither parent had been back to their perspective countries for more than 25 years. She did not speak Spanish except for a word here and there. Born and raised in the United States and attending both public and private schools, Connie never left the Cicero area (a suburb of Chicago). She took advanced English courses in high school, yet she scored low on her placement and was placed in Basic Writing.

Another entering freshman, Joe, categorized himself as Hispanic. Joe's participation in the course was limited to continued silence and frequent absences. At the urging of his instructor, Joe eventually dropped the course.

Lastly, there was Letty. Another 18–year–old entering freshman, she categorized herself as Mexican. Letty was born in the United States and attended school in both California and Chicago. Letty's parents were born and raised in Mexico and immigrated to the United States a year before Letty was born. She and her parents travel to Mexico on a regular basis, at least once a year. Letty did not score high enough on the written portion of her placement exam to take the required college–level composition class. Letty always appeared eager, interested, and willing to cooperate and worked hard at improving her essays. She came to the Writing Lab regularly. She always had an essay ready to discuss, and was active in the discussions. Letty also turned in all her work on time. I found Letty to be a wonderful student, and she did well. By the semester's end she received a B.

Once I identified my subjects, I followed them throughout the term and continued to collect data through audio taping, interviews, and fieldnotes. Additionally, throughout the semester, I interviewed or talked to the students and the instructor periodically (audio taping whenever I could). After each of the class sessions, I would review the audio tapes and make any adjustments in my fieldnotes I felt were necessary for the identification of the tapes and interpretation of the data.

**Letty**

Letty's biggest problem was writing her essays according to the structure the instructor (Pat) wanted students to follow. Interestingly, on Letty's first essay, the only comment Pat wrote was "Excellent" in bold lettering. On Letty's second essay, Pat had written this comment:

> Work on focusing everything you say through your thesis. Reread and #4 [Reread and work on paragraph number 4] ask yourself why you included that info [Next time, make info connection clear to reader].

On the third essay Pat wrote this comment: "Keep working on your flow of thought." Hence, most of my conversations with Letty dealt with structuring paragraphs and (as the following segment shows) Letty actively participated in class discussions:

> Pat: What would happen, Student 1, if everybody was born and we had people running around all over the place and there was no culture? What would happen?
>
> Student 1: /?/
>
> Pat: Okay, good. So you could tell people apart by culture. It gives you an identity. So it, it may, it may not be able to tell people apart—it may give you a sense of an identity. This is who I am. This is where I fit. Every single human being that is born into this world eventually gets old enough to look around and say: Where do I fit? Every single human being, from primitive men right on up: Where do I fit? What does this all mean? What, what's, what's this all about? Culture gives an answer to that. Yes?
>
> Letty: /?/ You're saying to yourself, even—
>
> Pat: Real loud so we can hear you.
>
> Letty: In the culture {clears throat} uh, even though those people that, like that, know what, like know what their real culture is, usually they're adopted. They grow up with the, the culture of that person that they grew up with.
>
> Pat: Exactly.
>
> Letty: They need that background in order to, they need it to fulfill something in their lives.
>
> Pat: Yeah, and, and fulfilling something in life might be—Where do I fit? What's expected of me? How am I supposed to act? What's important? It's the real thing. Like with my daughter in college last night. She was in tears and all upset. We talked about the basic questions in life: What's important? Its cultural values. Yes?

As this transcript shows, conversations with Letty frequently dealt with structuring paragraphs:

Raul: That's it. And now just go on from there. What it means, rules and how to behave. And you're dealing with this—

Letty: Like a lot of things. And it, and see that what I don't. She says to put a thesis based on sense of time.

Raul: Don't worry about the thesis now. You can always stick it at the very—

Letty: This is my thesis.

Raul: /?/.

Letty: Rules.

Raul: All right.

Letty: And it's because I have, like, first of all I'm, I'm doing it in general 'cause it—

Raul: Okay.

Letty: Like I have, "All parents have cultural expectations, but not everyone has the same one that all people are the same. My cultural expectations came from family background and myself."

Raul: There's your introduction to your thesis right there. Now you're ready to begin your paper.

Letty: But how do I fit everything under there, because then I start talking in general, like—

Raul: Okay, you don't—

Letty: Images of one should be?

Raul: No. See, you want to get away from general.

Letty: So, what would I do about the background? See, there's so many images of how one should be. How so we know which one is the best one?

Raul: Okay, that was a good start. Lets go back to your, to your thesis. What is it?

Letty: "All people have cultural expectations, but not everyone has the same ones because not all people are the same."

Raul: Okay.

Letty: What if I stated that—

Raul: Now read the whole thing.

Letty: Yeah, I will.

Raul: Read the whole thing.

Letty: My cultural expectations came form my family, friends, and myself.

Raul: Okay. Let's stop right there. Now, let's say this is the beginning of the paper. What are you going to write about in your paper?

Letty: I'm going to write about my cultural expectations, which came from my family and friends, and myself.

Raul: Yeah, you now need to expand on those three things. That's what you need to write on. See that. Everything goes back to that—

Letty: I mean I have all the ideas, but it's harder to put it down in words.

Raul: Well, except, look at your thesis. You have a nice thesis there. And I would start with that. The first thing, of course, I would start with yourself: "I." This is what? This is who I am. Introduce yourself. And then go from there.

Letty always appeared eager, interested, and willing to cooperate and worked hard at improving her essays. She always had an essay ready to discuss, and active in our discussions. Letty also turned in all her work on time. I found Letty to be a wonderful student, and she did well. By the semesters' end she received a solid B grade; I was surprised because I thought she would easily receive an A. She became what Fredrick Erickson (1993) describes as a student who fades "into the woodwork as an anonymous well-behaved, low achieving [student]" (p. 41).

## Negative Feelings About Basic Writing

I happened to run into Letty two semesters after she had completed Basic Writing and I took the opportunity to ask her about how she was doing— particularly in writing. She had completed her freshman writing requirement by this time (at UIC), as well as her research class at a community college over the summer.

Letty: Okay.
Raul: Have you taken English 160? [The Freshman Composition Course]
Letty: 160.
Raul: What grade did you get?
Letty: B.
Raul: How about 161? [The Research Composition Course]
Letty: 161—I took that over the summer. And I took that at a community college, and I got an A....

After a few minutes, when I thought she had relaxed enough, I focused on the Basic Writing course she had taken with Pat:

Raul: Why were you in 152? [The Basic Writing Course]
Letty: That's where I was placed.
Raul: Were you upset?
Letty: Oh yeah, because I was thinking, why do I have to go backwards instead of forward. Because, you know, everybody places in 160, and so just because of an essay that they give you, which is basically not all that great, you know. I ended up writing like a paragraph. And then it was timed, so I didn't have time. I was just trying to think about what to write about and time was up /?/. But I didn't do too bad. I didn't do as well as I expected. I was always used to doing really good in school, and in high school, I mean, so it was kind of like—it felt—it made me feel like things weren't going right. And like /?/ happen to me, and it's like—it made me feel like, I guess I can say, stupid. I'm used to doing so good. What's

happening? When I was in high school I always did really well—at least A's and B's. Last semester I ended up getting all A's and getting /?/ my final. So I guess I have that mentality where I would always do that way, do good, and I soon as I came here and classes were harder. I tried my best and everything, but still. I am always the kind of person that I tried to push myself to get real good grades and doing my best....

Raul: How did you feel going into English 152?

Letty: I was disappointed, I'm like, like /?/ how it felt going backwards. I was used to moving forward and doing really well, and I knew that 160 was basically where everybody started off. So it's like, great. I'm not even starting off /with/ everybody else. I'm going to a level back.

I was surprised about Letty's response to my questions concerning this Basic Writing course, but yet this was not a shock. Letty, although not happy about her placement into Basic Writing, accepted it. More importantly, although she appeared outwardly to accept her placement, as Kutz and Roskelly (1991) describe, she accepted and internalized "the school culture's assessment of [her] abilities" (p. 59). Inwardly she was hurt; this is clearly heard in her voice when she states:

I was disappointed, I'm like, like /?/ how it felt going backwards. I was used to moving forward and doing really well, and I knew that 160 was basically where everybody started off. So it's like, great. I'm not even starting off /with/ everybody else. I'm going to a level back.

This only brought out more questions: Why was Letty hurt at being placed in Basic Writing? Why did this hurt not go away when Letty did well throughout the course? Why did this feeling continue beyond her Basic Writing course and all her writing courses even though she continued to do well?

To address these questions and to help me understand Letty's frustrations, I went back to the instructor's syllabus, because as Stock and Robinson (1989) argue, a syllabus reflects an instructor's "beliefs about learning" (p. 315). Understanding the instructor's beliefs helps me to understand the vast gap that exists between the students and writing instructors.

## The Syllabus

When writing essays, students are expected to exhibit mastery of the grammatical and stylistic conventions, as well as to demonstrate an ability to organize the essay according to established patterns. These patterns are, typically: an introduction with a thesis statement that clearly explains the argument and purpose of the paper, the body of the text which contains paragraphs supporting the stated purpose, and a conclusion in which the purpose of the paper is restated. This pattern can be described simply as a beginning, middle, and end pattern. I do want to stress it is not simple by any means. As Farr (1992), Heath (1983), and Scollon and Scollon (1981) argue, this is a way of cognitively structuring and viewing the world. Farr (1992) points out that this discourse pattern is not only limited to written discourse. Other scholars, Heath (1983) and Hymes (1974), also stress that this style of discourse shapes speaking patterns as well, and makes this discourse style a distinctly identifiable register, which, according to Scollon and Scollon (1981) requires nothing outside the text...for interpretation (p. 48).

The codification of this three-part structure in both oral and written discourse suggests that it serves not only as a cognitive and linguistic frame, but also as ideological schemata for viewing the world. Scollon and Scollon (1981) have categorized it as a "complex of theoretical and educational positions of viewing the world...a 'reality set'" (pp. 41, 50). Stock and Robinson (1989) put it this way:

> Writers and readers behave in much the same way as speakers and listeners do; that individuals who speak and hear, and write and read, for and with one another over a period of time in a given context to constitute...an interpretive community. (p. 319)

Essayist literacy, then, is a way of thinking and a way of mapping the world. This is the type of discourse highly favored and valued in academic institutions, as well as the mainstream United States society. Members of this society in general, and college students in particular, must internalize this tripartite structure in order to "progress upward educationally and, in many cases, economically" (Farr, 1990, p. 9). Farr and Daniels (1986) argue that:

> [S]chool in our society is generally part of mainstream culture, the language practices in school are also closely tied to beliefs and conceptual principles by which a certain group of people live. (p. 31)

The possible link between this structural schemata and a host of culturally dominant ideological implications it may endorse suggests a rationale for the pervasiveness and function of this tripartite structure in education. To assess how the teaching of this culturally dominant structure affects the performance of culturally marginalized students, in particular, Latino students, I will begin this next section with an analysis of the instructor's syllabus.

As required by the English Department, the instructor (Pat) began the session by handing out a syllabus outlining what she hoped to accomplish for the entire term (for a copy of the syllabus, see Appendix 1, Syllabus). The instructor followed standard procedures as she moved mechanically from one ritual to the next. In addition to distributing the syllabus to the students, she also read it aloud and as required, submitted a copy to the Composition Office (Downs et al., 1991, p. 19).

The first section serves as the general introduction to the course. The instructor introduces herself by stating her name and announces conference times, office location, and the times and place for class meeting:

Syllabus

| | |
|---|---|
| UIC Fall 1991 | Office Hours: |
| Instructor: | M: 11:00–12:00 |
| English 152 | W: 2:00–3:00 |
| M,F 12:00–12:50 | F: 2:00–12:00 |
| W 11:00–1:50 | |

Pat wanted and expected to confer periodically and individually with her students throughout the semester; she wanted students to feel free to come to her office when they needed help. Thus, she listed the location of her office, along with times of her office hours and phone number because she wanted to convey to her students "that they are genuinely welcome to talk to [her]" (Fraher, 1984, p. 120).

The next section of the syllabus begins with "Aims of the Course." Here, Pat describes, in a general manner, her expectations of what she wishes her students to accomplish:

- To develop clarity of thought by reading, thinking, and rethinking, redrafting, revising, editing, and polishing prose.
- To organize and develop ideas in coherent writing.
- To become confident in writing academic discourse.

It is important that I stop here and note the extent to which the instructor sets up through the announcement of these course objectives the tripartite structure and the corresponding culturally dominant ideological assumptions embedded within it. First, note that the objectives mirror the tripartite structure not only in number (three objectives) but also in their relational interfacing with one another. "To develop clarity of thought" parallels the introduction of an essay where ideas and points are initially made, just as the second objective, by underscoring organization and development of ideas, mirrors the body and development of the thesis in an essay. The third objective mirrors the outcome of the conclusion of an essay which is a result of the introduction and the body. Please also note that the instructor assumes no previous knowledge or prior learning "to develop clarity of thought" just as an introductory paragraph of an essay usually assumes no prior knowledge of the argument to be made.

Here, I question the structural mirroring of the essay structure to be learned and internalized and its three objectives, especially the first. What does "clearly"" mean to the instructor when connected to thinking, speaking, and reading? What effect does this have on students? Certain students, especially those from ethnic groups repeatedly discriminated against in society (such as Latino students, who have experienced marginalization in 12 years of previous schooling) may see this as a hostile act. As Farr and Daniels (1986) state, these students (such as Letty, for example) continue to struggle with writing "despite the fact that they have spent up to 12 years in a context in which the standard is taught, or at least modeled" (p. 201). Yet these students still do not understand this structure. Why should they now believe that this instructor could help them?

Pat, however, sees all of this in another way. Pat's objective by the end of the semester is to get her students to write in academic discourse. Although Pat did not state this directly, the implication is made quite clearly by her three stated themes: "To develop clarity of thought" meaning to write clearly, directly, and concisely to avoid any "unnecessary complex prose" (Watkins & Dillingham, 1973, p. 5); "To organize and develop ideas" meaning to shape the ideas "to the larger intentions of the paper" without sacrificing clarity (Watkins,

& Dillingham, 1973, p. 39); finally, "to become confident in writing academic discourse." Pat is suggesting to her students that if they do what she has asked them to do they should be well on their way to writing academic prose on their own. This is important because Pat is letting her students know that she is aware that they must, in time, produce text that the academic community wants. As Bartholomae (1988b) writes, the student "has to do this as though he were easily and comfortably one with his audience, as though he were a member of the academy..." (p. 274).

To help the students become "members of the academy" Pat will use certain writing tools, namely those that she has listed: "reading, thinking, and rethinking, redrafting, revising, editing, and polishing prose." By performing each task, the students will thus eliminate unnecessary information, correct those features that are wrong, expand on what is correct or accepted, and also learn how to organize and structure their writing according to Western essayist literacy patterns. Moreover, the students will learn to become proficient in their critical thinking and uses of language because they will have been allowed time "to appropriate (or be appropriated by) a specialized discourse" (Bartholomae, 1988a, p. 274).

Pat herself stressed this idea of appropriating a specialized language to her students in her lectures. She stressed to her students, early in the semester in one of her lectures to the class, that they must start practicing how to use academic language:

> You can get rid of half that stuff and say what you want to say. Now, Letty does what a lot of you do, and in academic writing try not to do this, "in the ad I chose about the beer Michelob Light." I want you to focus on just telling it to me straight. A number of students in the other class, say, "Well I'm going to write about" or "this is what I think about." Don't do it. Just tell me your thoughts. I'm going to tell you about my thought, "I love _____'s cough drop she just gave me." Don't tell me to tell you about my thought I love _____'s cough drops. Just say "I love _____'s cough drops." So you're up here, you're now authority. Even if you don't know anything, act like the authority /?/. It's the mask that you got to put on. So what you're doing is just saying "In the in the ad of Michelob Light." Don't say the ad I chose. What you chose doesn't make any difference. You're the authority on this ad. And you're going to tell, tear this ad apart. Okay?

When she says, "So you're up here, you're now authority. In academic writing you act like authority. Even if you don't know anything," Pat is advising the students to take control of their own essays, to speak, or at least pretend to speak, with authority as though they were the experts (Bartholomae, 1988a, p. 274). Pat wanted her students to practice being writing experts to "dare to speak it or to carry out the bluff, since speaking and writing will most certainly be required long before the skill is 'learned'"(Bartholomae, 1988a p. 274). We can see then that beyond the surface structural mirroring of the essay structure to be learned and internalized and the three objectives to be satisfied is also a corresponding set of ideological assumptions on the authority of the instructor and hence sense of power. By trying, participation, and emulation the students will in time produce the type of text, and the sense of power, that the academic community wants.

This idea is supported by scholars such as Pascarella (1980), Valverde (1987), and Tinto (1993) who have shown that an important part of the students' integration into college is the interaction that takes place between students and between students and faculty. Both interactive modes play a major role in helping the student become a member of the school community. One affects the other. The interaction between students shows the student how to interact with faculty (Pascarella, 1980). Part of the interaction involves speaking and interpreting what is being spoken. This interaction is essential because it helps people establish social and ethnic identities and group membership (Jepp et al., 1993; Cazden, 1986; Gumperz, 1982). Pat wants her students to become members the academic community. To acculturate her students into the academic community this instructor knows that the student "must speak and write…toward such familiarity" (Stock & Robinson, 1989, p. 318). What better ways than to have the students interact with one another so as to practice. Interaction is the key by which the students are going to internalize the syntax of academic discourse. By conforming to this learning community, the students then would be well on their way to becoming members of the academic community.

In the middle section of the syllabus entitled "The Conduct of the Course" the instructor explains the procedures she will employ to teach the students to write to standard. Here she lists the class requirements:

**TEXTS**:
Bring both texts to every class meeting.
*Crossing Cultures: Readings for Composition.* Henry Knepler and Myrna Knepler, Eds. New York: Macmillan, 1989.

*The Bedford Handbook for Writers*. Diane Hacker, Ed. Boston: St. Martin's Press, 1991.

**ATTENDANCE AND PARTICIPATION:**
It is important that you attend regularly and participate in class activities. Class time will involve instruction, discussion, writing workshops, and individual assistance. All of these are essential to your growth as a writer. Therefore, more than four absences will be grounds for failure.

**READING**
All the reading assignments in *Crossing Cultures* must be completed by the beginning of the week for which they are listed. Our readings are selected to inform our discussions and writings. We will begin looking at culture and families. We then will continue with the struggle of the human spirit to fit in by conforming, stereotyping, scapegoating, destroying others, and destroying self. Our final segment of readings will deal with the survival of the human spirit. Throughout the semester, in-class impromptu writings on your reading assignments will be collected and evaluated.

The syllabus indicates that essay writing in this course will be personally focused and conform to a narrative structure that is mirrored in the assigned personal readings. Pat also assumes that students will locate versions of their own experiences and issues of concern in the essays she has selected.

The self-focused writing expectation required of the students through the reading section of the syllabus reveals the course theme as well as the underlying ideological assumptions and expectations. The purpose of the course is for the students to focus on themselves, their family, and cultural backgrounds with a shift to the internal struggles and conflicts they might have experienced in being asked to conform to external imposed expectations. The ideological assumptions indicate a prescribed homogeneity of experience and of expression. Pat even ends the thematic description of the course by talking about the struggle of human spirit and about self-destruction:

> ...the struggle to fit in by conforming, stereotyping, scapegoating, destroying others, and destroying self. Our final segment of readings will deal with the survival of the human spirit.

In writing about personal experiences and about struggling against conformity, students are then more likely to participate in written form because they start with what they know. Approaching writing with what the students know "is a workable concept which can help us teach writing.... It taps intuitive communication strategies writers already have, but are not adequately using" (Flower, 1986, p. 77). Basically, focusing on the personal essay becomes a starting point for the instructor to move into the more academic–type essays— the argumentative and persuasive essays.

These last two sections indicate how Pat is to evaluate the students on how well they complete the assignments listed in the course of study:

## GRADING

Attendance and participation in class are prerequisites for passing. The final grade for the course will be based on the six graded writings (90%) and in-class writing (10%).

## PROPOSED SYLLABUS:

| | |
|---|---|
| Week 1 | Read "Customs" (247–251) and "American Men Don't Cry" (209–292). |
| Week 2 | Read "Families" (85–89) and "Fitting In" (123–127). No class on Monday. |
| Week 3 | Read "Girlhood among Ghosts" (15–20) and "Halfway to Dick and Jane" (21–33). |
| Week 4 | Read "Hair" (120–122), "Shooting an Elephant" (228–235), and "The Village of Ben Suc" (209–215). |
| Week 5 | Writing #1 is due. |
| Week 6 | Read "Custer Died for Your Sins" (331–334) and "Incident" (37). |
| Week 7 | Read "When I Was a Child" (47–54). |
| Week 8 | Read "From Vietnam, 1979" (165–169). Writing # 2 is due. |
| Week 9 | Read "Arrival at Manzanar" (158–164). |
| Week 10 | Read "We Real Cool" (136). |
| Week 11 | Writing #3 and #4 are due. |
| Week 12 | Read "Graduation"(3–14) and "Alien Turf" (145–157). |
| Week 13 | Read "I Learn What I Am" (139–144). |
| Week 14 | Writing #5 is due. No class Friday, Nov. 29. |
| Week 15 | Writing #6: In-class essay. |

Breaking down the course of study apart from the rest of the syllabus is important because in case students do not see how thoroughly the ideological assumptions are structured and integrated a week–by–week description of the entire semester is provided. More importantly, Pat also shows how the reading assignments are sequenced with the writing assignments, which, in turn, are sequenced with her class objectives. This also allows students to see how each section of the syllabus can be distinctly identified, yet all the sections are nonetheless connected to each other from beginning to end in a sequential and hierarchical organizational type pattern (Mehan, 1979, p. 35–74). This sequential and hierarchical pattern allows for the syllabus to stand on its own as a separate text, to be understood as a completed text even outside the confines of the classroom (Scollon & Scollon, 1981, p. 48). Here, I use Meehan's (1979) definition of sequential and hierarchical: sequential referring to the continuity and connection of the parts of the syllabus as it unfolds through time from beginning to end, while hierarchal refers to how the syllabus is "nested" into its component parts, or units: "from the least important to the most important and from the most general to the most specific" (p. 35–74). Nested is: "A unit at a given rank is made of one or more units of rank below and combines with units of the same rank to make up a unit at the rank above"(p. 185–186).

The importance of the understanding why the syllabus, and ultimately the semester, is broken into these sequential and hierarchical patterns is further compounded because it is the instructor who is going to evaluate these students according to how many errors students make in structuring their essays. As she states in her "Grading" section of the syllabus: "The final grade for the course will be based on the six graded writings (90%) and in-class writing (10%)." This is further compounded by if they "miss more than four" class meeting, they will fail the course. Once again, the students are not being evaluated on how well they do, but on what they do wrong. Here is where we see that although the instructor has a broad understanding of essayist literacy, she has a somewhat ineffective interpretation of it. Thus, student reactions vary.

## The Academic Discourse Cultural Model

The instructor has successfully reduced teaching to "a narrowly defined concern with instrumental techniques, skills, and objectives" (Giroux, 1992, p. 98). But is memorizing the rules of academic discourse all there is to learning how to write? Obviously, the answer is a resounding no! For if this was the case, we wouldn't have what Pat Bizzell (1982) described as discrepancies in helping students to successfully complete composition courses. She points out that while some students are familiar and comfortable with academic discourse and excel in writing courses, others are not so familiar with this writing style and are even resistant to learning it. How well and how easily students learn this model depends on who the students are and where they come from (p. 225). Farr and Daniels (1986) further state when "Western schools attempt to teach students how to generate written language that displays these qualities [like] objectivity and explicitness" (p. 31), this is what it means to become literate in school; this translates into becoming successful in our society. When a student does not demonstrate these features, she is labeled as having something wrong, and that "wrong" must be "fixed." They then get placed in Basic Writing not so much to learn to write, but to understand the structure of writing (Ybarra, 1997).

Is this what happened to Letty? Yes. I suggest that the anger Latino students have about writing and English courses results from how we teach *beyond* writing skills; they result from how we as instructors treat students in writing courses. We treat them as if they are not very bright or intelligent. As a result, we unconsciously (or purposely) "water down the curriculum" (Moll, 1988). My answer is also supported by Paulo Freire (1997) in *Pedagogy of the Oppressed.* Freire is critical of mainstream teaching practices, referring to them as banking education. According to Freire (1997), in the banking approach to education, the teacher deposits information into an empty account because in this atmosphere, the student is seen as an object and is submersed in a culture of silence, resulting in the student feeling powerless because of his or her inability to change his or her life.

Letty is such an example. She increasingly became more silent as the semester progressed. Her silence alienated her from the classroom even more as she experienced "repeated failure and repeated negative encounters with her teacher" (Erickson, 1993, p. 41). Consequently, as a defensive mechanism, and "not necessarily within full reflective awareness," Letty's silence is because of her conflict with the process of her learning to write and this conflict is shown as an oppositional pattern, her "symbol of her disaffiliation with what she experienced" (Erickson, 1993, p. 41).

## Conclusion

"Teaching this culturally dominant structure to Latino students accounts for the assessment of their work as problematic in many writing courses because many Latinos don't think in this tripartite structure" (Ybarra, 2001, p. 48). Although understanding these parts are important when writing, as many scholars have pointed out for many years, writing is much more. The required tripartite structure conflicts with the oral discourse patterns that are influenced by

Spanish syntax, discourse rules, and cadence (Ybarra, 1997, 2001). As D. R. Randell (1998) argues, "When Anglo instructors ask students [Latinos] to state their thesis the beginning of the essay, they're asking students to go against their culture...." (p. 33). This is further compounded because we as teachers are going to evaluate how well these students write. Further compounding this matter, again, is the fact that students don't understand what we are teaching or why we are teaching writing in this way. This is so "despite the fact that they [may] have spent up to 12 years in a context in which the standard was taught" (Farr & Daniels, 1986, p. 201). Moreover, Latino students see school as trying to change them, but the personal costs of learning to become members of the school culture are often too high (Farr & Daniels, 1986; Ogbu, 1990). As a result, many of these students choose to reject school, and in doing so choose to fail. Many teachers see this response as "lazy or underachievers" and "fail to forge meaningful connections with their students" (Valenzuela, 1999, p. 5). Students, especially those from ethnic groups who have repeatedly been discriminated against in society, such as Latino students, will see this as a hostile act and resist learning.

Through an examination of this one syllabus I show how the teaching of writing, and the presentation on how to write, is organized according to a very specific model. I discuss how the instructor not only expects students to demonstrate this model in their writing, but also expects them to live within this model (Ybarra, 2000). Latino students feel they have very few options available to them. One option is that they accept that they are not very bright or intelligent; that they will never understand writing, so they shouldn't even try. Another other option is that they are different culturally and that writing and English courses are trying to change them, but this change is without guarantee. It is understandable why the students see learning to write academic discourse as a hostile and invasive course of action.

I should clarify at this point that I am not saying that we should not acculturate the nonmainstream student. I agree with scholars like Ogbu (1987) and Farr and Daniels (1986) that these nonmainstream students should understand the language and culture of the school because it will facilitate their economic improvement and perhaps their intellectual lives. But as teachers of writing we should be sensitive to the problems many of these students face when they encounter trouble according to mainstream standards (Ybarra, 1997). Furthermore, because we are teachers of writing and composition courses we have to locate our positions in what might be termed the conventional academic standards: the tripartite structure. We have to be aware, though, that we are not only suggesting change in discourse patterns, we are also suggesting change in a person's identity and culture (Scollon & Scollon, 1981; Ybarra, 2001).

Understanding that the model we use when we teach writing is as culturally and historically specific as is any other cultural language model will give us the insight we need to see how students from different ethnic groups and cultures respond to essayist literacy. However, there has been very little research done (to date) in this area. To understand how teaching writing affects nonmainstream students (specifically Latinos), we need to understand, describe, and analyze the culture of the classroom. We, the composition specialists, need to identify the cultural structures embedded in the writing so that we can then "adapt to make sure such tropes are conscious and use them to help revise our pedagogical assumptions" (Ybarra, 2001, p. 24). This then will help us better create an atmosphere that is conducive to learning for all students; a pedagogy of inclusion—what Lilia Bartholomae (1995) has termed a humanizing pedagogy that takes into account the cultural identities of the students.

To provide true learning access for all students in the composition classroom, writing and composition instructors must engage in a pedagogy that is inclusive and links cultural differences and approaches to learning objectives as those described above. That is to say, the concept of teaching standards and expecting students to perform at that level of standardization implies a learning objective of empowerment. Otherwise, the implicit objectives embedded within the notion of standardization of performance cannot be met, and many nonmainstream students will continue to fail.

# APPENDIX

## Syllabus

UIC Fall 1991                                    Office Hours: M: 11:00–12:00

Instructor:                                                                2:00–3:00

English 152 82714                                              W: 2:00–3:00

M, W, F: 12:00–12:50                                           F: 11:00–12:00

W: 11:00–1:50


AIMS OF THE COURSE

To develop clarity of thought by reading, thinking, and rethinking, redrafting, revising, editing, and polishing prose; to organize and develop ideas in coherent writing; to become confident in writing academic discourse.

TEXTS: Bring both texts to every class meeting.

*Crossing Cultures: Readings for Composition*. Henry Knepler and Myrna Knepler Eds. New York: Macmillan, 1989.

*The Bedford Handbook for Writers*. Diane Hacker, Ed. Boston: St Martin's Press, 1991.

ATTENDANCE AND PARTICIPATION

It is important that you attend regularly and participate in class activities. Class time will involve instruction, discussion, writing workshops, and individual assistance. All of these are essential to your growth as a writer. Therefore, more than four absences well be grounds for failure.

READING

All the reading assignments in *Crossing Cultures* must be completed by the beginning of the week for which they are listed. Our readings are selected to inform our discussions and writings. We will begin looking at culture and families. We then will continue with the struggle of the human spirit to fit in by conforming, stereotyping, scapegoating, destroying others, and destroying self. Our final segment of readings will deal with the survival of the human spirit.

Throughout the semester, in-class impromptu writings on your reading assignments will be collected and evaluated.

## WRITING

In addition to various short in–class and homework assignments, there will be six graded writings. Five of these must be typed double spaced, with one-inch margins. The sixth writing will be a final in-class essay. At announced times I will ask you to turn in all previous drafts with your final paper. Late papers lose one letter grade for each class meeting they are late.

## GRADING

Attendance and participation in class are prerequisites for passing. The final grade for the course will be based on the six graded writings (90%) and in-class writing (10%).

## PROPOSED SYLLABUS

Week 1    Read "Customs" (247–251) and "American Men Don't Cry" (209–292).
Week 2    Read "Families" (85–89) and "Fitting In" (123–127). No class on Monday, Sept. 2.
Week 3    Read "Girlhood Among Ghosts" (15–20) and "Halfway to Dick and Jane" (21–33).
Week 4    Read "Hair" (120–122), "Shooting an Elephant" (228–235), and "The Village of Ben Suc" (209–215).
Week 5    Writing #1 is due.
Week 6    Read "Custer Died for Your Sins" (331–334) and "Incident" (37).
Week 7    Read "When I Was a Child"(47–54).
Week 8    Read "From Vietnam, 1979" (165–169). Writing #2 is due.
Week 9    Read "Arrival at Manzanar" (158–164).
Week 10   Read "We Real Cool"(136).
Week 11   Writing assignments #3 and #4 are due.
Week 12   Read "Graduation"(3–14) and "Alien Turf" (145–157).
Week 13   Read "I Learn What I Am" (139–144).
Week 14   Writing #5 is due. No Class Friday, Nov. 29.
Week 15   Writing #6: In-class essay.

# Bibliography

Bartholomae, D. (1988a). Inventing the University. In E. R. Kintgen, B. M. Kroll, & M. Rose (Eds.), *Perspectives on Literacy* (pp. 273–285). Carbondale, IL: Southern Illinois University .

Bartholomae, D. (1988b). The Study of Error. In G. Tate & E. Corbett (Eds.), *The Writing Teacher's Sourcebook*, 2nd ed. (pp. 303–317). New York: Oxford.

Bartholomae, L. (1995). Beyond the Methods Fetish: Toward a Humanizing Pedagogy. *Harvard Educational Review, 64*, No. 2, 173–194.

Bizzell, P. (1982). Cognition, Convention, and Certainty: What We Need to Know About Writing. *Pre/Text 3*, No. 3, 213–243.

Cazden, C. (1986). Classroom Discourse. *Handbook of Research on Teaching* (pp. 432–463). New York: Macmillan.

D'Amato, J. (1993). Resistance and Compliance in Minority Classrooms. In E. Jacob & C. Jordan (Eds.), *Minority Education: Anthropological Perspectives,* (pp. 181–207). Norwood, NJ: Ablex.

Downs, N., et al. (1991). *A Syllabus for English 152*. Department of English. University of Illinois, Chicago.

Erickson, F. (1993). Resistance and Compliance in Minority Classrooms. In E. Jacob & C. Jordan (Eds.), *Transformation and School Success: The Politics and Culture of Educational Achievement* (pp. 27–51). Norwood, NJ: Ablex.

Farr, M. (1992). Essayist Literacy and Other Verbal Performances. *Written Communication, 10*, No. 1, 4–38.

Farr, M. (1990). *Oral Texts and Literacy Among Mexican Immigrants in Chicago*. Chicago: Spencer Foundation.

Farr, M., & Daniels, H. (1986). *Language Diversity and Writing Instruction*. New York: ERIC Clearinghouse on Urban Education Institute for Urban and Minority Education.

Flower, L. (1986). Writer–Based Prose: A Cognitive Basis for Problem in Writing. In T. Newkir (Ed.), *To Compose: Teaching Writing in High School* (pp. 76–103). Portsmouth, NH: Heinemann.

Fraher, R. (1984) Learning a New Art: Suggestions for Beginning Teachers. In M. Gullette (Ed.), *The Art and Craft of Teaching* (pp. 116–127). Cambridge, MA: Harvard University Press.

Freire, P. (1997). *Pedagogy of the oppressed*, 20th ed. Trans. Myra Bergman Ramos. New York: Continuum.

Giroux, H. A. (1992). *Border Crossings: Cultural Workers and the Politics of Education*. New York: Routledge.

Gumperz, J. J. (1982). *Discourse Strategies: Studies in Interactional Sociolinguistics*. New York: Cambridge University Press.

Heath, S. B. (1983). *Ways With Words: Language, Life and Work in Communities and Classrooms*. New York: Cambridge University Press.

Hymes, D. (1974). Introduction: Toward the Ethnographies of Communication. In J. Gumperz and D. Hymes (Eds.), *The Ethnography of Communication* (pp. 1–34). Washington, DC: American Anthropological Association.

Jepp, T.C, et al. (1993). Language and Disadvantage: The Hidden Process. In J. Gumperz (Ed.), *Language and Social Identity* (pp. 1–21). Cambridge, UK: Cambridge University Press.

Kutz, E. & Roskelly, H. (1991). *An Unquiet Pedagogy: Transforming Practice in the English Classroom.* Portsmouth, NH: Boynton/Cook.

Marin, G., & Marin, B. V. O. (1991). *Research With Hispanic Populations: Applied Research Methods.* Series. Vol. 23. Newbury Park, CA: Sage.

Mehan, H. (1979). *Learning Lessons.* Cambridge, MA: Harvard University Press.

Moll, L. C. (1988). Key Issues in Teaching Latino Students. *Language Arts, 65,* 465–472.

Ogbu, J. (1991). Immigrant and Involuntary Minorities in Comparative Perspective. In J. Ogbu & M. Gibson (Eds.), *Minority Status and Schooling: A Comparative Study of Immigrant and Involuntary Minorities* (pp. 3–33). New York: Garland.

Ogbu, J. (1990, Spring). Minority Status and Literacy in Comparative Perspective. *Dædalus,* 141–165.

Ogbu, J. (1987). Opportunity Structure, Cultural Boundaries, and Literacy. In J. Langer (Ed.), *Literacy and Culture: Issues of Society and Schooling* (pp. 149–177). Norwood, NJ: Ablex.

Pascarella, E. T. (1980). Student-Faculty Informal Contact and College Outcomes. *Review of Educational Research, 50,* No. 4, 545–595.

Randell, D. R. (1998). *The Logic of Indirection: The Polychronic Mode and Other Stories.* Unpublished Paper.

Rivera, L. ( 2001, October). *Can Adult Education Programs Provide a Way Out? A Study of Popular Education and Homeless Mothers.* Paper presented at the Trapped by Poverty/Trapped by Abuse Research Conference. Ann Arbor: University of Michigan.

Scollon, R. & Scollon, S. B. (1981). *Narrative, Literacy, and Face in Interethnic Communication.* Norwood, NJ: Ablex.

Stock, P., & Robinson, J. (1989). Literacy as Conversation: Classroom Talk as Text Building. In D. Bloome (Ed.), *Classroom and Literacy* (pp. 310–411). Norwood, NJ: Ablex.

Tinto, V. (1993). *Leaving College: Rethinking the Causes and Cures of Student Attrition,* 2nd ed. Chicago: University of Chicago.

Valenzuela, A. (1999). *Subtractive Schooling: U.S.–Mexican Youth and the Politics of Caring.* Albany: SUNY Press.

Valverde, S. A. (1987). A Comparative Study of Hispanic High School Dropouts and Graduates. *Education and Urban Society, 19,* 320–329.

Watkins, F. C. & Dillingham, W. B. (1973). *The Practical English Handbook.* Boston: Houghton Mifflin.

Ybarra, R. (2001). Cultural Dissonance in Basic Writing Courses. *Journal of Basic Writing, 20,* No. 1, 37–52.

Ybarra, R. (2000). Latino Students and Anglo–Mainstream Instructors: An Ethnographic Study of Classroom Communication. *Journal of College Student Retention: Research, Theory and Practice, 2,* No. 2, 161–171.

Ybarra, Raul. (1977). *Latino students and Anglo-mainstream instruction: An ethnographic study of classroom communication.* Ph.D. dissertation. Chicago: University of Illinois, Chicago.

. Ybarra, R. (1992). Western Essayist Literacy: A Way of Teaching. *College, Composition, and Communication Conference.* (ERIC Document. Reproduction Service No. ED. 346489)

# Chapter Six

# Academic Success
# and the Latino Family

*Roberto A. Ibarra*

My parents gave me the very best they had, but they couldn't give me what they didn't have... experience.

*Selena, a Chicana from Texas*

## Social Profile: Parents and the Family

Negative stereotypes shape our image of Latinos in the United States. What few outsiders see is how deeply these values permeate into that community. Latino family and social networks extend even beyond the nuclear parent–child group to include generations of cousins, in-laws, and even the fictive kin of god-parenting (Moore & Pachon, 1985, p. 96). Rarely portrayed are successful Latino families quietly achieving their goals by encouraging their offspring toward higher education. The common perceptions of Latino families by non-Latinos include the persistence of traditional patriarchal values, females who continue to encounter family roles subordinate to males, and Latinos who seek traditional family values; that is, they tend to be endogamous, or seek life partners within their group. Another common perception held by non-Latinos is that traditional Latino family patterns are unlikely to change as long as Latino families value pre-college education or 2–year, career–oriented degrees more than higher education. Non-Latino academics often refer to Latino traditional family values as serious barriers preventing access into higher education, especially for Latinas. But is this really the case? More specifically, what is the impact of traditional Latino family values on academic success in higher education?

## Research Design[1]

Preliminary answers emerged from research on Latinos pursuing graduate education and academic careers (Ibarra, 1996). In the study 77 individuals, 41 Latinos and 36 Latinas, were interviewed for a project for the Council of Graduate Schools (CGS) in 1994 and 1995. The primary objective was to explore all facets and elements of success for Latinos in graduate education and beyond. The strategy was to investigate social conditions, including characteristics associated with Latino families, communities, and other social systems, which could point to potentially significant influences for predicting success. The study focused on selected samples of Latino faculty, administrators, and graduate students working on master's or doctoral degrees. I also interviewed non-academics, individuals with doctoral degrees who either left academe or never pursued an academic position. Most non-academics were employed by private organizations either directly or indirectly affiliated with higher education.

I selected the participants to reflect, as much as possible, a cross-section of ethnicity, national origin, gender, generation, region, and institution. Latino faculty and administrators were those new and tenured, as well as seasoned deans, vice chancellors, and presidents.

My primary goal in selecting participants was to sample populations by ethnicity and region. The ethnicity and national origins of the study group were as follows: 41 Mexican Americans, four of whom were born in Mexico; 16 Puerto Ricans, among whom half were from the island; 12 Cuban Americans, including seven from Cuba; and eight "other" Latinos from the following origins: three from Costa Rica (including one international student), one each from Colombia, Venezuela, the Dominican Republic, California/Spanish American, and New Mexico/Spanish American. The last two individuals traced their ancestry back 200 years to the original Spanish land-grant families from Mexico and did not initially identify as Mexican Americans in the interviews.

A demographic profile of respondents shows the age range spans almost 5 full decades, beginning with the 1930s. The majority[2] were born between 1940 and 1960, with many born during the 1950s. All but one respondent were U.S. citizens, although 20% were immigrants who became naturalized U.S. citizens. Almost half the group were second-generation U.S. citizens; that is, native-born (including Puerto Rico) with foreign-born parents. Nearly a quarter of the respondents were third-generation (one or both parents born in the United States, including Puerto Rico) and only a few were from the fourth-generation or more. The majority of respondents (62%) were from predominantly first-generation (immigrant) and second-generation backgrounds. However, within each group only half the Mexican Americans and most of the Puerto Ricans, Cubans, and "other" Latinos were from first- or immigrant-generations.

## Factors for Academic Success

Research suggests that the common perception of a traditional and monolithic Latino family may be flawed from the start (Moore & Pachon, 1985; Vega, 1995). Even Latinos in this research project described their family life as somewhat nontraditional. Although many portrayed their families as holding onto some traditional beliefs, the patterns and incidents varied by ethnic group, and according to respondents, in some cases conditions were changing for the better. For example, according to some women in the study group, the influence of traditional patriarchal values favoring male over female siblings still exists, but is seems to be diminishing as more Latinas pursue higher education. While it may be true that more patriarchal traditions continue among Mexican American families, this is not the case for other Latino groups. Hidden by cultural misconceptions for over a century of American occupation, Puerto Rico has diminished the patriarchal family structure so much so that many no longer sustain traditional roles, even at the risk of declining economic well-being (Moore & Pachon, 1985; Ortiz, 1995). In fact, Puerto Rican women are anything but resigned to a submissive family role (Toro-Morn, 1995). It seems that at least some Latino family characteristics are changing from what the public commonly perceives. Clearly, to understand the Latino graduate experience academics would benefit greatly by examining the impact of the Latino family on the success of their offspring in higher education.

For Latinos in general the family and community play vital roles in building aspirations and preparing their members for entry into careers or higher education. At the core of the Latino cultures are family values that instill a preference for positive interpersonal interactions, a reliance on relatives as providers of emotional support, and family unity in times of need. Among Latinos in the study, the parental family was, indeed, a tight-knit unit. Only a small number had disrupted families or divorced parents, and almost all described the nurturing they received from their immediate and extended families. However, large family size and sibling order were not associated with reducing individual motivation and achievement according to Gándara's study of Chicano high achievers (1995, p. 35). Results from this study tend to corroborate her findings.

Latino participants in this study came from large families with at least five or more siblings. Almost 40% of the Mexican Americans were reared in families this size, compared to only 25% among Puerto Rican respondents. Regarding birth order, again, mainly Mexican Americans (42%) and Puerto Ricans (38%) tended to be the oldest or firstborns in their families, compared to very few firstborn among Cubans and "other" Latinos. This contrast may partially be due to the relatively larger sample size of the Mexican American cohort, and partially to the social and cultural differences between the various ethnic groups in the study. However, in contrast to Gándara's findings, in which none of her subjects were either disproportionately firstborns or lastborns, Mexican Americans and Puerto Ricans here stand out by their larger families and greater firstborn predominance. Though the potential exists for large families with limited resources to impede sibling success, none of the Latinos interviewed seemed affected by either family size or sibling order. These findings concur with Gándara's research which focused on "family dynamics and values across cultures" (1995, p. 35) as being far more significant than research focused on family structures in only one cultural context.

Language is another important factor for success. Most monolingual speakers assume that individuals reared in non-English speaking homes are at a disadvantage when they enter public schools or the workplace. Within the Latino study group Spanish was either the first language learned, or spoken, most often at home while growing up, which, not surprisingly, associates with the large number of first-generation Latinos in the study. Almost half of all those interviewed recall speaking only Spanish at home, while many (36%) recall using both Spanish and English, and only some (15%) spoke only English, meaning that they were exposed to Spanish but used it very little. The argument that bilingualism (Spanish in the home) causes language difficulties, poor test performance, and even educational underachievement is still being debated despite research showing there is no correlation or evidence to support the argument (see Gándara, 1995; Hurtado, 1995; Solis, 1995). Though nearly a majority of the Latinos interviewed in the study spoke only Spanish at home, most participants (86%) did not receive any bilingual education during their primary or secondary school years. Those who had some exposure to bilingual education were mainly educated outside the U.S. mainland, either in Puerto Rico, Cuba, or in some other country associated with their immigrant origins.

Most scholars agree that a family's socioeconomic well-being can, in our society, influence the outcome of its offspring. The combined occupational, educational, and social experiences of its members establish critical patterns that increase the chances for success among offspring. These family patterns also establish the cultural context, values, goals, and aspirations for preparing their offspring for entering higher education. The question then is: Are they being prepared well enough? One could assume that parents with more education are more likely to encourage their offspring to complete a degree and thereby increase their chances for success. Gándara (1995) found high parental aspirations, support, and encouragement toward educational achievement among the Chicanos she studied. Despite their low socioeconomic conditions, class status, and little parental involvement in their schools, her subjects eventually completed professional and doctoral degrees from academically challenging institutions.

Latinos in this study had very similar family profiles and the patterns were revealing in their diversity. Table 1 shows the level of parental experience in higher education by ethnic group. Overall, more than half the study group had one or more parents without any college experience, and most had never even completed a college degree. But the inter ethnic comparisons reveal significant inequities, which too often become masked by lumping together diverse ethnic data. For example, 71% of Mexican Americans in the group had parents with no college experience and over 65% of these parents never completed high school. In contrast, only some parents of Puerto Ricans, Cubans, and "other" Latinos had parents with no college training. In fact, only a few of the Mexican Americans interviewed had one or more parents with a college degree, whereas many Latinos from the other three groups had one or more parents with a college degree. Twice as many island Puerto Ricans had one or more parents with an advanced degree than Puerto Ricans from the mainland. Overall, Cuban Americans had the highest percentage of any group with parents earning advanced degrees. These patterns seemed to coincide with U.S. census data on the various Latino populations over age 25 (Hodgkinson & Outtz, 1996). It is easy to see how misconceptions about Latinos in higher education develop when too many administrators depend upon homogenized data to profile their various cultures. Unfortunately, they are missing the true picture of ethnic group diversity and their specific educational needs.

Table 1
Latino Project 1994–95 Parental Level of Higher Education
(Total of One or Both Parents and % of Total)

| CATEGORY | MEX AMER | PUERTO RICAN | CUBAN | OTHER LATINO | TOTAL N=77 |
|---|---|---|---|---|---|
| BOTH - NO COLLEGE | 71% (n=29) | 38% (n=6) | 30% (n=3) | 33% (n=3) | 54% (n=41) |
| SOME COLLEGE, NO DEGREE | 22% (n=9) | 25% (n=4) | 20% (n=2) | 22% (n=2) | 29% (n=17) |
| UNDERGRAD DEGREE ONLY | 2% (n=1) | 19% (n=3) | 30% (n=3) | 11% (n=1) | 10% (n=8) |
| ADVANCED DEGREES | 5% (n=2) | 19% (n=3) | 30% (n=3) | 25% (n=2) | 13% (n=10) |
| TOTAL RESPONSES | 41 | 16 | 11 | 8 | 76 |

Percentages are based on group totals and do not equal 100% due to rounding.
Total n will vary depending on whether focus groups were asked to respond.

Nearly everyone in the study provided information about their parents' work or occupations. Categorizing and arranging their responses into traditionally defined blue-collar (service sector, agricultural, and operative work) or white-collar (professional, executive, educational) occupational groups generated a clear picture of socioeconomic family conditions. Overall, the differences in these patterns (see Table 2) were similar to those on parents' education in Table 1. While the majority of those responding had parents with white-collar occupations, the inter ethnic comparisons presented a different picture. Over half the Mexican American parents held blue-collar jobs while the majority of Puerto Ricans, most of the "other" Latinos, and virtually all Cuban American parents came from white-collar backgrounds. Again, the patterns show that data masks the reality of socioeconomic and class differences. Yet despite these differences in parental backgrounds, Mexican Americans in the study achieved a high level of academic success by the fact that they were either in graduate programs, had received advanced degrees, or were successful in their academic careers. Another measure of their success is demonstrated by fact that of the seven respondents whose parents were agricultural migrants or subsistence farmers, six were Mexican Americans who achieved, or were nearing completion, of their doctoral degrees.

Table 2
Latino Project 1994–95 Parental Occupation
(Total of One or Both Parents and % of Total)

| CATEGORY | MEX AMER | PUERTO RICAN | CUBAN | OTHER LATINO | TOTAL N=77 |
|---|---|---|---|---|---|
| WHITE-COLLAR | 47% (n=16) | 67% (n=10) | 92% (n=11) | 86% (n=6) | 63% (n=43) |
| BLUE-COLLAR | 53% (n=18) | 33% (n=5) | 8% (n=1) | 14% (n=1) | 37% (n=25) |
| TOTAL RESPONSE | 34 | 15 | 12 | 7 | 68 |

Percentages are based on group totals and do not equal 100% due to rounding.
Total n will vary depending on whether focus groups were asked to respond.

## Social Profile: During Graduate School

By the time respondents entered graduate school, some of their parental family patterns had changed significantly, suggesting acculturation was changing the Latino social system. Some change is expected between families of orientation (where they were reared) and their own families. This would be especially true among first- or second-generation individuals who tend to make modifications in their lifestyle to fit their current professional status or career upward mobility. Some researchers have labeled these Latinos HUPPIES, or "Hispanic Upwardly-mobile Professionals, who want to integrate themselves into the mainstream and corporate cultures" (Cuello, 1996, p. 3).

Language is one of the first cultural characteristics to change for almost any immigrant group. In the study group, the predominance of using Spanish over English for communication in their parental home reversed dramatically for many individuals when they became adults. This was quite notable among those who now had life partners or families of their own. Not surprisingly, the majority (58%) admitted using only English with their families and partners at home today. While 36% spoke both English and Spanish at home, only a few (6%) spoke only Spanish. Perhaps this is related to the fact that over half of those currently living with a spouse or partner are paired with non-Latinos. And among those claiming to be bilingual at home, only two admitted to a habit of code switching. This common conversational practice among some Latinos can be a confusing event for most non-Latinos. It is an unconscious pattern of beginning a sentence or a phrase in either Spanish or English and then switching in mid-phrase to complete the idea in the other language.

Although participants seemed to speak more English in their own homes today than when growing up in their parents' homes, such language shifts are natural occurrences within first-generation populations (Moore & Pachon, 1995). None of this, however, signals impending doom for the use of Spanish among Latinos. In fact, a number of influences such as the continual replenishment from Spanish-speaking immigrations, the proliferation of Spanish language radio, television, newspapers, and magazines in the United States all contribute to language maintenance. The current positive attitudes toward the use of Spanish for general communication, and as ethnic identity in Latino families, may actually help significantly in sustaining current patterns of language use for future generations (Hurtado, 1995; Moore & Pachon, 1995). Whatever the future may hold for bilingual Spanish speakers, it did not seem to impede Latinos in the study from achieving their advanced degrees.

## The Latino Family and Cultural Context

One question about Latinos remains unclear: What impact does the family have on their progress through higher education? At the graduate level students are becoming more nontraditional, meaning that they are returning adults, or have families of their own, and less likely to be directly influenced by their parents. But, family ties that value mutual support still run deeply and a few questions in the study asked participants about financial obligations or other responsibilities between themselves and extended family members while in graduate school. A few participants mentioned extended family support, none of which was monetary. In Table 2, only eight of those interviewed, the majority being Mexican American, had parents or extended family members (i.e., grandparents) living with them while they were enrolled in a full-time graduate program. But many Latinos, again predominantly Mexican Americans, contributed to the financial support or care of family members beyond the immediate family. This did not seem to be a significant problem unless their graduate support was marginal. For those with a spouse or partner at the time, financial problems may not have been too severe. Over 80% of all of those interviewed mentioned that graduate funding was necessary but adequate (see Ibarra, 1996). But among those with families or committed relationships during graduate school, 75% had partners with steady employment and a good income. Among them, nearly 80% were in professional occupations or were also graduate students with an additional income to supplement support. There is no doubt that graduate education is a financial burden for Latinos, especially those from low-income backgrounds. But there are also many economic benefits associated with the family that present interesting implications that have yet to be fully explored by researchers in the field.

Two important patterns stand out among the differences in Latino family profiles. First, data aggregation, especially among Latinos, masks variations between ethnic groups that can create misconceptions about certain ethnic populations. Second, presuming that socioeconomic background is a variable that affects access to higher education, populations such as the Mexican Americans interviewed here could be facing greater adversity in obtaining advanced degrees than other Latino groups. Characteristics such as family size, language used in the home, class status, and levels of parental education and occupation could present barriers to educational achievement. This project confirms previous research findings (Gándara, 1982, 1993) that these characteristics did not seem to limit the participants' accomplishments. However, there is no reliable way to validate this conclusion without dependable, disaggregated ethnic data.

## Latino Family Values and Academic Success

My earlier comments suggest that some respondents and investigators believe the Latino family archetype is changing, and, indeed, a social transformation may be dawning (see Ibarra, 1996). Others in the study believe traditional family attitudes still have a strong grip on many Latino and Latina offspring. It was striking to see these contradictory perspectives, changing vs. traditional, on the family throughout the interviews. Participants painted portraits of contemporary families juxtaposed with fleeting images of traditional family values. One particular comment by a Latina university president states it quite succinctly:

> The average student comes to us still way under prepared...and once they get to us, they are bombarded with responsibilities of family, finances, and culture.... My family was an exception to what they believe a girl should do or what a kid should do. I still have students that I talk to who are wondering how to get permission to go to college

or to leave the [community]. How do you talk to your husband about going back to school? If things are still static in a great part of the masses, and we've not been successful in infiltrating some of those values that determine futures, then I think we do a lousy job of higher education.

Many would agree that we "do a lousy job of higher education." On our campuses, the common perception of Latino family values is riddled with stereotypes and misconceptions. Even campus administrators foster misinterpretations. In my previous role as a university administrator, many non-Latino colleagues, for instance, often discussed their "personal concerns" for Latino students. That phrase was often a euphemism for concealing their belief that Latino family customs created most of the problems for Latino students in higher education. We noted that usually near the end of each the academic year some Latino undergraduates approached their campus student service advisors pleading for help to deal with unexpected financial problems. I knew graduate students who seemed to face similar difficulties. Most undergraduates claimed they ran into bad luck or miscalculated their financial aid budgets. Some advisors were upset because these students were usually low-income freshman or sophomores who could not afford to give their money away. The students involved were mostly island Puerto Ricans, so advisors assumed they were still learning how to handle money. A few advisors suspected students had overspent budgets buying stereo systems or other expensive items for their residences. Actually, most of them ran out of funds because they felt a deep obligation to help support the family back home. Although few students would admit to it, throughout the year they would regularly send small portions of their financial aid funds home to assist their parents, who very likely needed the support. Program coordinators, however, could not be dissuaded from their belief that the students were being "pressured by traditional family customs" to send money to their parents.

The issue for my non-Latino colleagues was not about sending money back home, but rather about their belief that students were driven unduly hard by family pressure. As Manuel (not his real name), a Chicano doctoral student and former migrant worker attests, it was not family pressure but his own pressure and guilt that compelled him to send support:

When I got older I...would always give my money to my parents. When I went to [State College] I had to fill out all the financial aid forms myself because my parents didn't know how to do it. I felt guilty that I had left them behind in poverty—that I should be out there working in the fields because I knew what it was like. I took a job at the college work-study and then I took another job at [fast-food restaurant]. I would send the biggest paycheck home to my family and I lived off the smallest paycheck in order to compensate.

Poverty was a critical factor for Manuel and many like him, but I, too, remember an underlying sense of responsibility and duty to family. Many Latino students were just getting by on campus and could ill afford to send their financial aid or fellowship support to families back home. Nevertheless, they scrimped to avoid financial stress, until something happened to them or the family and their financial situation worsened. They were the Latino students caught financially short at years end. In most cases, their funds were grants, not loans, and a grant to support the family would also support their well-being on campus far away from home. It was not inappropriate; in fact, it was the right thing to do from their perspective.

## Cultural Context and Latino Family Values

Latino faculty in this study encountered similar misconceptions about Latino families from their administrative colleagues on campus. The following passage reveals a fresh perspective on the problem. Alfonso, a Cuban American professor at a southwestern university comments about non-Latino administrators and their perspective on the issue of "excessive connectedness" between Mexican American students and their families:

The university asked me to give talks on Latino history, Latino themes, Latino identity, and student life to their faculty, and to people who deal with student services. They have counselors and a whole group of people who work with the students. On two occasions they've asked me to come and give talks about Latino issues they're particularly interested in relating to Latinos and their families. One of the big problems they've had is what they seem to think is excessive connectedness between students and their families which creates barriers to the emergence of the individual. A lot of students feel constrained in developing their academic interests beyond undergraduate school because they feel like they have an obligation to go home whether it's in the Valley, or on the border, or wherever it might be. There is a very traditional family connection there which many of the counselors, who are mostly Anglo American, don't understand and don't know quite how to deal with it.... [A] lot of the Latino students, particularly from the more traditional families, seem to carry a tremendous burden. They feel that they're carrying their whole family name, their whole family honor with them when they come to the university. Usually they're the first generation and it's often a family event, so there's a sense that they can't fail which puts a lot of pressure on them. When they run into difficulties in school and in their classes the counselors talked about that kind of problem and how to deal with those kinds of issues. I was surprised but a lot of the counselors were just mystified by this very powerful family unit.

Alfonso describes not just cultural differences between Anglo American academics and Latino students, but also fundamental conflicts between High and Low Context cultures as described by anthropologist Edward T. Hall (1959, 1966, 1977, and 1984). Hall found that most Latino cultures, regardless of national origin, tended to be High Context (HC); they tend to imprint a wide variety of cultural values and cognitive patterns to help them perceive and interpret the world. As Hall tells us, HC cultures, with their high personal commitment to others, tend to value a group orientation to learning and prefer working in groups for problem solving. Singularly, these traits predict strong commitments toward family and community. In comparison, a Low Context (LC) population, which for Hall includes Northern Europeans and their ethnic counterparts in the United States, are not as deeply involved with people. Not surprisingly, Anglo American faculty and counselors would perceive the Latino student's high commitment to family as excessive connectedness, creating barriers to the emergence of the individual. Traditional Latino families are perceived as preventing growth in academic interests and individualism in their offspring by encouraging unnecessary obligations to remain close to the family both in values and proximity. But as Alfonso points out, higher education is a group process, a family event; the honor and the pressure to succeed rests on the shoulders of the offspring.

There are a number of issues and misconceptions involved here. Is an LC perspective the only legitimate learning mode? An HC group-oriented learning style does not automatically preclude personal independence. It would be a mistake to confuse the two, for Latinos cultivate a sense of independence in their attitudes toward work (Gándara, 1995) combined with the values of style or group-oriented learning. Latinos and Latinas learn a more individualistic learning style by conforming to the LC values of academia. The university, in Alfonso's situation, is missing a tremendous opportunity to understand group learning concepts, by encouraging families to become a part of their educational system. There might be new insights and broader applications in doing this. Rather than capitalizing on opportunities for life long learning through continuing education and outreach, colleges and universities (especially research institutions) tend to marginalize, segment, compartmentalize, or devalue these service-oriented missions in academia.

Meanwhile, Latino students are not just becoming bicultural; they are becoming bicognitive and multicontextual too (Ibarra, 2001). Despite mastering difficult cultural customs and linguistic behaviors, they also learn to live and function in hidden, opposing worlds of cultural context. While most students are taught to approach problem solving and academic studies from an individual LC perspective, Latinos and other HC cultures have learning modes which unconsciously trigger problem solving and academic learning in a group context. As Hall clearly describes (1959, 1966, 1977, 1984), these learning modes can be unconscious and, as I suggest, under certain conditions they even become default modes for perceptions of the world (Ibarra, 2001). Under duress the default mode of cultural context unconsciously dictates how one should react or behave, a situation describing bicognitive people in multicontextual circumstances. Latinos learn to balance and shift between the HC cultures of their family and community and then learn to maneuver through a maze of LC cultural values in their academic community.

These are not only conflicting learning modes, but also difficult modes to learn quickly or even completely. A fundamental misconception about ethnic populations is the assumption that if outsiders to the group exhibit fluency in language and overt customs, then the less visible underlying perceptions of the world are also identical to their own. This unspoken assumption carries over into education, especially higher education, with drastic consequences. Children enter public school or university systems with all the appropriate visible cultural signals that lead majority populations to think that their culturally diverse colleagues perceive the world as others do. But such assumptions are the basis for misunderstanding and misinterpreting academic performance, and are critical concerns in standardized testing and evaluation which predominantly favors LC capabilities.

Ramírez and Castañeda (1974) are quite clear about their findings on the lopsidedness of Euro-American public school systems, and they are not alone in their opinions. Cohen (1969) laid the groundwork for low-income populations in public schools and Hale-Benson (1986) presents very similar conclusions for African American children. Academic inability may not be the problem after all for Latinos and other HC populations. Instead, the complexity of cultural context embedded in academic culture may be hampering their ability to succeed academically. Consequently, this hidden HC/LC cultural conflict has a direct and negative impact on academic performance, and very likely it generates the negative perceptions of Latinos among university counselors who, for example, are mystified by the power of the family unit.

Evidence indicates that family values have a powerful impact in shaping cultural context and cognition in education (Cohen, 1969; Hale-Benson, 1986; Ramírez & Castañeda, 1974). In her study of high–achieving Chicanos, Gándara (1995) examines the influence of home and family on educational aspirations and academic achievement. She studied class values, work attitudes, support and encouragement, and family structure, among others. Applying research on parent-child interactions, teaching strategies (Laosa, 1978), and psychosocial factors relating to achievement motivation (Grebler, Moore, & Guzmán, 1970), Gándara concludes: 1. "[P]arents have a direct impact on the formation of the children's educational aspirations…." 2. "There are significant differences between non-Latino, majority middle-class parental teaching strategies and Mexican American teaching strategies in the home." 3. "These differences tend to disappear among middle-class Chicana mothers with higher levels of education" (1995, p. 26).

There are several dynamic interactions occurring simultaneously here. For instance, Laosa describes the teaching/learning strategies among the middle–class majority family as shaping "requirements for independent (as opposed to group) problem solving that are characteristic of American classrooms" (Laosa, 1978, in Gándara, 1995, p. 26–27). It also explains the conflict that occurs between HC/LC characteristics within the cultural domains, namely the association and learning described by Hall (1959). While HC individuals favor a group process and value the relationships between people for getting things done, LC individuals prefer learning and doing tasks individually. However, the concept of independence with regard to academic achievement may have a different meaning for Chicanos than other cultural groups. According to Grebler, Moore, and Guzmán, although "independence of the family *unit* might be valued within Chicano culture, family members are commonly rewarded for pursuing familial rather than personal goals" (1970, emphasis in Gándara, 1995, p. 27).

In other words, even though some Latino family values and behaviors may shift with upward socioeconomic mobility, there may be certain bicognitive values, in this case HC values, which either do not shift or are interlaced with the value and behavior changes associated with new class or educational status. Furthermore, these combinations of values and behaviors may be retained by family and community members as a function of ethnic maintenance and continuity. I view ethnicity and ethnic identity as reflecting a variety of social phenomena, which includes transforming human behavior into an expression of adaptive social strategies (Strickon & Ibarra, 1983). One could describe bicognition then as learning different sets of behaviors that one can choose to switch on or off depending on conditions and the appropriate ethnic or cultural contexts.

Psychologist Martin Ford (1992) has developed a "Living Systems Framework" that helps explain this phenomenon. Ford believes individuals develop and compile a repertoire of behavior episodes—temporary phenomena, like video news stories. Guided by these experiences, people tend to remember these episodes and other similar experiences. If they can be anchored by individual goals and contexts, these episodes can become reinforced as enduring behavior patterns (Ford, 1992). Over time, these behavior episodes tend to be linked together sequentially and can grow into elaborate scripts of habitual or automated behavior. Moreover, some individuals develop "a diverse repertoire of optional behavior patterns organized around a related set of goals and contexts" (p. 29). Combining these sets of behaviors generates governing (cognitive) functions, or adaptive strategies, which individuals can use for dealing with challenging conditions, adversity and multiple contextual environments.

Becoming multicontextual (Ibarra, 2001) is not only a process of developing behavioral flexibility and knowing when to use it, but also knowing how to apply the appropriate scripts to interact effectively within different sociocultural environments. In the case of multicontextual Latinos, different scripts are used when they are involved in HC family and community situations, and LC scripts are utilized in educational and academic settings. Those who learn and become adept at manipulating their behavioral scripts appropriately are more likely to adapt to the dominant LC culture of higher education and ultimately develop greater potential for success in achieving an advanced degree.

## Latino Family Values and School Support

Research on the patterns of parental support for school achievement among Mexican Americans (Okagaki & Frensch, 1995) reinforces the hypothesis of the Living Systems Framework and adds further evidence to confirm the multicontext model (Ibarra, 2001). In their study of the ways immigrant and nonimmigrant parents of Mexican descent differ in their parenting behavior, Okagaki and Frensch generated a number of conclusions: 1. Minority groups differ widely in the United States and to understand home-school relationships requires a greater understanding of the larger social context; 2. "The skills and behavioral norms of children at home may differ from the behavioral patterns and expectations of the classroom. Consequently, Mexican American students may have difficulty processing information and decoding cues…"; 3. These "context-specific differences may have more impact on young children than on adolescents…"; 4. Whether or not cultural differences among Mexican Americans is a factor in achievement, generational differences related to parental generation is a critical factor in school achievement (1995, p. 339). Based on my Latino interviews, I differ only with their third point: the difficulties processing information and decoding cues may have as much impact on graduate students as they do on young children.

These generational differences, according to Okagaki and Frensch, correlate directly with immigrant status. Nonimmigrant Mexican Americans were more like Euro-Americans in preferring autonomous parenting behavior over conforming parenting behavior, which was the preference closely associated with immigrant Mexican Americans. But when these same groups were asked about the importance of intelligence as defined by cognitive traits (problem-solving skills, verbal and creative abilities) and non-cognitive traits (social skills, motivation, practical skills), the groups of immigrant and nonimmigrant Mexican American parents were similar to each other in selecting non-cognitive traits, and different from Euro-Americans who selected the cognitive traits (Okagaki & Frensch, 1995, p. 337). I suggest these variable patterns not only reflect the changing dynamics of ethnicity in the United States, but more importantly, these similarities and differences reveal only one set of possible permutations associated with the multicontext model (Ibarra, 2001).

To illustrate, Okagaki and Frensch found that the primary difference between the two groups of Mexican Americans was that nonimmigrant parents valued teaching academic skills (how to ask questions and how to be creative) as more important than learning to print or work neatly. This can be directly associated with important LC cultural preferences toward analytical thinking found in North American schools (Cohen, 1969). Immigrant Mexican Americans, on the other hand, felt learning to "do work neatly and orderly as being more important than learning basic facts, developing problem-solving skills, and developing creativity" (Okagaki & Frensch, 1995, p. 338). This reflects values more closely aligned with Latin American educational systems in which the prevalent pattern is toward a more authoritarian teaching style that favors a combination of HC group learning processes intertwined with LC learning process of rote memorization and class recitations (see Hofstede, 1991). But the salient finding is that parents from both immigrant and nonimmigrant Mexican groups believed social skills (playing well with other children, showing respect, being sensitive to people's needs) are very important components in their concept of what is needed to demonstrate academic intelligence in schools. Characteristics emphasizing preferences toward group learning processes, associations, and personal commitment to people lends support to the hypothesis that HC cultural values are integral components in Mexican American and other Latino families. Moreover, the variability of preferences found among the immigrant and nonimmigrant Mexican groups in parental support and academic intelligence suggests that multicontextuality may also play a significant role in shaping Latinos in our educational systems.

Psychologist Robert J. Sternberg's study on successful intelligence (1996) confirms the pattern for parental concepts of intelligence and adds to it by describing the consequences for children when their parents and public schools value different perceptions of intelligence. With Okagaki as a coinvestigator, Sternberg studied parents from different ethnic groups, including Latinos, in California to compare their conceptions of intelligence (Okagaki & Sternberg, 1993). They found that public school systems in general value only certain kinds of intelligence and undervalue certain other forms of intelligence, causing schools to underestimate certain student abilities and peg them as much less intelligent than they really are. He learned

> that the more parents emphasize social competence skills—such as getting along with peers and helping out the family—in their conception of intelligence, the less bright their children look according to the standards of the schools. In other words, the missmatch between what the parents emphasized in their environment and what the schools required in theirs resulted in kids who might be quite competent in the home and community setting but would be judged as intellectually lacking in the school. (Sternberg, 1996, p. 143)

Sternberg's research has important implications for Latinos and other HC cultures involved throughout our secondary and higher educational systems in this country. He claims there are three kinds of intelligence: analytical, associated with academics, creative, the ability to formulate good problems and ideas, and practical, the ability to use these ideas and their analysis effectively in everyday life; and public schools as well as higher education in the United States ignores these important concepts to the detriment of many ethnic groups and women (1988, 1996). For Latino families, his research suggests that the origins of conflict between HC/LC cultures in our educational systems may run deep into the beliefs, values, and perceptions of human intelligence itself.

There is sufficient evidence to suggest that there is a multicontext model threaded into the fabric of Latino families (Ibarra, 2001). This means that the characteristics of HC cultural values and cognitive styles are fundamental forces shaping the perceptions of Latinos in the larger social and educational systems. Even within the same ethnic group, Latinos may differ by generation, but the influence of culture and cognition threaded through the dynamics of ethnic identity may be the adhesive components of Latino family infrastructures. No matter how much cultural change takes its toll on language, family, or even Latino cultural customs, the multicontext characteristics found within Latino cultures may play a greater role than was previously imagined within the hidden dimensions of success in our educational systems.

# Bibliography

Cohen, R. A. (1969). Conceptual Styles, Culture Conflict, and Nonverbal Tests of Intelligence. *American Anthropologist, 71*, 828–856.

Cuello, J. (1996). Latinos and Hispanics: A Primer on Terminology. *Midwest Consortium for Latino Research* (MCLR). Internet research publication, retrieved 12/22/96, at <jcuello@cms.cc.2wayne.edu>

Ford, M. E. (1992). *Motivating Humans: Goals, Emotions, and Personal Agency Beliefs.* Newbury Park, CA: Sage.

Gándara, P. (1995). *Over the Ivy Walls: The Educational Mobility of Low-Income Chicanos.* Albany: SUNY.

Gándara, P. (1993). *Choosing Higher Education: The Educational Mobility of Chicano Students.* California Policy Seminar Brief, Vol. 5, No. 10.

Gándara, P. (1982). Passing Through the Eye of the Needle: High Achieving Chicanas. *Hispanic Journal of Behavioral Sciences, 4*, 167–179.

Grebler, L., Moore, J., & Guzmán, R. C. (1970). *The Mexican American People: The Nation's Second Largest Minority.* New York: Free Press Press.

Hale-Benson, J. E. (1986). *Black Children: Their Roots, Culture, and Learning Styles.* Baltimore, MD: Johns Hopkins University.

Hall, E. T. (1984). *The Dance of Life: The Other Dimension of Time.* 2nd ed. Garden City, NY: Anchor Press/Doubleday.

Hall, E. T. (1977). *Beyond Culture.* 2nd ed. Garden City, NY: Anchor.

Hall, E. T. (1966). *The Hidden Dimension.* 2nd ed. Garden City, NY: Anchor.

Hall, E. T. (1959). *The Silent Language.* Greenwich, CT: Fawcett Publications.

Hodgkinson, H. L., & Outtz, J. H. (1996, January). *Hispanic Americans: A Look Back, a Look Ahead.* Washington, DC: The Institute for Educational Leadership, Center for Demographic Policy.

Hofstede, G. (1991). *Cultures and Organizations: Software of the Mind.* New York: McGraw-Hill.

Hurtado, A. (1995). Variations, Combinations, and Evolutions: Latino Families in the United States. In R. E. Zambrana (Ed.), *Understanding Latino Families: Scholarship, Policy, and Practice* (pp. 40–61). Thousand Oaks, CA: Sage.

Ibarra, R. A. (2001). *Beyond Affirmative Action: Reframing the Context of Higher Education.* Madison: University of Wisconsin Press.

Ibarra, R. A. (1996). Latino Experiences in Graduate Education: Implications for Change. *Enhancing the Minority Presence in Graduate Education, VII.* Washington, DC: The Council of Graduate Schools.

Laosa, L. M. (1978). Maternal Teaching Strategies in Chicano Families of Varied Educational and Socioeconomic Levels. *Child Development, 49*, 1129–1135.

Moore, J., & Pachon, H. (1985). *Hispanics in the United States.* Englewood Cliffs, NJ: Prentice-Hall.

Okagaki, L., & Frensch, P. A. (1995). Parental Support for Mexican American Children's School Achievement. In H. I. McCubbin et al. (Eds.), *Resiliency in Ethnic Minority Families: Native and Immigrant American Families*, Vol. 1 (pp. 325–342). Madison, WI: University of Wisconsin System Center for Excellence in Family Studies.

Okagaki, L., & Sternberg, R. J. (1993). Parental Beliefs and Children's School Performance. *Child

*Development, 64,* No. 1, 36–56.

Ortiz, V. (1995). The Diversity of Latino Families. In R. E. Zambrana (Ed.), *Understanding Latino Families: Scholarship, Policy, and Practice,* (pp. 18–39). Thousand Oaks, CA: Sage.

Ramírez, M. III, and Castañeda, A. (1974). *Cultural Democracy, Bicognitive Development, and Education.* New York: Academic Press.

Solis, J. (1995). The Status of Latino Children and Youth: Challenges and Prospects. In R. E. Zambrana (Ed.), *Understanding Latino Families: Scholarship, Policy, and Practice* (pp. 62–81). Thousand Oaks, CA: Sage.

Sternberg, R. J. (1996). *Successful Intelligence: How Practical And Creative Intelligence Determine Success in Life.* New York: Simon and Schuster.

Sternberg, R. J. (1988). *The Triarchic Mind: A New Theory of Human Intelligence.* New York: Viking.

Strickon, A. & Ibarra, R. A. (1983). The Changing Dynamics of Ethnicity: Norwegians and Tobacco in Wisconsin. *Journal of Ethnic and Racial Studies, 6,* No. 2, 174–197.

Toro-Morn, M. I. (1995). The Family and Work Experiences of Puerto Rican Women Migrants in Chicago. In H. I. McCubbin et al. (Eds.), *Resiliency in Ethnic Minority Families: Native and Immigrant American Families,* Vol. 1 (pp. 277–294). Madison: University of Wisconsin System Center for Excellence in Family Studies.

Vega, W. A. (1995). The Study of Latino Families: A Point Of Departure. In R. E. Zambrana (Ed.), *Understanding Latino Families: Scholarship, Policy, and Practice* (pp. 3–17). Thousand Oaks, CA: Sage.

Chapter Seven

# Literacy for Change: Latina Adult Learners and Popular Education

*Lorna Rivera*

## Introduction

This chapter examines the experiences of a group of Latina adult learners who participated in a shelter-based popular education program located in one of Boston's poorest neighborhoods. When I first visited The Family Shelter, I met with a group of homeless mothers who were each studying for their General Education Diploma (GED). They said they were returning to school to improve their economic opportunities and to provide a better life for their children. They also said they were fortunate to be participants in the Family Shelter's unique popular education program because they were learning more than basic literacy skills. The program inspired them to become community leaders, and the women described it as a "family." The popular education classes at The Family Shelter were rooted in a model of pedagogy that involved problem-posing and consciousness-raising activities based upon the problems (generative themes) found in the lives of the low-income women. Popular education is a methodology of teaching and learning through dialogue that directly links curriculum content to people's lived experiences, in turn inspiring political action (Beder, 1996; Freire, 1990; Williams, 1996). Drawing upon ethnographic research with Latina adult learners, this chapter will examine the following questions: Why do they drop out of school? What obstacles to participation in education do they face? What motivates low-income Latinas to participate in adult literacy education? What is the impact of popular education on Latina adult learners and its potential to foster community change?

This chapter will also critique the public discourse regarding the meaning and purposes of literacy. Most research about literacy concentrates on the early childhood, elementary, secondary, or higher education systems, while the adult literacy education system is largely neglected (Sticht, 1998). According to a report from the Council for the Advancement of Adult Literacy (CAAL), the adult literacy education system is severely underfunded because "we place all of our money on children's education to prevent literacy problems in the future" (CAAL, 2002, p. 13). D'Amico (1998) argues that the adult education field is currently being driven by welfare reform and its practices have become "impoverished by flawed assumptions about the relationships among literacy, poverty, education and work.... [T]he purpose of education is being increasingly defined as quick job placement" (p. 12). In this chapter, I propose that popular education approaches challenge the mainstream discourse regarding what it means to be literate and the purposes of adult literacy. In my research, I observed how Latina adult learners learned more than important reading and numeracy skills in their shelter-based popular education classes. I present the voices of Latina adult learners who describe why they were motivated to return to school, what obstacles they faced, how they worked to help other women like themselves, and how they became more involved with their children's education. The popular education classes inspired the women to become more critically conscious about their social problems and to participate in activities to address these problems.

## Theoretical Framework

### Literacy and Social Change

Since the enactment of the U.S. Adult Education Act in 1966, participation rates in adult education have grown steadily. From 1979 to 1993, Latino enrollments in adult education increased from 21% to 31%, while white and black enrollments declined, and Latinos tend to be enrolled in the lowest levels of adult basic education (NCES, 2000). The U.S. Department of Education estimates that less than half of Latino adults have finished high school (Carnevale, 1999). According to the 2000 U.S. Census, the number of Latinos who dropped out or never attended high school increased by 53% since the 1990s.[1] The Latinos who participate in AELS are typically school dropouts who are seeking their GED, low–skilled workers enrolled in workplace education programs, or immigrants who enroll in English for Speakers of Other Languages (ESOL) classes (NCES, 2000).

In the adult literacy education field, "conventional" literacy refers to "the ability to read, write, and comprehend texts on familiar subjects and to understand whatever signs, labels, instructions, and directions are necessary to get along in one's environment" (Brodkey, 1991, p. 162). Since the 1980s, conventional literacy has been redefined as "functional" literacy in the United States. According to a definition offered by Hunter and Harmon (1979) in *Adult Illiteracy in the United States:*

> functional literacy: [is] the possession of skills *perceived as necessary by particular persons and groups* to fulfill their own self-determined objectives as family and community members, citizens, consumers, job-holders, and members of social, religious, or other associations of their own choosing. (emphasis in original, quoted in Brodkey, 1991, p. 162)

In 1991, Congress defined the functional purposes of literacy as follows: "an individual's ability to read, write, and speak in English, and compute and solve problems at levels of proficiency necessary to function on the job, and in society, to achieve one's goals, and to develop one's knowledge and potential" (National Institute for Literacy, 1998). In 1998, the federal Workforce Investment Act (WIA) consolidated over 50 employment, training, and literacy programs into three state block grants (MDOE, 1999). Under Title II of the Adult Education and Family Literacy Act, one primary goal for adult education and literacy is to assist adults in becoming literate and obtaining the knowledge and skills necessary for employment and self-sufficiency. The passage of the WIA further fueled a long–standing debate in the field of adult literacy education regarding the purposes of literacy and what it means to be literate (Beder, 1987; Heaney, 1996; Hunter & Harmon, 1979; Macedo, 1994).

According to Brodkey (1991), proponents of adult literacy programs often view literacy as the "solution to many of the social and economic problems to which large cities are subject" and "in this country literacy programs are funded because of a presumed relationship between illiteracy and unemployment" (1991, p. 164, 166). Heaney (1996) studied the history of adult education in the United States and writes:

> Under the expanding influence of capitalism, Human Capital Theory became the dominant rationale for most public adult education—a theory which holds that long-term benefits or rate of return from an individual's investment in education are superior to other forms of investment. Learners became "human capital" and the function of adult education was instrumentally reduced to the development of human (as distinct from natural or technological) resources.... Adult education no longer emphasized reflection, but rather the diffusion of knowledge. Adult education, which

was first conceived as a tool for social change, became a functional tool. It became an enterprise determined by the market, without clear social goals. (p. 15)

Beder (1987) similarly argues that "Human Capital Theory has become the dominant rationale for all public subsidies of adult education including adult literacy, job training programs and to a large extent, even the Cooperative Extension Service. From a public policy perspective, the overriding purpose of adult education is to enhance economic productivity" (p. 109). However, supporters of literacy as "good for the economy" often do not question the conditions that create the need for literacy education. According to Giroux (1981):

> In spite of its appeal to economic mobility, functional literacy reduces the concept of literacy and the pedagogy in which it is suited to the pragmatic requirements of capital; consequently, the notions of critical thinking, culture and power disappear under imperatives of the labour process and the need for capital accumulation. (in Macedo, 1991, p. 151)

Since the 1970s there has been a growing critical literacy movement that questions the conditions that create the need for literacy programs and explores adult literacy as a tool for social change (Aronowitz & Giroux, 1993; Lankshear & McLaren, 1993). According to Degener (2001),

> Critical theorists believe that critical education should guide students toward becoming political. Different theorists have different names for this process—emancipatory education, liberatory education, democratic education, transformative education—but it all boils down to the importance of moving students beyond learning content and toward taking political action. (p. 37)

The Center for Popular Education and Participatory Research (CPEPR) states that the following are central themes in popular education:

> First, popular education is community education, aimed at empowering communities through cooperative study and action. Secondly, popular education is political education, with a stated goal of collective social action toward a more equitable society. Thirdly, popular education is people's education, traditionally aimed at marginalized and disenfranchised communities. (2001, p. 1)

Popular education's roots can be found in Brazil in the late 1950s and early 1960s during a period of political reform, industrialization, and great social changes (Ferreira & Ferreira, 1997). In 1961, the Catholic Church in Brazil sponsored a national literacy program based on the work of Paulo Freire, who had been developing literacy programs using popular education methods (Ferreira & Ferreira, 1997; Freire, 1990; Gadotti, 1994). Freire was influenced by Catholic, existentialist, phenomenological, and Marxist philosophies (Berryman, 1987; Gadotti, 1994; Giroux, 1981; Gramsci, 1971; McLaren, 1989).[2]

In Freire's best-known work, *Pedagogy of the Oppressed*, he argues that humans name the world through dialogue. He opposes situations in which some humans "name" on the behalf of others and criticizes "banking" methods of education that treat learners as if they are empty objects into which the teacher "deposits" knowledge (Freire, 1990). Banking education fosters "cultures of silence" in learners and in order to break through the cultures, the issues discussed in educational activities must relate to the reality of the learners. These issues or problems then become generative themes and teachers and learners develop "codes," which are concrete representations of the themes, such as photographs, drawings, poems, films, or skits. The generative themes and codes form the basis for discussion, reflection, and action in classes (Freire, 1990). This dialogic process inspires conscientization, the development of a "critical consciousness" (Freire, 1990; Shor, 1992).[3] According to Degener (2001),

> When students begin to understand the reasons behind their problems, they begin to understand their world and what they need to do to change it. When disadvantaged learners are able to reflect on their commonsense knowledge and get beyond it, they begin to understand that they can take action to transform their lives. (p. 36)

It is this rationale that influenced the development of the popular education program at The Family Shelter.

In October 1990, at the request of former shelter residents, The Family Shelter began its own on-site adult literacy education program. The volunteer teachers were Catholic nuns who recognized that for the homeless mothers a traditional GED program had little sense of context. The sisters chose popular education methods because they wanted to help the women gain literacy skills in a meaningful context. In addition, the design of the popular education program was influenced by the Catholic sisters' beliefs in liberation theology and the principles and practices of the Catholic Action method that emphasized a "historical process of reflection and action" and a mission to help others see reality, articulate experience, judge, interpret, act, plan, decide, organize, evaluate, and celebrate (Berryman, 1987; Rivera, 2001a).

## Latinas and Popular Education

Much of the academic research about the education of Latinos focuses on children, and there is a lack of inquiry regarding the specific educational experiences of Latina adult learners who are homeless. Though findings from research on Latino children's schooling are relevant for understanding the educational experiences of Latino adult learners, Olivas (1997) argues that most of the literature on education and Latinos "falls into two conceptual categories: studies that blame Hispanics for their own school failures and studies that articulate a deficiency model of minority education, a model of remediation, or one of compensation" (p. 470). Research shows that language barriers, cultural assimilation, institutional racism, poverty, identity conflicts, family and community networks, and social capital affect the academic achievements of Latino students (Darder, Torres, & Gutierrez, 1997; Flores-Gonzalez, 2002; Garcia, 2001; Nieto, 1996; Slavin & Calderon, 2001; Stanton-Salazar, 2001; Walsh, 1991). Studies of adult learners suggest that culturally relevant, participatory literacy practices are most empowering for Latinos and other immigrant adult learners (Auerbach, 1989; Fingeret, 1990; Jurmo, 1989; Reder, 1987, 1990; Spanos, 1991; Sparks, 1998, 2002; Wallerstein, 1983).

While there is a growing body of literature about popular education in the United States (McLaren & Giarelli, 1995; Williams, 1996), few adult literacy programs identify their approach as popular education and much of the current literature about popular education focuses on the work of nongovernmental organizations in developing nations (Torres, 1995).[4] Notable exceptions include research studies by Young and Padilla (1990) and Benmayor (1991). Young and Padilla (1990) investigated popular education at Mujeres Unidas en Accion (MUA), a nonprofit agency that offers educational programs to low-income Latina women in Boston. They examined how popular education influenced the agency's collective approach to decision making and community development and how the use of participatory approaches led to the development of "community affairs" activities. MUA originally offered English as a Second Language classes but later expanded to offer a range of support services including childcare, support groups for battered women, and a community forum with topics proposed by participants. Through popular education approaches the material needs of the MUA students were incorporated into the educational process (Young & Padilla, 1990).

Another study about Latina adult learners and popular education focused on the El Barrio Popular Education Program in New York City's East Harlem neighborhood (Benmayor, 1991). The El Barrio program was a community-based program originally developed to promote empowerment through native-language literacy training and education for Spanish-speaking adults. Benmayor (1991) examined how oral history projects in the Puerto Rican community and other popular education activities in the El Barrio program inspired community activism. She argues that "community" in the program "is created through common circumstances and common struggle. It builds on common histories and on bonds of national origins, class, gender, and becomes more concretely expressed through the educational initiative in which participants are collectively involved"(p. 167). Benmayor's (1991) as well as Young and Padilla's (1990) research provide strong evidence about the empowering effects of popular education on the lives of low-income Latina adult learners.

## Methodology

For this chapter, I focus on a subset of data from a larger study (Rivera, 2001a).[5] Between January 1995 and June 1998, I gathered data from 50 current and formerly homeless women about their classroom experiences in popular education classes at The Family Shelter. I conducted over 1,500 hours of participant observation in popular education classes at the shelter. Most of the observations occurred in classrooms as women participated in discussions based on subject material provided by the teachers or interjected by the women into the program planning. Research also included an open-ended education history questionnaire I administered to the women between January 1995 and June 1998.

Over three years I collected a significant amount of data from fieldnotes, education histories, and transcripts from interviews. In analyzing the data, I looked for the frequencies in which several women came up with similar comments and observations. Specifically, I examined whether there was an order or process that led to a particular action or event (Lofland & Lofland, 1995). I also cross-referenced fieldnotes and interview data from the same women as a way of conducting "consistency checks" (Carspecken, 1996, p. 166). I organized recurring themes into conceptual categories using the three broad categories of School-, Family-, and Community-Life. Under the category of School-Life, I examined the women's educational histories before they entered the program. With Family-Life, I analyzed the poverty-related obstacles in the women's lives based upon in-depth interviews. Regarding Community-Life, I examined how the women related to one another within the context of the popular education classes and how they were affected by popular education. This chapter specifically examines the education experiences of 11 Puerto Rican women who participated in The Family Shelter's popular education classes for at least 3 months between 1995 and 1998.

**Table 1**
**Profile of Sample**

| Pseudonym | Age | Children | Homeless | Reading Level |
|:---:|:---:|:---:|:---:|:---:|
| Elsie | 22 | 1 | 1995–1998 | 9–12th grade |
| Magdalena | 23 | 3 | 1990–1995 | 9–12th grade |
| Margarita | 22 | 1 | 1995–1998 | 5–8th grade |
| Norma | 26 | 4 | 1995–1998 | 9–12th grade |
| Octavia | 26 | 4 | 1990–1995 | 5–8th grade |
| Rayna | 21 | 2 | 1995–1998 | 9–12th grade |
| Rosario | 32 | 3 | 1990–1995 | 5–8th grade |
| Soledad | 28 | 4 | 1990–1995 | 0–4th grade |
| Sylvia | 23 | 2 | 1995–1998 | 5–8th grade |
| Yolanda | 29 | 4 | 1990–1995 | 9–12th grade |
| Yvette | 30 | 3 | 1990–1995 | 9–12th grade |

## Findings

### Motivations for "Going Back to School"

Beder and Valentine's (1990) research finds that there are several basic motivations for adults who attend adult education classes; these are, namely, self-improvement, family responsibilities, diversion, literacy development, community or church involvement, job advancement, economic need, educational advancement, and at the urging of others. The experiences of the low-income Latina adult learners in this research are consistent with Beder and Valentine's research. The women participated in The Family Shelter's popular education classes because they believed they were setting an example for their children. Margarita, a 22 year-old mother of one, said she returned to school because of her daughter:

> I decided to go back to school not only for myself but for my baby. I feel if I go back to school, get my GED, and find myself a good job, or get into a training, my daughter and I would be living lovely, but right now we're not. We are struggling for every little thing we got and it's hard. I would go a day or two without eating just so she could have a little something to eat except milk all the time.

All of the women also said that they returned to school because they believed that once they obtained their high school diplomas they would have increased access to decent jobs, get off of welfare, or be accepted into a good job training program or college. Sylvia, a 23 year-old mother of two, said:

> No matter where you go, you're gonna need that piece of paper! And that's something that I need for myself, you know, because I never finished high school. I never even got my diploma from middle school because of one point. You know? So it's like I want my diploma. I mean, I go to my sister's house and I see her diploma up against the wall and I'm like, wow.

Wikelund (1993) studied welfare recipients who were required to participate in "Career and Life Planning" and "Pathways to Progress" programs. Although these low-income mothers were mandated to enroll in these educational programs—otherwise they risked losing their welfare benefits—Wikelund found that the women were motivated to attend because of concrete basic needs as well as "individual and symbolic motives" (1993, p. 27). The women in Wikelund's (1993) study were motivated to participate in adult education because they needed "income for basic survival," they were concerned with their "children's well-being," they wanted "better jobs," they wanted "independence," they wanted to be "good role models for their children," and they wanted to be "doing something for themselves" (1993, pp. 27–28). In this research, Norma, Sylvia, Octavia, Rayna, and Elsie were mandated by the Department of Transitional Assistance (DTA), the Department of Social Services (DSS), or their shelters, to enroll in an educational activity. Although these women were mandated to return to school, they still said that they were going to school for their children and to "better" themselves. Norma, a 26 year-old mother of four, said:

> I went to the welfare office and they gave me the runaround. I didn't do nothing that first year. And I went again this year and Ms. Murphy gave me this number. She told me to go for it. She said this was a good program. She said if I was serious about doing it then this was the place to be. But I wanted to get out of the house anyway and do something for myself.

## Dropping Out of School

In a writing class, I observed how the women talked about the negative effects of dropping out, and Sylvia wrote the following story:

> Dropping out is the dumbest thing a person can do. When I was in the eighth grade and I thought about dropping out of school. Which in the long run I did drop out. I thought I could make it on my own. Which I thought wrong. I couldn't hold a job because I didn't have a high school diploma. Now I'm twenty three and in a GED program. If I wouldn't of dropout of school I could have been done with school, would've had my diploma and have a good job. It's like they say you learn from your mistakes. This is one mistake I wouldn't advice someone to do.

There are multiple factors that have been linked to a student dropping out including recent migration, having been retained in a grade, and family poverty (Dodson, 1999; Fine, 1991; Fine & Zane, 1991; Lockwood, 1996). Other research examines why some high school dropouts, especially racial and ethnic minorities, may resist participating in adult education because they have had negative experiences in school (Cervero & Fitzpatrick, 1990; Quigley, 1992; Sparks, 1998). Recent research by Reder and Strawn (2001) challenges the conception of "school resister" and the notion that most high school dropouts have had negative schooling experiences. They argue that efforts to increase recruitment and retention of adult learners should not "assume that negative experiences are a common barrier" (p. 4).

This was the case with the Latina adult learners in this research at the Family Shelter. The majority of the women said that they really liked elementary school and described themselves as good students. They had fond memories of elementary school, but when they went to high school, they faced many poverty–related problems. This is consistent with much research on urban high school dropouts (Fine, 1991; Way, 1998). Yvette, a 30 year–old mother of three, said she used to be a good student, but family problems led her to drop out:

> Math and reading was my favorite subject and I had certificates and awards and all that. All my awards was for math, you know. Because I was a math crazy freak right then! I don't understand why I am doin' so bad on it now, you know? But back then, it was my favorite subject and I used to get awards from it.

Elsie described herself as a teacher's pet, but said that she experienced tension with other girls in high school. Sylvia described herself as lazy and boy–crazy. Although Margarita, Rosario, Yolanda, and Rayna said that they were involved in gangs while in high school (and that they had skipped school on a regular basis), they dropped out because they got pregnant and did not have childcare. All of the women regretted dropping out of high school, but they felt pressured to drop out. Yvette said:

> If my mom still would've been alive and all that, I don't think I would've went in the direction I went. I don't think I would've went with Aida's father. I would still stayed home even though I was pregnant. And I think I still would've completed school, you know. I would've finished school and done better now.

## Obstacles that "Get in the Way"

I want to succeed in life
but
So many obstacles get in my way
it makes me give up
But I am trying very hard

To go on and ignore my obstacles
that keep getting in my way
So I can achieve what I started

–Soledad, a shelter participant

The education histories and interviews with these Latina adult learners revealed childhood trauma in which parents were killed, or died from drug abuse or family violence. The death of a mother or father had a profound impact on Soledad, Margarita, Yolanda, Rosario, and Rayna. According to Soledad:

> My father passed away when I was a child. When I grew up I started asking questions about my father, and my mother told me that he had killed himself when I was very small. I asked her, "Why did he kill himself?" But she did not give me any information about what really happened. So I never asked any questions about his death because she looked very sad.

Yvette was deeply hurt when her mother died and had only recently learned that her mother had died of AIDS. She said:

> I guess my family didn't really want me to be hurt. But, you know, back in eighty-seven we really didn't know what AIDS was. And my mom used to use a lot of drugs and she was out there you know, hanging with the wrong crowd. And, back then they told me that it was pneumonia…. It hurts me because I could just imagine what my mother was going through, the pain that she was feeling. Knowing that she was gonna die and that we was there. And she always used to tell us that she loved us. Every day we used to go over there and she used to tell us that she loved us, you know. And I kinda knew that, you know, she was gonna die but I didn't think that it was gonna happen all so soon.

Elsewhere, I examine the prevalence and persistence of violence in the lives of these homeless mothers and the impact of trauma and violence on learning (Rivera, 2001a; Rivera, 2001b). My data clearly suggest a pattern of physical, emotional, and sexual violence beginning in childhood and continuing to the present. I learned that many of the women had been physically abused by their partners (this was the primary reason they became homeless), and they were afraid and ashamed to disclose incidents of violence in their lives (Brandwein, 1999).

It is likely that the extent of domestic violence among the women was much higher because some women like Octavia and Magdalena repeatedly denied experiences with domestic violence. For example, Octavia dropped out of the program for a few months because she was ashamed that the other women at The Family Shelter knew that she was in an abusive relationship. The week before she dropped out, Octavia had missed school for a week. When I saw her one evening on Central Street, I noticed she had a bruise on the right side of her face near her eye. Although she said that she burned herself while cooking, a neighbor told me that Octavia's boyfriend had broken into her apartment through the bedroom window and attacked her. The next day, at The Family Shelter, the Children's Center teachers asked the children to draw pictures of their families and Octavia's son drew a picture of his mother with a bruised eye. Octavia was furious that the women were gossiping about her, saying, "They should just mind their own business." She withdrew her son from the Children's Center and did not return to The Family Shelter for 3 months. Soledad, Norma, Magdalena, Elsie, and Yvette were also battered by their partners. Some of them stayed in abusive relationships for the sake of their children, because they wanted their children to have relationships with their fathers.

In this research, the homeless shelter was, for the women, a last resort. The majority of them came to The Family Shelter because they had already exhausted their other networks of support. Former students and shelter residents told other women about their positive experiences at The Family Shelter and it became recognized as being better for mothers and a place where you don't even have to ask for help. In the following excerpt, Yvette explains how she learned about The Family Shelter:

I seen Letty [another student] and then I started telling her about me going back to school. And then she said, "Well, there's this great place you could go named The Family Shelter. And you can put your daughter in daycare." And I was like, "For real?" And she said, "Yeah, you can come by. I'll speak to the lady for you. Her name is Sister Lois." And then when I, when she called me back and she was like, "Yeah, they're gonna take you." I was so happy. I was like, oh my God! Finally I found a place! This place is so nice. And then, coming here everyday, I learned that, you know, it wasn't nice because it was my first day. It was nice because it is nice. This is what they really do. They help people.

The Family Shelter addressed some of the women's problems by providing comprehensive social services, such as counseling, domestic violence support groups, childcare, a food pantry, clothing fund, after school youth programs, healthcare, and housing/legal advocacy. According to Beder (1996), "Although the intrinsic benefits that derive from community, dignity and empowerment are important in popular education, meeting participants' basic material needs through popular education is also important" (p. 78).

## The Impact of Popular Education

The majority of the popular education classes I observed in The Family Shelter focused on generative themes related to motherhood and parenting, and social inequality. The generative themes were also linked to subject matter that developed and strengthened reading and mathematical skills. Teachers used stories written by homeless women, neighborhood newspapers, and photographs as codes to represent the generative themes in the lives of the women. In their classes, the women discussed the problems represented in these codes, how they had experienced these problems, why the problems existed, and what they could do to address them. I observed how the popular education classes inspired the women to become actively involved in changing their community, both inside and outside of The Family Shelter (Rivera, 2001a).

A commonly shared theme expressed by all of the women was their desire to provide a safe environment and a "better life" for their children. As I stated earlier, the majority of the women returned to school for the sake of their children. All of them wanted their children to do well in school, and they wanted their children to go to college. Yvette said she told her daughter, "I want you to be somebody." She went on to explain,

> My youngest daughter, she wanna work at the fire department and she wants to be a nurse. And then Aida, she wants to be a cop and she wants to be a lawyer. So they have expectations. They, they know what they wanna be. You know what I'm sayin'? I'm just there to make sure that they follow up on it.

My findings are consistent with Bingman, Ebert, and Smith's (1999) research, as well as other studies that link parental involvement and literacy practices in the home to the academic achievements of children (Fingeret & Drennon, 1997; Purcell-Gates, 1995; Ripke & Crosby, 2002; Taylor & Dorsey-Gaines, 1988; Valdes, 1996). The Latina adult learners described how they did homework together with their children. As the women and their children learned together, education became a common bond for the family. In addition, the women held high expectations for their children's education. They wanted their children to have opportunities that were not accessible to them. Several studies confirm that parents from low-income and minority groups have high expectations for their children's education and their involvement in schools has a positive impact on their children's academic achievements (Ada & Zubizarreta, 2001; Delgado-Gaitan, 1990; Nieto, 1996; Trueba, 1988; Valdes, 1996).

The women also drew upon their experiences to help other women in similar situations. For example, Yvette remarked, "I love to help people. It's like it's difficult for me to, to see somebody, you know, and not help them. Because it's just that I been through so much. Pain strikes me easy." The women helped one another by providing support in the form of childcare, transportation, other basic necessities, and emotional strength. The Latina adult learners also worked as advocates for other women on issues related to welfare rights, housing, health, and education. These advocacy activities were an extension of lessons learned in popular education classes and they went beyond the provision of immediate basic needs. For example, I observed how the women circulated petitions to extend the 2–year Massachusetts welfare term limit. Some of them wrote letters to state and federal legislators protesting changes in welfare policies. Others attended lobby days at the State House and spoke at rallies about affordable housing and welfare reform. All of the women worked as educators in information booths at local health fairs and neighborhood festivals (Rivera, 2001a).

I observed how participation in popular education activities increased the women's sense of community, personal power, and social activism. When they first enrolled in the program, they talked about changing their individual "attitude" and needing to change from within, before they were "ready to learn," or to commit to learning. At first, the majority of them believed that their life struggles were due to personal failures. Yvette, Norma, Soledad, and Margarita often talked about the mistakes and "bad choices" they had made. At first, the women internalized widely held assumptions regarding their "personal responsibility," but the problem-posing popular education approaches enabled them to break through the prejudice they held against themselves. The popular education classes helped them understand how social forces impacted their everyday lives and how their problems were linked to socioeconomic inequalities. They learned that the discourse regarding individual choices is woven into a hegemony that oppresses them.

## Conclusion

### Recreating Alternatives to Literacy

As states implement educational reforms such as high-stakes testing, the failures of the elementary and secondary education systems to meet the needs of Latinos are already being reflected in the "third branch" of public education in the United States, the Adult Education and Literacy System (AELS).[6] Indeed, Latinos are the fastest growing and youngest U.S. ethnic group and they have the highest poverty and dropout rates (NCES, 2000; U.S. Census Bureau, 2001). Given the Latino population's increasing participation rates in adult literacy education, more research is needed about the educational experiences of Latino adult learners. What adult education programs best help Latinos meet their personal and social goals? Currently in Massachusetts there is anecdotal evidence to suggest that the state's Massachusetts Comprehensive Assessment System (MCAS) high-stakes test will result in high failure rates for Latinos and may increase enrollments in Adult Secondary Education programs that offer high school equivalency degrees such as the GED.[7] Latino educators in Greater Boston are already reporting an influx of younger students in GED classes. One educator argues, "Because of the pressure of MCAS that's going on in our schools, some students may be deciding it would be easier to get a GED" (Allen, 2000). Some researchers recommend that the Massachusetts Department of Education "use intensive GED classes to help prepare for the unexpected increase in dropouts resulting from K–12 education reform" (Comings, Sum, & Uvin, 2000, p. 85). GED classes can serve as a "safety net" for the 25,000 students who are expected to fail the MCAS exams. Comings, Sum, and Uvin (2000) propose that "intensive GED classes may offer an effective, albeit not ideal, short-term alternative to a high school diploma" (p. 85). But according to Hayes (2000), "If adult literacy education becomes more like a traditional school, will it simply recreate the conditions that led these youth to drop out in the first place" (p. 107; see also Fernandez, this volume, Chapter 4)?

When the U.S. Congress passed the 1996 Personal Responsibility and Work Reconciliation Act, it posed additional barriers to low-income students' educational aspirations. The changes in U.S. social welfare policies were shaped by the discourse of the "other" and a political climate in which it is acceptable to blame, even hate, the low–income for being poor. The majority of Americans see poverty as a personal problem and "its causes are rooted in failed individuals, failed families, and moral degeneration rather than in a failed public economy and a discriminatory public policy" (Polakow, 1993, p. 46). The Latina adult learners in this study had also internalized these beliefs. Although 50% of welfare recipients have less than a high school education, under "work-first" policies, welfare recipients were mandated to find employment as soon as possible. However, research studies show that welfare-to-work programs do not lift people out of poverty, and welfare recipients with low literacy levels are pushed further into poverty when they are forced into low–paying jobs and denied access to education (D'Amico, 1998; Sparks, 1999). Many of the adult education programs that had the greatest decline in enrollments were intensive (20 hours a week) community-based programs like The Family Shelter's popular education program that offered classes during the morning hours to accommodate the schedules of mothers with school-aged children. These programs had therefore offered a real possibility of change for the women who attended (Sparks, 1999).

We continue to ignore the structural causes of poverty when we adopt policies that do not aim to eliminate poverty, but only to perpetuate it. According to popular educator Myles Horton: "The ordinary schools want the future productive workers to learn discipline, to learn authority, to accept regimentation; it's a training ground for what they are going to do later in life" (in Graves, 1979, p. 5). The discourse that defines the primary purpose of literacy as "worker training" fails to address the unequal socioeconomic conditions that create the need for literacy. Punitive social welfare policies and public education programs must change fundamentally if we are to meet the needs of low-income Latina adult learners. I argue that popular education approaches have great potential for addressing the personal, academic, and community goals of this group. Based upon my observations and interviews with the women, The Family Shelter's popular education classes had a positive impact on the women's lives. In their popular education classes, the women discussed strategies and took actions both individually and collectively to address their commonly shared problems. As a result of their participation in popular education classes, their efforts and desires to help other impoverished women increased. The women's levels of participation in their children's education increased and their ability to advocate for their basic legal rights with regards to welfare, housing, health, and education was also strengthened. Most importantly, through popular education their "cultures of silence" were broken when they understood how their individual problems were connected to social problems (Freire, 1990).

# Bibliography

Ada, A. F., & Zubizarreta, R. (2001). The cultural bridge between Latino parents and their children. In M. Reyes & J. Halcon (Eds.), *The best for our children: Critical perspectives on literacy for Latino students*. New York: Teachers College Press.

Allen, M. (2000, May 7). Latino educators discuss the effect of MCAS. *Standard Times, pp 1–2* .

Aronowitz, S., & Giroux, H. (1993). *Education still under siege*. 2nd ed. Westport, CT: Bergin and Garvey.

Auerbach, E. (1989). Toward a socio-contextual approach to family literacy. *Harvard Educational Review, 59*, No. 2, 165–181.

Beder, H. (1996). Popular education: An appropriate educational strategy for community-based organizations. *New Directions for Adult and Continuing Education, 70*, 73–83.

Beder, H., & Valentine, T. (1990). Motivational profiles of adult basic education students. *Adult Education Quarterly, 40,* No. 2, 78–94.

Beder, H. (1987). Dominant paradigms, adult education, and social justice. *Adult Education Quarterly, 37*, No. 2, 105–113.

Benmayor, R. (1991). Testimony, action research, and empowerment: Puerto Rican women and popular education. In Gluck and Patai (Eds.), *Women's words*. New York: Routledge.

Berryman, P. (1987). *Liberation theology*. Philadelphia: Temple University Press.

Bingman, M. B., Ebert, O., & Smith, M. (1999). *Changes in learners' lives one year after enrollment in literacy programs: An analysis from the longitudinal study of adult literacy participants in Tennessee*. (Report). NCSALL No. 11. Cambridge, MA: National Center for the Study of Adult Learning and Literacy.

Brandwein, R. A. (1999). *Battered women, children, and welfare reform*. Thousand Oaks, CA: Sage.

Brodkey, L. (1991). Tropics of literacy. In C. Mitchell & K. Weiler (Eds.), *Rewriting literacy: Culture and the discourse of the other*. Westport, CT: Bergin and Garvey.

Carnevale, A. P. (1999). *Education = success: Empowering Hispanic youth and adults*. Princeton, NJ: Educational Testing Service.

Carspecken, P. F. (1996). *Critical ethnography in educational research*. New York: Routledge.

Center for Popular Education and Participatory Research (CPEPR). (2001). What is popular education? *Voices,1*, No. 1, 1.

Cervero, R.., & Fitzpatrick, T. (1990). The enduring effects of family role and schooling on participation in adult education. *American Journal of Education, 99*, No. 1, 77–94.

Comings, J., Sum, A., & Uvin, J. (2000). *New skills for the new economy: Adult education's key role on sustaining economic growth and expanding opportunity*. Boston: Mass, Inc.

Council for Advancement of Adult Literacy (CAAL). (2002). *Research on research mini-survey*. New York: Council for Advancement of Adult Literacy.

D'Amico, D. (1998). *Writing poverty, politics, policy, practice and personal responsibility: Adult education in the era of welfare reform*. (Unpublished paper). Presented at the National Center for the Study of Adult Learning and Literacy, July 19–21, 1998. New Brunswick, NJ: Rutgers University, .

Darder, A., Torres, R., & Gutierrez, H., (Eds.). (1997). *Latinos and education*. New York: Routledge.

Degener, S. C. (2000). Making sense of critical pedagogy in adult literacy education. In J. Comings, B. Garner, & C. Smith (Eds.), *Annual review of adult learning and literacy, Vol. 2*. San Francisco: Jossey–

Bass.

Delgado-Gaitan, C. (1990). *Literacy for empowerment: The role of parents in children's education.* Bristol, PA: Falmer Press.

Dodson, L. (1999). *Don't call us out of name.* Boston: Beacon Press.

Ferreira, E. C., & Ferreira, J. C. (1997). *Making sense of the media: A handbook of popular education techniques.* New York: Monthly Review Press.

Fine, M. (1991). *Framing dropouts: Notes on the politics of an urban public high school.* Albany: SUNY Press.

Fine, M., & Zane, N. (1991). Bein' wrapped too tight: When low-income women drop out of high school. *Women's Studies Quarterly, 19,* 80.

Fingeret, H. A. (1990). Changing literacy instruction: Moving beyond the status quo. In F. P. Chisman (Ed.), *Leadership for literacy: The agenda for the 1990s.* San Francisco: Jossey–Bass.

Fingeret, H. A., & Drennon, C. (1997). *Literacy for life: Adult learners, new practices.* New York: Teachers College Press.

Flores-Gonzalez, N. (2002). *School kids/street kids: Identity development in Latino students.* New York: Teachers College Press.

Freire, P. (1990). *Pedagogy of the oppressed.* 20th ed. New York: Continuum.

Freire, P. (1985). *The politics of education: Culture, power, and liberation.* Westport, CT: Bergin and Garvey.

Gadotti, M. (1994). *Reading Paulo Freire: His life and work.* Albany: SUNY Press.

Garcia, E. (2001). *Hispanic education in the United States.* Lanham, MD: Rowan & Littlefield.

Giroux, H. A. (1981). *Ideology, culture, and the process of schooling.* Philadelphia: Temple University Presss.

Gramsci, A. (1971). *Selections from the prison notebooks.* Q. Hoare & N. Smith (Eds.). New York: International Publishers.

Graves, B. (1979). What is liberatory education? A conversation with Myles Horton. *Radical Teacher, 12,* 3–5.

Hayes, E. (2000). Youth in adult literacy education programs. In J. Comings & C. Smith (Eds.), *The annual review of adult learning and literacy, Vol. 1.* San Francisco: Jossey-Bass.

Heaney, T. (1996). *Adult education for social change: From center stage to the wings and back again.* ERIC Clearinghouse on Adult, Career, and Vocational Education. (ERIC Document No. ED 396190)

Hunter, C., & Harmon, D. (1979). *Adult illiteracy in the United States: A report to the Ford Foundation.* New York: McGraw Hill.

Jurmo, P. (1989). The case for participatory literacy education. In H. A. Fingeret & P. Jurmo (Eds.), *Participatory literacy education.* San Francisco: Jossey-Bass.

Lankshear, C., & McLaren, P. (Eds.). (1993). *Critical literacy: Politics, praxis, and the postmodern.* Albany: SUNY Press.

Lockwood, A. T. (1996). *Caring, community, and personalization: Strategies to combat the Hispanic dropout problem advances in Hispanic education.* Washington, DC: U.S. Department of Education.

Lofland, J., & Lofland, L. (1995). *Analyzing social settings.* 3rd ed. Belmont, CA: Wadsworth Publishers.

Macedo, D. (1994). *Literacies of power: What Americans are not allowed to know.* Boulder, CO: Westview Press.

Macedo, D. (1991). The politics of emancipatory literacy in Cape Verde. In C. Mitchell & K. Weiler (Eds.), *Rewriting literacy: Culture and the discourse of the other.* Westport, CT: Bergin and Garvey.

Martin, R. (2001). *Listening up: Reinventing ourselves as teachers and students.* Portsmouth, NH: Boynton/Cook Publishers.

Massachusetts Department of Education (MDOE). (1999). *Workforce investment act.* Retrieved Oct. 22, 1999, Available online <http://www.doe.mass.edu/ACLS>

McLaren, P. (1989). *Life in schools: An introduction to critical pedagogy in the foundations of education.* White Plains, NY: Longman.

McLaren, P. L., & Giarelli, J. M. (Eds.). (1995). *Critical theory and educational research.* Albany: SUNY Press.

National Center for Education Statistics (NCES). (2000 March). *Participation in adult education in the United States: 1998–1999.* Office of Educational Research and Improvement. Washington, DC: U.S. Department of Education.

National Institute for Literacy. (1998). *Literacy it's a whole new world.* (Campaign kit materials). Washington, DC: National Institute for Literacy.

Nieto, S. (1996). *Affirming diversity: The sociopolitical context of multicultural education.* 2nd ed. New York: Longman.

Olivas, M. A. (1997). Research on Latino college students: A theoretical framework and inquiry. In A. Darder, R. D. Torres, & H. Gutierrez (Eds.), *Latinos and education: A critical reader.* New York: Routledge.

Polakow, V. (1993). *Lives on the edge: Single mothers and their children in the other America.* Chicago: University of Chicago Press.

Purcell-Gates, V. (1995). *Other people's words: The cycle of low literacy.* Cambridge, MA: Harvard University Press.

Quigley, B. A. (1992). Looking back in anger: The influences of schooling on illiterate adults. *Journal of Education, 174,* No. 1, 104–121.

Reder, S. (1990). *Literacy across languages and cultures.* (Unpublished paper). Presented at the 3rd Gutenberg Conference, Ithaca, NY. (ERIC Document Reproduction Service No. ED 318279)

Reder, S. (1987). Comparative aspects of functional literacy development: Three ethnic communities. In D. Wagner (Ed.), *The future of literacy in a changing world.* Oxford: Pergamon Press.

Reder, S., & Strawn, C. (2001, December). The K–12 school experiences of high school dropouts. *Focus on Basics 4,* 1–5. Retrieved: 01/01/01. Available online. <http://ncsall.gse.harvard.edu/fob/2001/reder.html>

Ripke, M. N., & Crosby, D. A. (2002). The effects of welfare reform on the educational outcomes of parents and their children. In W. Secada (Ed.), *Review of Research in Education, 26,* No. 1, 181–261.

Rivera, L. (2001a). *Learning community: An ethnographic study of popular education and homeless women in a shelter-based adult literacy program.* Ph.D. Dissertation. Boston: Northeastern University.

Rivera, L. (2001b). *Can adult education programs provide a way out? Popular education and homeless women.* (Unpublished paper). Presented at the biannual Trapped by Poverty/Trapped by Abuse conference. Ann Arbor: University of Michigan.

Schugurensky, D. (1998). The legacy of Paulo Freire: A critical review of his contributions. *Convergence, 31*, Nos. 1–2, 17–29.

Shor, I. (1992). *Empowering education.* Chicago: University of Chicago Press.

Slavin, R. E., & Calderon, M. (2001). *Effective programs for Latino students.* Mahwah, NJ: Lawrence Erlbaum.

Spanos, G. (1991). *Cultural considerations in adult literacy education.* Washington, DC: National Clearinghouse on Literacy Education. (ERIC Document Reproduction Service No. ED 334866)

Sparks, B. (2002). *The struggles of getting an education: Issues of power, culture, and difference for Mexican Americans of the southwest.* DeKalb, IL: Educational Studies.

Sparks, B. (1999). Critical issues and dilemmas for adult literacy programs. In L. G. Martin & J. C. Fisher (Eds.), *The welfare to work challenge for adult literacy educators. New directions for adult and continuing education, No. 83.* San Francisco: Jossey–Bass.

Sparks, B. (1998). The politics of culture and the struggle to get an education. *Adult Education Quarterly, 48,* No. 4, 245–259.

Sticht, T. (1998). *Moving adult literacy education from the margins of educational policy and practice.* Office of Vocational and Adult Education. Washington DC: U.S. Department of Education.

Stanton-Salazar, R. (2001). *Manufacturing hope and despair: The school and kin support networks of U.S. Mexican youth.* New York: Teachers College Press.

Taylor, D., & Dorsey-Gaines, C. (1988). *Growing up literate: Learning from inner city families.* Portsmouth, NH: Heinemann.

Torres, C. A. (1995). Participatory action research and popular education in Latin America. In P. McLaren & J. Giarelli (Eds.), *Critical theory and educational research.* Albany: SUNY Press.

Trueba, H. T. (1988). Culturally based explanations of minority student's academic achievement. *Anthropology and Education Quarterly, 19,* 270–287.

United States Census Bureau. (May, 2001). *The Hispanic population: Census 2000 brief.* Washington, DC: U.S. Census Bureau.

Valdes, G. (1996). *Con respeto: Bridging the distances between culturally diverse families and schools.* New York: Teachers College Press.

Wallerstein, N. (1983). *Language and culture in conflict: Problem-posing in the ESL classroom.* Don Mills, Ontario, Canada: Addison-Wesley. (ERIC Document Reproduction Service No. 221043)

Walsh, C. (1991). *Pedagogy and the struggle for voice: Issues of language, power, and schooling for Puerto Ricans.* Westport, CT: Bergin and Garvey.

Way, N. (1988) *Everyday courage: The lives and stories of urban teenagers.* New York: New York University Press

Weiler, K. (1994). Freire and a feminist pedagogy of difference. In P. McLaren & C. Lankshear (Eds.), *Politics of liberation: Paths from Freire.* New York: Routledge.

Wikelund, K. (1993). *Motivations for learning: Voices of women welfare reform participants.* Philadelphia: National Center on Adult Literacy. (ERIC Document Reproduction Service No. ED 364748)

Williams, L. (1996). First enliven, then enlighten: Popular education and the pursuit of social justice. *Sociological Imagination, 33,* No. 2, 94–116.

Young, E., & Padilla, M. (1990). Mujeres Unidas en Accion: A popular education process. *Harvard Educational Review, 60,* No. 1, 1–17.

Chapter Eight

# The Effects of Family Background, Immigration Status, and Social Context on Latino Children's Educational Attainment

*Gabriella C. Gonzalez*

## Introduction

Differing fertility rates, immigration patterns, and age distributions among ethnic minorities suggest that by the year 2030 the United States elementary school population could be divided equally between white children and children of all other racial and ethnic groups combined (Edmonston, 1996). This minority subgroup, assuming current levels of immigration, fertility, and mortality, is expected to outnumber the white subgroup by the year 2050 (Hodgkinson, 1992). Latinos represent the most rapidly growing part of the school age population. Unfortunately, Latino students have a higher dropout rate than any other minority subgroup population in our schools, and this rate is growing (Secada et at., 1998). Their overall high school graduation rate of 53% is the lowest of all major ethnic groups in the Unites States. One reason for the difficulties Latino students face in school is the lower socioeconomic standing of their families, thus restricting access to quality schools or tangible resources in the home. Another reason may be that more than half of the Latino population is foreign-born, or the children of foreign-born parents. In 1990, 7.9% (19.8 million people) of the United States population was foreign-born (Lapham, 1993). In 2000, this proportion increased to 10.4%, or 28.4 million people. Of our current foreign-born, 51% were born in Latin America, Central America, or the Caribbean (Lollock, 2001). Thus, Latino students may have the double burden of being economically disadvantaged and newcomers to our society and our schools.

The analyses in this chapter expand the research on the educational attainment of Latino children by examining how a Latino student's socioeconomic status, immigration status, and community context affect the amount of schooling the child acquires. I use contextual data from zip code files from the 1990 U.S. Census and data from the 1988 to 1994 National Education Longitudinal Study (NELS) to focus my analyses on children of Cuban, Puerto Rican, and Mexican descent, as compared to white, black, and Asian children.

I found that Cuban, Puerto Rican, and Mexican students progress less far in school than white students do. The current literature documents this trend. Yet, any ethnic differences in educational attainment disappear when I control for family background. I also find that the socioeconomic status of the community in which a child attends school indeed affects his or her years of schooling, but that this effect also disappears when we consider that child's family background. In addition, children with one immigrant parent are not as likely to progress as far through school as children with two native parents. Conversely, children with two parents who are foreign-born are more likely to progress farther. From these findings I explore how immigration status relates to the low retention rate of Latinos. By much the same way we know the Latino population is not a homogenous subpopulation group, it is important that we not assume that immigrants and children of immigrants in our schools are a homogenous group. Students from different countries of origin, those who grow up in households with two foreign parents (or one foreign parent), assimilate to schooling practices quite differently than children outside of these stipulations. I conclude with a discussion of how density of ties in a community, coupled with family home environment and the parents' education, act to foster or hinder the educational attainment of Latino students.

## The Status Attainment Process Between Latino Immigrant Adults and Their Children

Three realms of the adult immigrant Latino's life interact to affect his or her child's performance in school. Foremost is the family background: the adult's pre-arrival social status, the occupation, and earnings once in the United States. Second, community context: the ties that bind the community where the family lives and the socioeconomic role models available to the students in that community. Finally, the social and cultural assimilation of the immigrant family into that community. I discuss each realm in turn below.

**Family Social Status: The Role of Pre–Arrival Educational Attainment**

Social stratification research consistently finds that a person's social and economic position is linked to his or her parents' education and occupation (e.g., Blau & Duncan, 1967). However, this traditional status attainment literature does not give adequate attention to immigrants to the United States who have arrived since the 1965 Family Reunification Act; a large portion of whom are from the Caribbean, Central, and Latin America and have a different profile from previous immigrant groups (Betts & Lofstrom, 1998). The potential status attainment patterns of the children of this "new wave" of post-1965 immigrants will determine whether a family, or particular country-of-origin group, will economically or socially assimilate to the prevailing labor market and social structures in American society—that is, whether the family or group will "succeed." The potential status attainment patterns of the children of Caribbean, Central, and Latin American immigrants thus deserves special attention if we want to make claims about whether immigration as a whole contributes to our economy and if immigrants as people are succeeding in the labor market. Recent studies that investigate the intergenerational transmission of status for immigrants do not adequately address the pre-arrival social status of immigrant parents. Knowing this pre-arrival information could well be central to understanding how a student will approach schooling.

Figure 1 uses data from the March 1998 Current Population Survey to display the variation in educational attainment of recently arrived adults from different countries of origin. From this figure, we see that many recent immigrants from Mexico, Central America, and the Caribbean enter the United States without a high school diploma. As traditional status attainment models would predict, the lower educational attainment of some immigrant adults from Mexico, the Dominican Republic, and Guatemala currently entering the United States could translate into the future lower educational attainment for their children. However, the community context in which the family finds itself, and the capacity to assimilate into the mainstream educational system, may temper any effects of parents' pre-arrival educational attainment.

**Figure 1:**
**Percent of Immigrants with less than a high school diploma by country of origin**

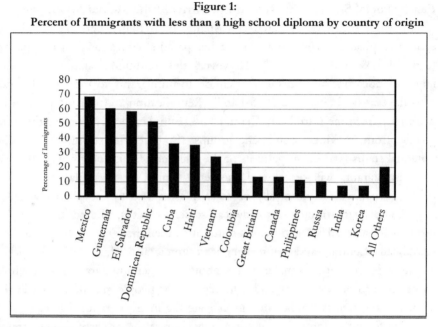

Source: 1998 Current Population Survey

## Geographic Concentration and Density of Ties

The immigrant population tends to be concentrated in certain parts of the United States and often resides in immigrant ghetto neighborhoods. In Figure 2 I use data from the 2000 U.S. Census and use the zip code, a relatively broad geographic boundary, to delineate a community. Even with this rather broad geographic setting, we see that there are striking differences between immigrants and native-born people with whom they choose to live.

Immigrants reside in zip codes with greater heterogeneity than their native-born counterparts do. The mean percentage of zip code inhabitants who are of the same ethnicity as the respondent is 36% for immigrants, compared to 79% for natives. Conversely, immigrants who live among their foreign peers is 33% compared to less than 5% for natives. Ethnic plurality is a distinctive, yet common feature of today's immigrant neighborhood, indicating that a group of single national origin no longer dominates the new immigrant enclaves as they did at the turn of the twentieth century. Immigrant families today are living in more ethnically mixed neighborhoods as compared to native families (Zhou, 2001).

**Figure 2:**
**Geographic Concentration of Immigrant and Native Residents**

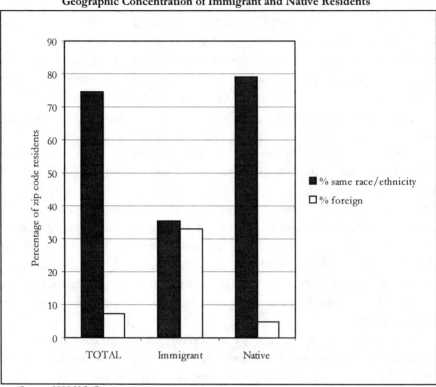

Source: 2000 U.S. Census

This raises the points: Does the community into which the immigrant groups assimilate affect their children's schooling success? Are the contextual advantages or disadvantages experienced by the immigrant adults transmitted to their children?

To answer these questions researchers turn to the theory of segmented assimilation (Portes & Zhou, 1993). This theory helps to explain the role geographic concentration plays in determining the educational attainment of children. Segmented assimilation posits that the type of community in which the immigrant groups live determines the social and economic assimilation patterns of the individuals and the group as a whole (Rumbaut, 1994). Distinct forms of adaptation emerge from the acculturation and assimilation of an immigrant group into a specific social and economic sector of American society, which in turn shapes intergenerational mobility (Portes & Rumbaut, 1996; Portes & Zhou, 1993). Accordingly, children of immigrants from Mexico have lower educational attainment due to realistic appraisals of the relatively lower return to educational investment in the United States for their ethnic group (Kao & Tienda, 1995; Portes & Zhou, 1993; Suárez-Orozco & Suárez-Orozco, 1995). Underachievement located within the structure of co-ethnic peer communities absorbs succeeding generations of Mexican origins not into the mainstream, but into an adversarial stance of impoverished groups confined to the bottom of the economic hourglass (Suárez-Orozco & Suárez-Orozco, 1995).

The theory of segmented assimilation seems to explain the variety of assimilation patterns for students and adults of different ethnicities. Unfortunately, much of the research that tests segmented assimilation fails to delve deeply enough into the characteristics of the community into which the immigrant adult or child assimilates. Instead, researchers claim to uphold the theory of segmented assimilation whenever a racial or ethnic effect is present in regression analysis of a child's academic achievement or educational attainment after controlling for parents' educational attainment (e.g., Portes & MacLeod, 1996; Kao & Tienda, 1995; Hao & Bornstead-Bruns, 1998). The theory of segmented assimilation is a valuable contribution to understanding the assimilation patterns of Latino immigrant adults and children, and needs to be properly tested.

Whether the concentration of an immigrant community serves as a springboard for economic advancement, or as a trap into a downward spiral of immobility, it is determined in part by the social capital and ethnic capital of that community. According to James Coleman, social capital "[I]nheres in the structure of relations between persons and among persons…. The function identified by the concept 'social capital' is the value of those aspects of social structure to actors, as resources that can be used by the actors to realize their interests" (1998, pp. 302, 305). The idea here is of a "dense set of associations" within a social group promoting cooperative behavior that is advantageous to group members. Social capital appears not simply in the individual, but in the structure of social organizations, patterns of social relationships, and processes of interaction among individuals and organizations.

Social capital has two basic functions, both of which are applicable in a variety of contexts, as a source of social control and as a source of benefits through extra-familial networks (Portes, 1998). A close-knit community, measured in terms of the proximity of other immigrants or of co-ethnic peers, could negatively, or positively, affect a child's schooling depending on these two functions of social capital. First, having fellow immigrants, or co-ethnic peers, could be beneficial because of the social control developed and ensured by close ties of family members with other community members. Zhou and Bankston (1994) exemplify this form of social capital as social control in their study of Vietnamese in New Orleans, in which "both parents and children are constantly observed as under a 'Vietnamese microscope'" (p. 207). The source of this type of social capital is found in bounded solidarity and enforceable trust, and its main result is to render formal or overt controls unnecessary (Portes, 1998).

The second, and most common function attributed to social capital, is as a source of network mediated benefits beyond the immediate family that enhances access to employment, mobility through occupational ladders, and entrepreneurial success (Portes, 1998). Granovetter (1974) on this point coined the term "strength of weak ties" to refer to the power of indirect influences that serve as an informal employment referral system. Social capital (as social control), family connections, and networking opportunities are often perceived as positive influences in the educational and economic life of a person. Social capital, however, does have a potential "dark side" (Fiorina, 1999; Putnam, 2000). Strong community ties could be detrimental to the occupational success of the immigrant adults because the lack of occupational or language opportunities may have a negative impact on the academic potential of their children. Another term for this is "institutional completeness" which refers to the extent to which an immigrant ethnic group can meet the needs of its members (Breton, 1964). If an ethnic group can meet those needs, then its members will have little contact with non-group members. Additionally, close ties within a group will not provide much of an advantage for the schooling of the children if group members do not hold much "capital" or resources to share.

**Sociocultural and Economic Assimilation**

Another theory that can help us understand how the community affects the intergenerational transmission of status for Latino children in immigrant households is ethnic capital (Borjas, 1994). Derived from the theory of social capital, ethnic capital refers to "the characteristics of the ethnic environment such as the skills and economic opportunities that permeate the ethnic networks" (Borjas, 2000, p. 14). In line with much of the present literature on neighborhood effects, we can think of this concept in terms of availability of role models specific to that immigrant and ethnic group. The theory's logic is stated as follows: immigrants who originate in countries that have abundant human capital and higher levels of per capita income tend to perform better in the United States. Borjas explains that those immigrants with lower education levels or literacy rates have children with lower educational attainment and lower wages. The economic impact of immigration obviously depends not only on how well immigrants adapt, but also on the adjustment process experienced by their offspring. Borjas then turns to the characteristics of the ethnic environment, or ethnic capital, in immigrant communities to explain why economic disparities persist through generations. He surmises that the characteristics of the ethnic environment influence the skills and economic performance of the children in the ethnic group above and beyond the influence of the parents. These characteristics include the culture, attitudes, and economic opportunities that permeate the ethnic networks. Exposure to an advantaged ethnic environment (in the sense that the environment has abundant human capital) has a positive influence on the children in the group, while exposure to a disadvantaged environment has a negative influence. Because few people in disadvantaged ethnic groups can afford to escape the ethnic ghetto, these enclaves make it easy for ethnic capital to influence the social mobility of individuals who reside there and help to perpetuate the generational socioeconomic differences observed across ethnic groups. Ethnic ghettos provide the social and economic networks that will influence the lives of the children and grandchildren of these immigrants far into the next century.

When combined with the theory of segmented assimilation, the increase in available social capital, coupled with ethnic capital, may positively affect children's educational attainment, even after controlling for parents' socioeconomic status. Conversely, offspring of disadvantaged immigrants would be expected to be caught in the double bind of slower socioeconomic mobility, because of the family living in an area with low community-level human capital (ethnic capital), and weak, unstable personal and community bonds (social capital).

In addition to the important potential effects of immigrant adults to assimilate into the social and economic structure of the United States labor market is the effect immigration has on the classroom experience of the child and their subsequent educational attainment. As a whole, immigration has had a significant effect on the size of the school age population. During the 1990s, U.S. public schools have seen an increase of almost 1 million immigrant students, approximately 5.5% of the public school population. A growing number of recent immigrant students are entering middle and high schools with little or no prior formal schooling and low literacy rates (Broeder, 1998). For these students to succeed in school they must learn to read, write, understand, and speak English; develop academic literacy in English to make the transition to the labor force or into other educational programs; and become socialized into American society during adolescence, a time of major emotional, physical, and psychological change (Mace-Matluck, Alexander-Kasparik, & Queen, 1998).

Specifically, many of these children are English–language learners and have greater difficulty in subject-related classes than students whose first language is English. One reason for this is that English learners face the double challenge of learning English while simultaneously learning content (Bennici & Strang, 1995). The Council of Chief State School Officers stated that immigrant children are more likely to be retained and placed in low academic tracks on the basis of insufficient English–language skills and low academic progress (Stewart, 1993).

The classroom difficulties encountered by English–language learners are most pronounced for Latino students. By the year 2010, Latinos are expected to be the largest minority group in the United States, making up 21% of the population and having the highest rate of Limited English Proficient youth (Del Piñal & Garcia, 1994; Holman, 1997). According to Kaufman, Chaves, and Lauren (1998), about 18% of Latino children are born outside of the United States and 66% of Latino children come from a home that speaks a language other than English. Youth from non–English–language backgrounds are 1.5 times more likely to leave school before high school graduation than those from English–language backgrounds (Driscoll, 1999; Secada et al., 1998). Though dropout rates have declined overall in recent years, especially among African Americans and whites, the trend for Latino students is quite the opposite (Fernandez, Paulsen, & Hirano-Naknishi, 1989; Hugh, 1997). In 1992 roughly half the of Latinos age 16–24 dropped out of high school, and this amount rose to about 60% in 1998 (Vaznaugh, 1995; Secada et al., 1998). This higher dropout rate among Latino high school students is cause for growing concern because future earnings are linked to educational attainment. Providing appropriate instruction to immigrant students who are English–language learners has become an issue of particular concern to educators across the country (Hurtado & Garcia, 1994).

Even though researchers are giving greater attention to the educational needs of students in immigrant households, there has not been a serious commitment to disentangle the effects of language ability, minority status, and immigrant status on educational attainment. Much of the present research focuses either on one aspect of these three interrelated characteristics or on a combination of just two (e.g., Buriel, Raymond, & Cardoza, Desdemona, 1988; Portes & MacLeod, 1996; Warren, 1996; Mau, 1997; Bhattacharya, 2000).

## Data and Methods

The National Education Longitudinal Study (NELS) provides data that are invaluable to investigating roles of ethnicity, family background, community context, and a family's assimilation and immigration status. NELS utilizes a two stage probability sampling design that selects a nationally representative sample of 24,599 students from 1,057 random schools. Within each school, approximately 26 students were randomly selected with a typical selection of 24 regularly sampled students, with an over-sample of Hispanic or Asian/Pacific Islander students. The study also surveys parents, teachers, and school administrators. It began with a cohort of 8th graders in 1988 and followed them at 2–year intervals. I use data from the first stage of sampling in 1988 through the fourth stage in 1994.

Because the NELS sample design was stratified, disproportionate sampling of certain strata (e.g., over sampling of Asian and Hispanic students) and clustering probability sampling (e.g., students within a school), the resulting statistics are more variable than they would have been had they been based on data collected from a simple random sample of the same size. Because of this sampling design, observations in the same cluster are not independent.[1] In order to accommodate the sampling design of the NELS, I use pertinent weights to account for the probability of subpopulation selection in the sample in each of the three stages and I use Huber–White (or Sandwich) standard errors to account for the cluster sampling methods.[2]

I match the individual-level student and parent data from the study to contextual data from the 1990 U.S. Census based on the zip code of the student's school. My final sample is 10,395 students from 761 schools that have zip code information linked to them.[3]

## Variables

A student's educational attainment in 1994 is a categorical variable that measures what type of schooling, if any, an 8th grader in 1988 attends by 1994. The categories used are: The categories used are: not a high school graduate; high school graduate and no postsecondary education; high school graduate and entered either a 2–year associates or vocational degree program; and, high school graduate and entered a 4–year bachelor's degree program. Because the 1994 data does not account for whether the students graduated from their postsecondary education institution, I consider their educational attainment in categories that measure what type of school students decide to enter or not enter. The outcome categories are clearly in a ranked order, yet the intervals among the categories cannot be treated as uniform. I analyze the likelihood for a student to be in one of the categories of the dependent variable with ordered logistic regression. [4]

I use three main variables to define family background: father's and mother's occupational status (post-arrival if the parents are foreign-born), number of years of parents' education (pre-arrival if the parents are foreign-born), and log of income from all contributors in the household. I use the parent's self-report, or the report of a spouse, to determine educational attainment and occupation. If this parent–level information is missing, I use the student's response. I chose parents who came to the United States at age 23 or above to capture pre-arrival education with some accuracy. Family education is a linear variable that uses the higher of the mother's or father's pre-arrival education.

I code the father's and mother's occupations based on their 1988 Duncan socioeconomic index (SEI) scores. The classification of occupations constitutes the backbone of much, if not most, stratification research. "Ever since it was recognized that the division of labor is the kernel of social inequality and occupation therefore is the main dimension of social stratification, stratification researchers have developed ways to derives status measures from information on occupations" (Ganzenboom & Treiman, 1996, p. 202). SEI scales are more widely used by stratification researchers than are prestige scales or ordinal class categorizations because they better capture the basic parameters of the process of stratification (Featherman, Jones, & Hauser, 1975). For those parents who marked "homemaker" or "never worked," they were matched with their spouse's occupational codes. If there was no spouse before arriving to the

United States, or if the spouse also marked "homemaker" or "never worked," then I coded the occupation as 0 (zero) for "unemployed." The occupations are coded as:

| | |
|---|---|
| 29.44: laborer | 38.51: craftsperson |
| 30.46: service sector | 48.40: protective services |
| 34.10: operative/machinist | 50.64: proprietor/owner |
| 35.57: farmer/farm manager | 51.21: technical |
| 35.77: sales | 53.52: manager/administration |
| 38.16: clerical | 64.38: professionals: lawyer, school teacher |

Another family background component used is family income. I used the log of the income from all contributors in the household rather than from individual contributors to assess the overall household environment in which the student lives.

To define segmented assimilation, I match the student-level data from the 1988 NELS file with 1990 U.S. Census information to construct four variables that measure the type of social community in which the family lives. They are: percentage of residents in the student's school's zip code who are of the same race or ethnicity as the student, percentage of zip code residents who are foreign-born, percentage of that foreign-born group who arrived between 1987–1990, and the percentage of zip code residents who have lived in the same residence for the last 5 years. With these variables I am able to directly measure the social context in which a family lives rather than simply use the student's race or ethnicity as a proxy for the social environment, as some segmented assimilation research has (Kao & Tienda, 1995; Hao & Bornstead-Bruns, 1998).

In order to test the availability and effects of social capital on the children's educational attainment, I measure that the parents of the child know: (1) many, (2) some, or (3) none of their child's friends' parents.[5] I also measure community-level social capital with a standardized index of upper-middle class neighbors, defined as the proportion of residents aged 25 or over in a neighborhood who are college graduates, are employed with a professional occupation, and are in the median household income of zip code residents. This index measures the availability of role models in the community. If I find that the more of one's child's friends a parent knows, the greater probability of that child attending postsecondary schooling, it can safely be said that social capital in the form of networks, connections, and the density of ties among families in the community has a positive affect on child's schooling. Alternatively, I may find that the presence of social control due to tight bonds within the community negatively effects a child's educational attainment, resulting in a negative coefficient for this variable. I expect that given the previous literature on ties within immigrant communities, the greater the social capital, the better the child will do in school.

I operationalize ethnic capital with the interaction of student's race or ethnicity with the index of upper–middle–class neighbors. If there is a high level of human capital available in an immigrant community, as Borjas' theory of ethnic capital suggests, then we should find that these variables increase a student's probability of attaining an education beyond their parents' educational credentials. Conversely, if I find that these variables do not influence a child's educational attainment significantly more than their parents' educational attainment, then there may be reason to believe that the occupational opportunities in a community are not the relevant factors that determine a child's status attainment potential. In fact, there would be reason to believe that a child is not hampered by a low amount of community human capital.

In the following analyses, I also consider certain variables that impart an understanding of how assimilated into the American social and cultural mainstream the parents are. Of particular concern for educational attainment of children is a family's immigration status. "Immigrant" families are those in which both parents are immigrants. "Combined" families have only one foreign-born parent. "Native" families are those with two native-born parents. My analyses center upon the differences among these three family types. Unfortunately, "Immigrant" and "Combined" families are often presented together in current scholarly work, defining them both as immigrant families. I choose to differentiate these two family types because the amount of resources available to them may differ. It is possible that linguistic or economic resources available to children who have one native-born parent are greater than those available to children who have two immigrant parents because of the implied social and economic assimilation of the family with a native-born parent. Conversely, if the family lives in a highly concentrated immigrant neighborhood the social capital available to the child (in the form of close ties amongst adults in the community) may be greater than for children of mixed parentage. The parents in a mixed marriage may not be privy to the social connections or occupational opportunities that an immigrant or native family may have access. Another assimilation variable I include is the number of years the mother and father have been in the United States (age, if the parent is native-born). I expect that if a family has been in the United States longer, it will be more accustomed to the school system and labor market, and is better equipped to navigate the child through school; the parent, better equipped to navigate the employment sector. Likewise, the older the parent, the more financially solvent and accustomed to the labor market the parent will be. I also control for years that a student has lived in the United States (age if native-born) and in what grade the student started his or her schooling in the United States (kindergarten if native-born).

Another possible assimilation mechanism that I consider is English ability, or "language capital" (Borjas, 1994), which can be a determinant in how well an immigrant does in the labor market and affects how well an immigrant student may do in school (White, 1997; White & Kaufman, 1997). I construct a 5-point scale (0-limited to 5-fluent) of the parents' English ability, based on a self-report, of how well the responding parent speaks, understands, reads, and writes English. I also control for whether the child is considered limited English proficient. I mark a student as limited English proficient based on whether the child attended an English as a Second Language (ESL) or a bilingual education class in 8th grade (the first year of the survey), or whether the student ranks him or herself as "poor" on writing, speaking, reading, or understanding English.

Table 1 provides a full description of the variables I used in this analysis with means and standard errors.

**Table 1:**
**Variable Description, Mean, and Standard Deviations**

| Variable | Description | Mean | s.d. |
|---|---|---|---|
| **Educational Attainment** | 0: did not complete high school; no postsecondary schooling<br>1: completed high school, no postsecondary schooling<br>2: entered 2–year degree program<br>3: entered 4–year bachelor's degree program | 1.78 | 1.02 |
| **Family Background** | | | |
| Parents' years of educ. | Higher of father or mother's | 13.47 | 2.53 |
| Father's occupation | Duncan SEI coding | 42.30 | 10.92 |
| Mother's occupation | Duncan SEI coding | 41.61 | 11.51 |
| Household income | Parent response of yearly household income | 34,484 | 28,129 |

Table 1—*Continued*

Table 1—*Continued*

| Variable | Description | Mean | s.d. |
|---|---|---|---|
| **Segmented Assimilation** | | | |
| Percent same race/ ethnicity in zip code | Percent of householders in 8th grader's zip code with the same race or ethnicity as the 8th grader | 69.55 | 35.51 |
| Percent foreign in zip code | Percent of householders in 8th grader's zip code born outside of the United States | 7.29 | 10.88 |
| Recent arrivals in zip code | Percent of foreign born in zip code who arrived between 1987 and 1990 | 30.03 | 18.56 |
| **Social Capital** | | | |
| Ties among families | 1: child's parents' know many or some of friends' parents 0: child's parents' don't know any of friends' parents | 0.40 | 0.43 |
| Index of upper– middle–class residents | Standardized composite of: a) Proportion of college graduates among persons age 25, or over b) Proportion of employed persons with professional occupations c) Median household income | 0.00 | 0.99 |
| Residential stability | Percent of householders in 8th grader's zip code who lived in the same zip code for at least 5 years | 70.38 | 13.21 |
| **Family "Assimilation"** | | | |
| Immigration Status | Immigrant: both parents are foreign | 0.08 | 0.28 |
| | Combined: one parent is foreign | 0.13 | 0.33 |
| | Native: both parents are native | 0.77 | 0.41 |
| Parents' English ability | Index of parents' self-reported ability to speak, read, write, and understand English | 4.58 | 0.99 |
| Child is LEP | Dummy variable categorizing: a) Child's self-reported ability to speak, read, write, and understand English b) Whether child was in a LEP class in past year | 0.21 | 0.40 |
| Parents' years in US | Higher of father or mother's years in U.S. (age if native-born) | 37.79 | 11.84 |
| Child's years in US | Number of years in U.S. (age if native-born) | 13.88 | 1.90 |

*Continued next page*

Table 1—*Continued*

| Variable | Description | Mean | s.d. |
|---|---|---|---|
| Generation of child | First: Child is foreign with at least one foreign parent | 0.05 | 0.21 |
| | Second: Child is native with at least one foreign parent | 0.16 | 0.37 |
| | Third plus: Child is native with two native parents | 0.77 | 0.41 |
| Years of child's schooling in US | Grade 8th grader started schooling (kindergarten if native-born) | 0.62 | 0.71 |
| **Race/Ethnicity** | | | |
| | Mexican | 0.09 | 0.29 |
| | Puerto Rican | 0.009 | 0.09 |
| | Cuban | 0.004 | 0.06 |
| | Other Latino | 0.023 | 0.15 |
| | Asian | 0.06 | 0.24 |
| | Black | 0.11 | 0.32 |
| | White (reference) | 0.65 | 0.47 |
| | Other race/ethnicity | 0.015 | 0.12 |
| **Student Achievement** | Mathematics score in 8th grade | 34.82 | 11.59 |
| | Reading score in 8th grade | 25.93 | 8.38 |

*Sources:* 1988–1994 National Educational Longitudinal Study (NELS).

1990 STMP3 zip code files from the United States Census.

## Understanding the Roles of Family Background, Ethnicity, and Community Context

Table 2 offers a complex account of how race and ethnicity, family background, community context, and family immigration relate to educational attainment. This table compares the means of the dependent and the main independent variables in this analysis separated by race/ethnicity and family immigration status. Differences in racial and ethnic background and immigration status have striking relationships with just about all of these important contextual and family background variables.

Whites in particular live with other whites (mean percentage of white people in a white respondent's zip code is 90.45%). No other ethnic group lives so closely among its own ethnic group. Mexican, Cuban, and black students live in areas with a relatively high mean percentage of neighbors with the same ethnicity, but their numbers pale in comparison to whites. For a Mexican person, the mean percentage of their co-ethnics in the respondent's zip code is

43.73%, and for blacks, it is 39.83%, Cubans, 27.05%. It is also clear that certain ethnic groups live in predominantly immigrant communities. The total mean percent foreign-born in a zip code is 7.14%. All ethnic groups in my sample, except whites, live in areas that house a larger percentage of foreign-born than this overall percentage of 7.14%. Mexican, Puerto Rican, and Cuban students, in particular, live in neighborhoods with a high proportion of immigrants (19.22%, 29.22%, and 46.07%, respectively). Mexican students also live in communities in which there is a relatively high percentage of recent arrivals to the United States (39.66% of the foreign-born in the zip code arrived in the 3 years before the 1990 Census). Index of upper-class residents in a zip code also differs by race or ethnicity. Cubans and Asians, in particular, seem to live in more advantaged areas than other ethnic groups do. Conversely, blacks and Mexicans have significantly less role models living in their zip codes than whites.

Mexican, Puerto Rican, and Cuban students live in communities that have a high concentration of immigrants. Additionally, Mexican and Cuban students live among their co-ethnic peers to a greater degree than do Puerto Ricans or any other ethnicity. One would think that if the ties that bind a community were based on ethnicity, then Mexicans and Cuban students would be succeeding in school at a greater rate than any other ethnicity. Conversely, one would hypothesize that Puerto Rican and Asian students would not go as far in school because the ethnic supports are not as tight in the zip codes in which they go to school (7.03% and 3.32%, respectively). However, in this sample, Asian and Cuban students on a whole have greater years of educational attainment than Mexicans and Puerto Ricans. We can diffuse this dilemma by looking to the parents' years of education and the proportion of residents with a professional occupation or with a bachelor's degree and the median household income, measured as the index of upper–middle–class residents. Correlation analyses (not shown) indicate that these two indicators are strongly positively associated with a child going far in school. Mexican and Puerto Rican students have relatively low parental education (13.10 years and 12.82 years, respectively) and Asian parents have the highest parental education level. Years of education of the parents of Cuban students (13.11 years), however, is not higher than it is for the parents of Mexican students (13.10 years). Cuban students are living in zip codes that have a high index of upper-middle class neighbors. This is also apparent for Asian youth. Mexican students, however, live in neighborhoods that have less availability of role models than any other ethnic group.

*The Effects of Family Background*

**Table 2:**

**One–Way Analysis of Variance of Mean Differences**

| | TOTAL | White | Black | Mexican | Puerto Rican | Cuban | Other Latino | Asian | Both Foreign | One Foreign | Both Native |
|---|---|---|---|---|---|---|---|---|---|---|---|
| Percent same race/ethnicity | 69.55 (35.51) | 90.84 (11.25) | 36.94 (28.77) | 38.16 (28.77) | 7.03 (8.84) | 35.87 (29.28) | 10.44 (16.56) | 3.32 (7.39) | 23.32 (31.08) | 52.48 (38.74) | 77.74 (29.88) |
| Percent foreign residents | 7.29 (10.88) | 4.13 (5.53) | 7.26 (12.18) | 19.22 (14.98) | 29.22 (14.03) | 46.07 (26.07) | 14.41 (15.91) | 15.24 (14.00) | 22.84 (17.21) | 12.23 (13.79) | 4.67 (6.86) |
| Percent recently arrived | 30.03 (18.56) | 26.97 (18.77) | 33.08 (18.82) | 39.66 (13.48) | 32.24 (13.34) | 32.66 (10.85) | 36.28 (15.04) | 37.78 (14.81) | 39.74 (13.36) | 33.23 (17.32) | 28.37 (18.85) |
| Percent same residence in last 5 years | 70.38 (13.21) | 69.30 (13.63) | 72.94 (12.18) | 72.30 (11.87) | 76.80 (8.37) | 78.45 (7.68) | 70.37 (13.08) | 72.68 (11.43) | 74.59 (10.04) | 71.72 (12.83) | 69.66 (13.49) |
| Parents know many of friends' parents | 0.35 (0.43) | 0.39 (0.44) | 0.31 (0.39) | 0.25 (0.36) | 0.21 (0.36) | 0.26 (0.41) | 0.29 (0.39) | 0.19 (0.37) | 0.21 (0.37) | 0.24 (0.37) | 0.38 (0.43) |
| Parents know some of friends' parents | 0.48 (0.44) | 0.47 (0.45) | 0.50 (0.41) | 0.51 (0.40) | 0.58 (0.40) | 0.51 (0.43) | 0.51 (0.42) | 0.54 (0.46) | 0.51 (0.44) | 0.53 (0.42) | 0.47 (0.44) |
| Index of upper-middle class neighbors | 0.00 (0.99) | 0.04 (0.91) | -0.28 (0.83) | -0.35 (0.78) | 0.07 (0.93) | 0.21 (0.75) | 0.04 (0.95) | 0.59 (1.10) | 0.31 (1.12) | 0.00 (0.99) | -0.03 (0.89) |
| Father's occupation | 42.30 (10.92) | 43.35 (10.92) | 38.32 (9.10) | 37.29 (8.95) | 40.02 (10.38) | 43.19 (10.78) | 42.91 (11.37) | 46.63 (12.10) | 42.50 (12.19) | 40.31 (10.36) | 42.62 (10.83) |
| Mother's occupation | 41.61 (11.51) | 42.50 (11.56) | 40.03 (11.14) | 37.09 (9.69) | 37.71 (9.23) | 38.85 (10.05) | 40.97 (11.95) | 43.70 (12.23) | 40.12 (11.66) | 39.03 (10.81) | 42.22 (11.54) |
| Parents' years of education | 13.47 (2.53) | 13.71 (2.37) | 13.04 (2.14) | 3.10 (1.50) | 12.82 (2.70) | 13.11 (3.13) | 13.29 (2.78) | 14.68 (3.01) | 13.02 (3.65) | 13.12 (2.66) | 13.58 (2.33) |
| Parents' number of years in the US | 37.79 (11.84) | 41.19 (8.15) | 38.85 (10.18) | 29.70 (14.13) | 22.20 (12.85) | 19.34 (10.88) | 30.34 (15.28) | 20.13 (15.14) | 11.38 (5.08) | 30.91 (11.24) | 41.99 (7.06) |
| Parents' English ability | 4.58 (0.99) | 4.93 (0.34) | 4.90 (0.39) | 3.10 (1.50) | 3.32 (1.31) | 2.69 (1.52) | 3.78 (1.37) | 3.25 (1.38) | 2.39 (1.47) | 4.12 (1.07) | 4.90 (0.35) |
| | N=10,547 | N=6,958 | N=1,233 | N=978 | N=101 | N=48 | N=245 | N=697 | N=948 | N=1,379 | N=8,220 |

*p<.05, **p<.01, *** p<.001 standard deviations in parentheses

*Source*: 1988–1994 National Educational Longitudinal Study.

1990 STMP3 zip code files from the United States Census.

These mean percentages weave a complicated tapestry. The Latino students who are concentrated in areas with large numbers of their co-ethnics (Mexicans and Cubans) or immigrants (Puerto Ricans and Cubans) have different educational attainments, leading us to question whether social capital, as measured by tight ethnic or immigrant bonds, can help or hinder a student's advancement in school. The advantages of living in a community with a high proportion of upper–middle–class residents, however, are clear. This is apparent with Cuban students. Their parents' years of schooling are not much higher than Mexicans, yet they live in areas with a larger index of upper–middle–class residents. It is quite possible that the overall socioeconomic status of the community may help students succeed in school.

Native families are more likely than foreign families to live with their own race or ethnicity (77.74% as compared to 23.32%) and foreign families live in communities with a higher percentage of foreign-born than native families do (22.84% as compared to 4.67%). Unlike the differences for ethnic groups, the index of upper–middle–class residents in a zip code does not differ based on family's immigration status. Immigrants are living in zip codes with similar levels of role models as native-born families. Although they are living in largely immigrant neighborhoods, they are not living in necessarily more depressed neighborhoods than native–born people. Additionally, the neighborhoods they choose to live in are relatively more ethnically heterogeneous than the communities in which native-born families live in. How is it possible (as a whole) children in immigrant households have higher rates of school completion and more years of schooling than children in native households, yet they don't live in communities that are any more or less privileged than native-born students? Evidently, these simple mean differences in ethnicity and immigration status obscure the interaction between ethnicity and immigration. Students from different ethnic, immigrant, and social status backgrounds will have a varied high school experience. Whether this experience is dependent on the socioeconomic status of the community in which the student lives or on the density of the ties within that community can be determined in the multivariate analyses below.

Table 3 elaborates how ethnicity of the child determines how far he or she will go in school when controlling for family background, the community in which he or she attends school, and the assimilation and immigration status of the family. I first test the effects of family background on Latino children's educational attainment (Model 2). Second, I include the effects of community context, segmented assimilation, social capital, and ethnic capital (Model 3), and then the effects of "assimilation" of the family into the mainstream American society (Model 4). In Model 5, I interact family immigration status with the other independent variables to test the relative predictive capabilities of family's immigration status on the Latino child's educational attainment. For each regression I control for various parental and child characteristics and use "white" student as the reference category. Because ordered logistic regression analysis uses cut points to determine the probability of a child continuing from one category of educational attainment to the next, the interpretation may not be that clear in these multivariate analyses. To alleviate this problem I interpret the results (with caution) using relative terms.

**Table 3:**
**Ordered Logistic Regression Analyses of Family Background, Community Context, and Immigration Status on Latino Child's Educational Attainment**

| | Model 1 | Model 2 | Model 3 | Model 4 | Model 5 |
|---|---|---|---|---|---|
| Child Characteristics | | | | | |
| Mexican student | -0.799*** | 0.069 | 0.255 | 0.081 | 0.118 |
| | (0.102) | (0.113) | (0.205) | (0.228) | (0.277) |
| *Mexican * both parents are foreign* | - | - | - | - | -0.573 |
| | - | - | - | - | (0.503) |
| *Mexican * one parent is foreign* | - | - | - | - | 0.253 |
| | - | - | - | - | (0.403) |
| Puerto Rican student | -1.168*** | -0.643* | -0.467 | -0.618 | -1.420* |
| | (0.338) | (0.278) | (0.359) | (0.399) | (0.688) |
| *Puerto Rican * both parents are foreign* | - | - | - | - | 0.094 |
| | - | - | - | - | (1.134) |
| *Puerto Rican * one parent is foreign* | - | - | - | - | 1.625 |
| | - | - | - | - | (0.864) |
| Cuban student | -0.389* | -0.015 | 0.039 | -0.253 | 0.606 |
| | (0.194) | (0.247) | (0.410) | (0.435) | (0.812) |
| *Cuban * both parents are foreign* | - | - | - | - | -1.656 |
| | - | - | - | - | (1.033) |
| *Cuban * one parent is foreign* | - | - | - | - | -0.337 |
| | - | - | - | - | (1.064) |
| Other Hispanic student | -0.076 | 0.196 | 0.503 | 0.232 | -0.049 |
| | (0.108) | (0.143) | (0.269) | (0.275) | (0.335) |
| *Other Hispanic * both parents are foreign* | - | - | - | - | -0.074 |
| | - | - | - | - | (0.717) |
| *Other Hispanic * one parent is foreign* | - | - | - | - | 0.976* |
| | - | - | - | - | (0.472) |
| Asian student | 0.758*** | 0.772*** | 1.022*** | 0.464 | 0.149 |
| | (0.116) | (0.127) | (0.288) | (0.291) | (0.379) |
| *Asian * both parents are foreign* | - | - | - | - | 0.018 |
| | - | - | - | - | (0.646) |
| *Asian * one parent is foreign* | - | - | - | - | 0.773 |
| | - | - | - | - | (0.513) |

*Continued next page*

Table 3—*Continued*

|  | Model 1 | Model 2 | Model 3 | Model 4 | Model 5 |
|---|---|---|---|---|---|
| Black student | -0.575*** | -0.011 | 0.134 | 0.172 | 0.171 |
|  | (0.108) | (0.136) | (0.285) | (0.288) | (0.354) |
| *Black * both parents are foreign* | - | - | - | - | -0.048 |
|  | - | - | - | - | (0.689) |
| *Black * one parent is foreign* | - | - | - | - | 0.229 |
|  | - | - | - | - | (0.424) |
| Student of "other" ethnicity | -0.761*** | -0.390* | 0.014 | -0.040 | 0.307 |
|  | (0.181) | (0.174) | (0.317) | (0.312) | (0.334) |
| *"Other" * both parents are foreign* | - | - | - | - | -0.649 |
|  | - | - | - | - | (0.650) |
| *"Other" * one parent is foreign* | - | - | - | - | -0.705 |
|  | - | - | - | - | (0.571) |
| **Family Background** |  |  |  |  |  |
| Parents' years of education | - | 0.174*** | 0.164*** | 0.176*** | 0.201*** |
|  | - | (0.019) | (0.018) | (0.019) | (0.023) |
| *Parents' education * both parents are foreign* | - | - | - | - | -0.173*** |
|  | - | - | - | - | (0.047) |
| *Parents' education * one parent is foreign* | - | - | - | - | -0.103* |
| Father's occupation | - | 0.022*** | 0.020*** | 0.019*** | 0.015*** |
|  | - | (0.003) | (0.003) | (0.003) | (0.003) |
| *Father's occupation * both parents are foreign* | - | - | - | - | 0.030** |
|  | - | - | - | - | (0.011) |
| *Father's occupation * one parent is foreign* | - | - | - | - | 0.023* |
|  | - | - | - | - | (0.010) |
| Mother's occupation | - | 0.013*** | 0.012*** | 0.011*** | 0.011** |
|  | - | (0.003) | (0.003) | (0.003) | (0.003) |
| *Mother's occupation * both parents are foreign* | - | - | - | - | -0.023 |
|  | - | - | - | - | (0.012) |
| *Mother's occupation * one parent is foreign* | - | - | - | - | 0.003 |
|  | - | - | - | - | (0.009) |
| **Segmented Assimilation** |  |  |  |  |  |
| % same–race residents in zip code | - | - | 0.003 | 0.002 | 0.002 |
|  | - | - | (0.002) | (0.002) | (0.003) |
| *% same–race * both parents are foreign* | - | - | - | - | -0.008 |
|  | - | - | - | - | (0.006) |
| *% same–race * one parent is foreign* | - | - | - | - | 0.001 |
|  | - | - | - | - | (0.004) |
| % foreign residents in zip code | - | - | 0.005 | -0.003 | -0.002 |
|  | - | - | (0.004) | (0.004) | (0.005) |
| *% foreign * both parents are foreign* | - | - | - | - | 0.002 |
|  | - | - | - | - | (0.009) |
| *% foreign * one parent is foreign* | - | - | - | - | -0.004 |
|  | - | - | - | - | (0.012) |

*Continued next page*

Table 3—*Continued*

| | Model 1 | Model 2 | Model 3 | Model 4 | Model 5 |
|---|---|---|---|---|---|
| % of recently arrived | - | - | -0.002 | -0.001 | -0.002 |
| | - | - | (0.001) | (0.001) | (0.001) |
| *% recent foreign * both parents are foreign* | - | - | - | - | -0.016 |
| | - | - | - | - | (0.007) |
| *% recent foreign * one parent is foreign* | - | - | - | - | 0.003 |
| | - | - | - | - | (0.004) |
| % same residence in last 5 years | - | - | 0.0007 | 0.0001 | 0.0008 |
| | - | - | (0.002) | (0.002) | (0.002) |
| *% same residence * both parents are foreign* | - | - | - | - | -0.003 |
| | - | - | - | - | (0.007) |
| *% same residence * one parent is foreign* | - | - | - | - | -0.008 |
| | - | - | - | - | (0.006) |
| **Social Capital** | | | | | |
| Parents know many of friends' parents | - | - | 0.710*** | 0.183*** | 0.815*** |
| | - | - | (0.112) | (0.050) | (0.132) |
| *Many friends * both parents are foreign* | - | - | - | - | -0.866** |
| | - | - | - | - | (0.261) |
| *Many friends * one parent is foreign* | - | - | - | - | -0.130 |
| | - | - | - | - | (0.241) |
| Parents know some of friends' parents | - | - | 0.424*** | 0.721*** | 0.537*** |
| | - | - | (0.101) | (0.112) | (0.123) |
| *Some friends * both parents are foreign* | - | - | - | - | -0.499 |
| | - | - | - | - | (0.269) |
| *Some friends * one parent is foreign* | - | - | - | - | -0.210 |
| | - | - | - | - | (0.232) |
| Index of upper-class neighbors in zip code | - | - | 0.176*** | 0.453*** | 0.177** |
| | - | - | (0.049) | (0.102) | (0.051) |
| *Upper-class neighbors * both parents are foreign* | - | - | - | - | 0.025 |
| | - | - | - | - | (0.120) |
| *Upper-class neighbors * one parent is foreign* | - | - | - | - | 0.015 |
| | - | - | - | - | (0.099) |
| **Ethnic Capital** | | | | | |
| Mexican upper–class neighbors | - | - | 0.062 | 0.021 | -0.044 |
| *Mexican*Index of upper–class neighbors* | - | - | (0.135) | (0.148) | (0.163) |
| Puerto Rican upper–class neighbors | - | - | 0.664* | 0.625* | 0.623* |
| *Puerto Rican*Index of upper–lass neighbors* | - | - | (0.261) | (0.249) | (0.279) |
| Cuban upper–class neighbors | - | - | -0.076 | 0.033 | 0.132 |
| *Cuban*Index of upper–class neighbors* | - | - | (0.442) | (0.473) | (0.357) |
| Other Hispanic upper–class neighbors | - | - | -0.158 | -0.127 | -0.191 |
| *Other Hispanic*Index of upper–class neighbors* | - | - | (0.164) | (0.144) | (0.169) |

*Continued next page*

Table 3—*Continued*

|  | Model 1 | Model 2 | Model 3 | Model 4 | Model 5 |
|---|---|---|---|---|---|
| Asian upper–class neighbors | - | - | 0.182 | 0.146 | 0.160 |
| *Asian\*Index of upper–class neighbors* | - | - | (0.104) | (0.099) | (0.121) |
| Black upper class neighbors | - | - | -0.268 | -0.297 | -0.300 |
| *Black\*Index of upper–class neighbors* | - | - | (0.242) | (0.246) | (0.265) |
| "Other" race upper–class neighbors | - | - | 0.197 | 0.175 | 0.293 |
| *"Other"\*Index of upper–class neighbors* | - | - | (0.218) | (0.228) | (0.243) |
| Family's Assimilation and Immigration Status |  |  |  |  |  |
| Both parents foreign | - | - | - | -0.077 | 3.695** |
|  | - | - | - | (0.314) | (1.308) |
| One parent foreign | - | - | - | -1.262*** | -0.710 |
|  | - | - | - | (0.341) | (0.844) |
| Cut point 1 | -1.804*** | 5.880*** | 6.120*** | 2.516** | 3.152** |
|  | (0.060) | (0.462) | (0.575) | (0.801) | (0.905) |
| Cut point 2 | -0.632*** | 7.204*** | 7.456*** | 3.884*** | 4.528*** |
|  | (0.043) | (0.478) | (0.590) | (0.814) | (0.919) |
| Cut point 3 | 0.742*** | 8.828*** | 9.106*** | 5.561*** | 6.218*** |
|  | (0.043) | (0.495) | (0.601) | (0.822) | (0.929) |

N= 10,395
*p<.05, ** p<.01, *** p<.001
[Huber/White standard errors]

Notes:
Dependent Variable = Postsecondary education in 1994.
Weights to account for probability of being sampled employed.
Sample is all public school students.
All models control for parent's English ability, child is Limited English Proficient, family's years in the US (age if native–born parent), child's years in US (age if native-born child), grade when child started schooling in the US, generation of child, and family's household income.

In Model 1 (no controls), we see that compared to white students, Mexican (b= -0.799), Puerto Rican (b= −1.168), Cuban (b= −0.389), and black students (b= −0.575) do not go as far in school. Asian students, however, are more likely to be in a higher category of educational attainment than whites are (b= 0.758). When I control for family background, in Model 2, we see that all differences between Mexican, Cuban, and black students relative to white students disappear, but the differences for Puerto Rican students and Asian students remain. All of these ethnic differences disappear once I test for the effects of community context (Model 3) and family's assimilation and immigration status (Model 4). It is apparent, then, that much of the differences that we associate with different ethnic groups can be explained when we consider the interaction of ethnicity with socioeconomic status of the community (ethnic capital), and the connections among parents and their child's friends' parents (social capital), family background, and assimilation of the family. Most striking in Model 4 is that parents' educational attainment (b= 0.176) and the community level socioeconomic status, the index of upper–middle–class neighbors (b= 0.183), have similar predictive value for a child's educational attainment.

The family's immigration status has a clear negative association with how far the child goes in school when all else is controlled. Children growing up in a "combined" family, a family in which only one parent is foreign-born, progress less far in school than children in a household with two native-born parents and in an "immigrant" household (b= −1.262). This finding runs counter to the a straight-line assimilation hypothesis (Park, 1914; Gordon, 1964; Matute-Bianchi, 1986) that the more assimilated a student's family is to the prevailing mainstream culture and norms the farther that student will go in school because of the greater knowledge of how to navigate the schooling and labor market systems. Instead, this finding supports the idea that these families may not be linked to either the immigrant or native population in meaningful ways, and may be detracting from the child's educational attainment. These families should be considered more "assimilated" into the mainstream culture and should know how to navigate the system better than their immigrant counterparts. Since I control for assimilation of the family, we see that the children in combined families are at a detriment, and may be falling into the trap of the second-generation decline; they are not progressing as far in school as their counterparts in immigrant and native households.

Model 5 examines the relationship between family immigration status and ethnicity more closely. In this model, I include the interactions between ethnicity, family background, and community context with family's immigration status to test the relative effects of being in one family versus another. Once again the one ethnic group that continues to have lower educational attainment than white students is Puerto Rican students (b= −1.420 for Puerto Rican students born of native parents). As Model 1 showed, Puerto Rican students do not go as far in school as white students, but that this disparity disappeared when the community context, family background, and assimilation effects were controlled. In Model 5, however, it is evident, all else being equal, Puerto Rican children in native-born households do not go as far in school as their native-born white counterparts.

Three possible characteristics of Puerto Rican students may cause them still to do less well in school than their white counterparts. One possible factor is that Puerto Rican students straddle the two worlds of the mainland and the island—the United States and Puerto Rico, respectively. The commonwealth status of Puerto Rico contributes to great amounts of migration to and from the island. Return migration to Puerto Rico has been a significant component of its demographic picture since the 1950s (Rivera-Batiz & Santiago, 1998). Circular migration is a phenomenon not peculiar to Puerto Ricans, but certainly dominates the cultural landscape. Census data show that as many as 130,000 circular migrants moved back and forth between the United States and Puerto Rico in the 1980s (Rivera-Batiz & Santiago, 1998). This constant movement of the families may have deleterious effects on the children. Unfortunately, the data I used did not ask students or parents about the family's circular migration patterns, so I cannot test this theory.

Second, Puerto Ricans are officially citizens of the United States, yet the island of Puerto Rico, the country of origin, is not culturally similar to the mainland. In fact, Puerto Ricans often feel more culturally aligned with Latin America than with the United States (Morris, 1995). Third, the cultural divide attached to mainland Puerto Ricans, from both mainstream American culture and their island culture, may contribute to the disturbing lack of educational attainment for Puerto Rican children. The difficulty to form a coherent identity around a country may shroud the students' abilities to use ethnic or social capital in their communities to their benefit.

There are also differences in the effects of social ties among parents in a student's circle of friends. Table 2 shows that native–household parents know "many" of their children's friends' parents than do immigrant–household parents. The social capital hypothesis would lead us to believe that these ties enhance the parent capacities to watch over their children's schooling. In fact, for children in native households, the closer the social ties between parents in their circle of friends, the farther in school they will go. However, an immigrant parent's knowing "many" or "some" of his or her children's friends' parents does not seem to matter. We see this same effect for parents' educational attainment.

Social capital, the ties that bind a family to the community, does not make a large difference in the educational attainment of children in immigrant households for a number of reasons. One, the community into which they are making these ties consists of other foreign-born people. Table 2 shows that immigrant households live in communities where the mean percentage of foreign-born residents is 22.84%, and one third of those foreign-born arrived within the 3 years prior to the 1990 Census, whereas native-born households live in zip codes with about 5% foreign-born population. The concentration of immigrant householders into communities in which most people are newcomers may not offer immigrants with a great opportunity structure of employment or information networks that native householders may have. The ties that bind parents together in a student's community may not factor as much into that child's schooling success because the ties do not hold as much capital for the parents. Secondly, the friends of students may not necessarily be of the same ethnicity or immigration status as their parents. Parents would then be reluctant and uncomfortable to reach out to the parents of their child's circle of friends. Because of these two reasons, parents may be more reliant on the family itself to help construct the learning environment for their children. Family support may be acting as a counterweight to the loss of community bonds.

Studies suggest (Stanton-Salazar & Dornbush, 1995; Valenzuela & Dornbush, 1994) that immigrant families compensate for the absence of social capital in outside networks with an emphasis on social capital in the form of familial support including preservation of the cultural orientation of their home country (Gibson, 1988). Relations inside the family would be a strong predictor of how far Latino immigrant children go in school when controlling for the ties that bind a community together, for "Parental support leads to higher educational achievement, both directly and indirectly through compensating for the loss of community among migrants" (Portes, 1998, p. 11).

Because of the potential for immigrant adults to rely more heavily on within-family communication, we might expect to find that the higher the parents' educational attainment for native households, the farther in school the child will progress. Immigrant parents' years of schooling, however, does not have the same predictive value for a child's educational attainment as it does in native families. Instead, father's occupation and the household income have a significant effect on an immigrant household child's educational attainment.

Pre-arrival educational attainment for immigrant adults may not have the same effects as the post-arrival social status of the family.

## Discussion

Similar to the native-born population in the United States, the foreign-born population is a heterogeneous group. In addition to cultural and religious differences, there are great differences in the levels of social status (years of education, occupation, and income) within the foreign-born population. From the previous set of analyses, it is clear that not only can we not make global statements about Latinos and their educational attainment, it is also impossible to make global statements about immigrants. Differences in the years of educational attainment among students of Mexican, Puerto Rican, and Cuban descent rely on the differences in parents' educational attainment, coupled with the socioeconomic context and density of ethnic and immigrant community in which the family lives.

Most research on the effects of neighborhood context (see Jencks & Mayer, 1990 and Brooks-Gunn et al., 1997) suggests that neighborhood effects tend to disappear when we consider the family's social status background. When I control for community context, all the differences between the different ethnic groups disappear. It is quite clear that any cultural or religious differences that ethnicity may proxy for are not apparent when community context is constant. However, community context variables may serve as a proxy for linguistic and social practices of Latino families and classroom interactions between student and teachers.

In the United States, linguistic and social practices of ethnic and linguistically different groups often differ considerably from the expected mainstream educational values and behaviors (Delgado-Gaitan & Trueba, 1991, p. 26). Culture is now considered a dominant explanation of achievement differences between limited and non-limited English proficient students and among different racial and ethnic groups and has been defined in many terms. For example, language proficiency (Cheng, 1987; White & Kaufman, 1997; Wang & Goldschmidt, 1999), norms of appropriate behavior (Ogbu & Simons, 1998; Ogbu, 1991; Hayes, 1992; Fuligni, 1997), socially shared cognitive codes, maps, and assumptions about worldviews and lifestyle in general (Delgado-Gaitan & Trueba, 1991; Farkas et al., 1990; Farkas, 1996), heritage from country of origin (Caplan, Choy, & Whitmore, 1991), classroom-based differences between teacher and student (Stanic, 1989; Vasquez, 1990; Ray & Poonwassie, 1992; Malloy & Malloy, 1998), and psychological adjustment (Portes, 1999; Kao, 1999). The differences in learning style of racial or ethnic minority groups from the mainstream and predominantly used model of teaching or home culture are two ways to think about how culture can influence student achievement beyond the usual family influences of parental education or occupation, family income, or family structure.

According to Vasquez (1990), certain cultural values may influence the learning process of Hispanic students such as "family commitment," which includes loyalty, a strong support system, a belief that a child's behavior reflects on the honor of the family, a hierarchical order among siblings, and a duty to care for family members. Apparently, this strong sense of "other directedness" may conflict with the country's mainstream emphasis on individualism. The emphasis on cooperation in the attainment of goals can result in Hispanic students' discomfort with this nation's conventional classroom competition. Some children have been raised in the cultural tradition of cooperative work. Therefore, they have a difficult time assuming competitive attitudes. Hesitancy to engage in competitive behavior eventually gives way to a sort of cultural code switching from cooperation to competition (Delgado-Gaitan & Trueba, 1991; Azmitta et al., 1994).

Hispanic adolescent students are also more inclined than Anglo adolescents to adopt their parents' commitment to religious and political beliefs, occupational preferences, and lifestyle (Black, Paz, & DeBlassie. 1991), suggesting that they may be more complacent to their parents' demands or susceptible to their parents' lack of demands. In addition, learning alone, as opposed to in groups, was preferred more by white students than by Mexican Americans (Dunn and Dunn, 1992, 1993), and preferred more by Mexican Americans than by African Americans (Dunn, Griggs, & Price, 1993; Jalali, 1988). These learning style differences may influence students' abilities to perform in the mathematics classroom if teachers are not aware of, or not prepared for, these differences. In addition to differences in learning styles or in familiarity with formal schooling techniques, some studies have found general differences in home culture that seems to affect students' achievement (Wong, 1987; Yao, 1987; Smith & Hausafus, 1998).

Hickey's (1998) study on classroom instructional practices of teachers in high–proportion immigrant Asian and Hispanic schools, found differences in achievements based on the children's respective religious traditions. Like the study on Southeast Asian student achievement by Caplan, Choy, and Whitmore (1991) she found that Asian students were heavily influenced by the Hindu, Buddhist, and Islamic value systems that emphasized group orientation. They were also influenced by an emphasis on family relationships and familial responsibility, respect for authority and reverence for the elderly, self-control, and personal discipline. They placed a high value on educational achievement, and shame was utilized to control behavior. Latino students, heavily influenced by their Catholic traditions, also emphasize familial responsibilities and have a group orientation. Yet, there is a stronger emphasis on traditional family and gender roles. These traditional expectations may hinder student achievement (Hickey, 1998, pp. 443–444). Indeed, Hickey found that teachers often unprepared for different cultures in their classrooms. U.S. models of learning were not appropriate: students were not used to challenging authority and performing in ways that would put the individual above the group (p. 446).

Steinberg, Dornbusch, and Brown (1992) challenged these widely held explanations for the superior school performance of Asian American adolescents and the inferior performance of African and Hispanic American adolescents: parenting practices, familial values about education, and youngster's beliefs about the occupational rewards of academic success. Their focus on the familial values is interesting in light of the common conception that Asian families have higher educational expectations than other racial or ethnic subgroups. They find that there is strong support for the power of authoritative parenting (parental acceptance or warmth, behavioral supervision and strictness, and democracy or granting psychological autonomy) in the socialization literature, but that Asian American students have the highest academic performance and their parents are among the least authoritative. African American and Hispanic parents are considerably more authoritative than Asian American parents are, but their children do less well in school on average.

In addition, Steinberg, Dornbusch, and Brown find that in contrast to the differential cultural values hypothesis, which suggests that ethnic differences in achievement can be explained in terms of ethnic differences in the value placed on education (see Caplan, Choy, and Whitmore, 1991; Schneider and Lee, 1990). Steinberg, Dornbusch, and Brown find that African American and Hispanic students are just as likely as other students to value education. This theory suggests that ethnic differences in achievement can be explained in terms of ethnic differences in the value placed on education (see also, Caplan, Choy, & Whitmore, 1991; Schneider & Lee, 1990), and African American and Hispanic students are just as likely as other students to value education. Their parents are just as likely as other parents to value education as well. Also students' beliefs about the relation between education and life success influence their performance and engagement in school; it may be students' beliefs about the negative consequences of doing poorly in school, rather than their beliefs about the positive consequences of doing well, that matter.

There are interesting ethnic differences in the relative influence of parents and peers on student achievement: parents are more potent sources of influence on white and Hispanic youngsters than they are on Asian American or African American youngsters. In comparison with white youngsters, minority youngsters are more influenced by their peers (and less by their parents) in matters of academic achievement. One can't simply say "parents need to be more involved in schooling of their children." Although parents are the most salient influence on youngster's long-term educational plans, peers are the most potent influence on their day-to-day behaviors in school (e.g., how much time they spend on homework, whether they enjoy coming to school each day, how they behave in the classroom).

Research on teacher/student classroom interactions further enhances the ongoing debate about the effect different learning styles and family cultural values have on Latino students' educational attainment. For example, Delgado-Gaitan and Trueba (1991) look at language and cultural conflicts in classrooms. They found that bilingual students, who were fluent English speakers, had better grades and a higher rate of educational stability and were more likely to complete a quarter more of their high school credits by the end of 9th grade than limited English proficient, or non-bilingual English—only speakers. They attribute these differences to the social behaviors of the students. The very act of learning English as a second language is a cultural variation, but it does not necessarily create distress for children. A conflict ensues when children, limited in English, are taught their English curriculum in such a way that their native language and culture are invalidated. They conclude, although English is necessary to the children's successful and meaningful participation in the classroom and in society, the language must be taught appropriately in the context of real experience.

## Conclusion

Even though researchers are giving greater attention to Latino students' educational attainment and the large amounts of immigrant students into the U.S. school population, a serious commitment to disentangle the effects of community context, language ability, minority status, and immigrant status is still missing. Much of the present research focuses either on one aspect of these four interrelated characteristics or on the combination of just two of them (see Buriel & Cardoza, 1988; Portes & MacLeod, 1996; Warren, 1996; Mau, 1997; Battacharya, 2000). It is difficult to decipher the effects of immigrant status or language ability or minority status from one another, particularly because the dominant form of research is limited to either one-community case studies or national data analyses with a small number in each subgroup population. This analysis aimed to overcome these methodological problems in order to dissect the various roles that socioeconomic status, ethnicity, immigration status, and community context play in the educational attainment of Latino youth. In doing so, I highlighted the differences in educational attainment among students of Mexican, Puerto Rican, and Cuban descent.

The ties that bind immigrant parents of children to other parents in the child's circle of friends do not seem to affect how far a student will go in school. However, children in native-born households are very strongly positively affected by the density of ties between their parents and their friends' parents. We need to reframe our conceptions of social capital for the children of immigrants. Evidently, the links parents have with the community do not seem to affect their likelihood of continuing on to postsecondary education as they do for children of native parents.

These analyses also point to a reconsideration of how parental education affects the educational attainment of Latino youth. For children in native households, parental education has a strong positive relationship to that child's educational attainment, even when language ability, community context, and other social status variables such as occupation and income are included in the model. For children in immigrant households, however, the relationship between parental educational attainment and child's educational attainment is not apparent. Instead, father's occupation and the household income are positively related to a child's years of schooling. One reason for this could be that educational credentials from another country are not often recognized in the United States, and a parent may be forced to accept a job that is "below" his or her skill level. In analyses of Latino youth we need to consider the role of the parents' and family's social status not only in this country, but also in the country of origin if the parents are foreign-born.

The one message of these analyses is that we often fall into the trap of "statistical discrimination," that is, applying overall trends of achievement of a group to an individual. In this case, the overall trend that Latinos are doing poorly and do not have high levels of engagement or retention in high school, in particular, should not be projected onto each individual student of Mexican, Puerto Rican, or Cuban descent. In order to turn around the low retention rate of Latinos in school, we need to understand the heterogeneity of the Latino community and try to understand the cultural differences of children from different ethnic backgrounds. What kind of educational background do their parents have? What kind of community is the student living in?

While the focus of this study has been on Puerto Rican, Mexican, and Cuban students in immigrant households, as compared to student of other ethnicities in immigrant households, it is important to consider other Latino groups—particularly the fastest–growing populations immigrating from Central America, South America, and the Dominican Republic. These countries have their own unique history of immigration to the United States that we cannot discount.

# Bibliography

Azmitta, M., et al. (1994). *Links between home and school among low-income Mexican-American and European-American families.* Educational Practice (Report No. 9). National Center for Research on Cultural Diversity and Second Language Learning. University of California: Santa Cruz.

Bennici, F. J., & Strang, W. E. (1995). *An analysis of language minority and limited English proficient students from NELS: 88.* Task Order D100. Office of Bilingual Education and Minority Language Affairs. Washington, DC: U.S. Department of Education.

Betts, J., & Lofstrom, M. (1998, October). *The educational attainment of immigrants: Trends and implications.* Working Paper No. W6757. Washington, DC: National Bureau of Economics Research.

Bhattacharya, G. (2000). The school adjustment of south Asian immigrant children in the United States. *Adolescence, 35,* No. pp. 137, 77–85.

Black, C., Paz, H., & DeBlassie, R. (1991). Counseling the Hispanic male adolescent. *Adolescence, 26,* 223–232.

Blau, P., & Duncan, O. D. (1967). The process of stratification. In *The American Occupational Structure* (pp. 163–205). New York: Wiley and Sons.

Borjas, G. (2000). *Issues in the economics of immigration: A National Bureau of Economics research conference report.* Chicago: University of Chicago.

Borjas, G. (1994). The economics of immigration. *Journal of Economic Literature, 32,* pp. 1667–1717.

Buriel, Raymond, & Cardoza, Desdemona, 1988. Socio-cultural correlates of achievement among three generations of Mexican American high school seniors. *American Educational Research Journal, 25,* No. 2, 177–192.

Breton, R. (1964). Institutional completeness of ethnic communities and the personal relations of immigrants. *American Journal of Sociology, 70,* No. 2, pp. 193–205.

Broeder, P. (1998). *Language, ethnicity, and education: Case studies on immigrant minority groups.* London: Taylor & Francis.

Brooks-Gunn, J., Duncan, G., & Lawrence Aber, J. (Eds.). 1997. *Neighborhood poverty: Vol. I. Context and consequences for children.* New York: Russell Sage Foundation.

Caplan, N., Choy, N., & Whitmore, J. K. (1991). *Children of the boat people: A study of educational success.* Ann Arbor: University of Michigan Press.

Cheng, L. R. L. (1987, June). Cross-cultural and linguistic considerations in working with Asian populations. *ASHA, 29,* pp. 33–38.

Coleman, J. (1988). Social capital in the creation of human capital. *American Journal of Sociology, 94,* 95–120.

Crandall, T.C. et al. (1985). The language of mathematics: The English barrier. In *Proceedings of the 1985 Delaware Symposium on Language Studies,* VII (pp. 129–150). Newark, DE: University of Delaware Press.

Delgado-Gaitan, C., & Trueba, H. (1991). *Crossing cultural borders: Education for immigrant families in America.* Bristol, PA: Falmer Press.

Del Piñal, J., & Garcia, J. (1994). *Hispanic Americans today: A report from census data.* Upland, CA: Diane.

Driscoll, A. (1999). Risk of high school dropouts among immigrant and native Hispanic youth. *International Migration Review, 33*, No. 4, pp. 857–875.

Dunn, R., & Dunn, K. (1993). *Teaching secondary students through their individual learning styles: Practical approaches for grades 7–12.* Boston: Allyn and Bacon.

Dunn, R., & Dunn, K. (1992). *Teaching elementary students through their individual learning styles: Practical approaches for grades 3–6.* Boston: Allyn and Bacon.

Dunn, R., Griggs, S., & Price, G. (1993). Learning styles of Mexican-American and Anglo-American elementary school students. *Journal of Multicultural Counseling and Development, 21* No. 4, pp. 237–247.

Edmonston, B. (Ed). (1996). *Statistics of immigration: An assessment of data needs for future research.* Washington, DC: National Research Council.

Farkas, G. (1996). Human Capital or Social Capital? New York, NY: Aldine de Gruyter Press.

Farkas, G., et al. (1990). Cultural resources and school success: Gender, ethnicity, and poverty groups within an urban school district. *American Sociological Review, 55*, pp. 127–142.

Featherman, D. L., & Hauser, R. (1976). Prestige or socioeconomic scales in study of occupational achievement. *Sociological Methods and Research, 4* No. 4, pp. 403–422.

Featherman, D., Jones, F., & Hauser, R. (1975). Assumptions of social mobility research in the U.S.: the case of occupational status. *Social Science Research.4*, No. 4, pp. 329-360.

Fernandez, R., Paulsen, R., & Hirano-Naknishi, M. (1989). Dropping out among Hispanic youth. *Social Science Research, 18*, pp. 21–25.

Fiorina, M. (1999). Extreme voices: A dark side of civic engagement. In T. Skocpol and M. Fiorina (eds.) *Civic engagement in American democracy.* Washington, DC: Brookings Institution Press and New York,: Russell Sage Foundation.

Fuligni, A. (1997). The academic achievement of adolescents from immigrant families: The roles of family background, attitudes, and behavior. *Child Development, 68*, pp. 351–368.

Ganzenboom, H., & Treiman, D. (1996). Internationally comparable measures of occupational status for the 1988 International Standard Classification of Occupations. *Social Science Research 25*, No. 3, pp. 201–239.

Genesee, F. (Ed.). (1999). *Program alternatives for linguistically diverse students.* Santa Cruz, CA: Center for Research on Education, Diversity, and Excellence.

Ghasarian, C. (1995, February). Education and its consequences: Value conflicts in an immigrant community. *Social Education, 59*, pp. 78–81.

Gibson, M. (1988). *Accommodation without assimilation: Punjabi Sikh immigrants in an American high school and community.* Ithaca, NY: Cornell University Press.

Gordon, M. (1964). *Assimilation in American life: The role of race, religion, and national origin.* New York: Oxford University Press.

Granovetter, M. (1974). *Getting a job: A study of contacts and careers.* Cambridge, MA: Harvard University Press.

Hafner, A., et al. (1990). *National education longitudinal study of 1988: A profile of the American eighth grader.* NELS:88 Student Descriptive Summary. National Center for Education Statistics. (Report No. 90-458). Washington, DC: U.S. Department of Education.

Haggerty, C. et al. (1996, March). *National education longitudinal study: 1988–1994*. (Methodology Report No. 96-174). National Center for Education Statistics. Washington, DC: U.S. Department of Education.

Hao, L., & Bonstead-Bruns, M. (1998, July). Parent-child differences in educational expectations and the academic achievement of immigrant and native students. *Sociology of Education 71*, No. 3, pp. 175–198.

Hayes, K. (1992, September). Attitudes toward education: Voluntary and involuntary immigrants from the same family. *Anthropology and Education Quarterly, 23*, pp. 250–267.

Henderson, R. W. (1980). Social and emotional needs of culturally diverse children. *Exceptional Children, 46*, pp. 598–604.

Hickey, M. G. (1998, Nov./Dec.). "Back home, nobody's do that": Immigrant students and cultural models of schooling with emphasis on Asian and Hispanic children. *Social Education, 62*, No. 7, pp. 442–447.

Hodgkinson, H. L. (1992). *A demographic look at tomorrow*. Washington, DC: Institute for Educational Leadership, Center for Demographic Policy.

Holman, L. J. (1997, April). Meeting the needs of Hispanic immigrants. *Educational Leadership, 54*, pp. 37–38.

Hurtado, A., & Garcia, E. (1994). *The educational achievement of Latinos: Barriers and successes*. Santa Cruz, CA: University of California Press.

Inger, M. (1992, August). *Increasing the school involvement of Hispanic parents*. (ERIC Digest: Clearinghouse on Urban Education, No. 80)

Jacobs, J. (1983, October). Equity through mathematics: Everyone's responsibility. *Mathematics Teacher, 76*, pp. 463–464.

Jencks, C., & Mayer, S. (1990). The social consequences of growing up in a poor neighborhood. In L. Lynn & M. McGeary (Eds.), *Inner-city poverty in the United States*. Washington, DC: National Academy Press.

Kao, G. (1999). Psychological well-being and educational achievement among immigrant youth. In J. Hernandez (Ed.), *Children of immigrants: Health, adjustments, and public assistance*. Washington DC: National Academy Press.

Kao, G., & Tienda, M. (1995, March). Optimism and achievement: the educational performance of immigrant youth. *Social Science Quarterly, 76*, No. 1, pp. 1–20.

Kaufman, P., Chavez, L., & Lauren, D. (1998, September). *Generational status and educational outcomes among Asian and Hispanic 1988 eighth graders*. (Report No. 1999–020). National Center for Education Statistics Statistical Analysis. Washington DC: U.S. Department of Education.

Lapham, S. (1993). *We, the American foreign-born*. Ethnic and Hispanic Branch, Population Division. Washington, DC: Bureau of the Census.

Lareau, A. (1989). *Home advantage: Social class and parental intervention in elementary education*. Philadelphia, PA: Falmer Press.

Lollock, L. (2001). The foreign-born population in the United States: March 2000. (Current Population Reports P20–534). Washington, DC: U.S. Census Bureau.

Lucas, T. (1996, December). Promoting secondary school transitions for immigrant adolescents. *High School Magazine, 6*, No. 4, pp. 40–41.

Mace-Matluck, B., Alexander-Kasparik, R., & Queen, R. M. (1998, November). Qualities of effective programs for immigrant adolescents with limited schooling. From *Through the golden door: Educational approaches for immigrant adolescents with limited schooling.* ERIC Digest: Clearinghouse on Languages and Linguistics. Delta Systems, Co., Inc.

Malloy, C. E., & Malloy, W. (1998, September). Issues of culture in mathematics teaching and learning. *The Urban Review, 30*, No. 3, pp. 245–257.

Matute-Bianchi, M. E. (1986, November). Ethnic identities and patterns of school success and failure among Mexican-descent and Japanese-American students in a California high school: An ethnographic analysis. *American Journal of Education, 95*, N 1, pp. 233–255.

Mau, W. C. (1997, July). Parental influences on the high school students' academic achievement: A comparison of Asian immigrants, Asian Americans, and white Americans. *Psychology in the Schools*, 34, pp. 267–277.

McCargo, C. (1999). Addressing the needs of English-language learners in science and math classrooms. *The ERIC Review: K–8 Science and Mathematics Education, 6*, Issue 2, pp. 52–54.

McDonnell, L., & Hill, P. T. (1993). *Newcomers in American schools: Meeting the educational needs of immigrant youth.* Santa Monica, CA : RAND.

Morris, N. (1995). *Puerto Rico: Culture, politics, and identity.* Westport, CT: Praeger.

Morse, S. (1990, January). The non-schooled immigrant child. *Thrust, 19*, pp. 36–38.

Ogbu, J. (1991). Immigrant and involuntary minorities in comparative perspective. In M. Gibson & J. Ogbu (Eds.), *Minority status and schooling: A comparative study of immigrant and involuntary minorities* (pp. 3–33). New York: Garland.

Ogbu, J., & Simons, H. (1998). Voluntary and involuntary minorities: A cultural-ecological theory of school performance with some implications for education. *Anthropology and Education Quarterly, 29*, No.2, pp. 155–188.

Park. R. (1914). Racial assimilation in secondary groups with particular reference to the Negro. *American Journal of Sociology, 19*, No. 5, pp. 606–623.

Portes, A. (1998). Social capital: Its origins and applications in modern sociology. *Annual Review of Sociology, 24*, pp. 1–24.

Portes, A. (1996). The educational progress of children of immigrants: The roles of class, ethnicity, and school context. *Sociology of Education, 69*, No. 4, pp. 255–276.

Portes, A., & MacLeod, D. (1996). Educational progress of children of immigrants: The roles of class, ethnicity, and school context. *Sociology of Education, 69*, pp. 255–275.

Portes, A., & Rumbaut, R. (1996). *Immigrant America: A portrait.* Berkeley: University of California Press.

Portes, A., & Zhou, M. (1993). The new second generation: Segmented assimilation and its variants. *Annals of the American Academy of Political and Social Sciences*, Vol. 530, 75–96.

Portes, P. R. (1999). Social and psychological factors in the academic achievement of children of immigrants: A cultural history puzzle. *American Educational Research Journal, 36*, No. 3, pp. 489–507.

Putnam, R. (2000). *Bowling alone: The collapse and revival of American community.* New York: Simon and Schuster.

Ray, D., & Poonwassie, D. (Eds.). (1992). *Education and cultural differences: New perspectives.* New York: Garland.

Rivera-Batiz, F., & Santiago C. (1998). *Island paradox: Puerto Rico in the 1990s.* New York: Russell Sage Foundation.

Rong, X. L., & Hickey, M. G. (1998). Focusing on new immigration. *Social Education, 62,* No. 7, pp. 390–392.

Rong, X. L., & Preissle, J. (1998). *Educating immigrant students: What we need to know to meet the challenges.* Thousand Oaks, CA: Corwin.

Rumbaut, R. (1994). The crucible within: Ethnic identity, self-esteem and segmented assimilation among children of immigrants. *International Migration Review, 28,* No. 4, pp. 748–794.

Schneider, B., & Yongsook L. (1990). A model for academic success: The school and home environment of east Asian students. *Anthropology and Education Quarterly, 21,* pp. 358–377.

Secada, W., et al. (1998, February). *No more excuses: The final report of the Hispanic dropout project.* Washington, DC: U.S. Department of Education.

Smith, F. M., & Hausafus, C. (1998). Relationship of family support and ethnic minority students' achievement in science and mathematics. *Science Education, 82,* pp. 111–125.

Stanic, G. (1989). Social inequality, cultural discontinuity, and equity in school mathematics. *Peabody Journal of Education, 66,* No. 2, pp 57-71.

Stanic, G., & Hart Reyes, L. (1986). Minorities and mathematics. *Arithmetic Teacher, 33,* p. 12.

Stanton-Salazar, R., Dornbusch, R. & S. (1995). Social capital and the reproduction of inequality: Information networks among Mexican-origin high school students. *Sociology of Education, 68,* No. 2, pp. 116–136.

Steinberg, L., Dornbusch, S., & Brown, B. B. (1992). Ethnic differences in adolescent achievement: An ecological perspective. *American Psychologist, 4,* No.6, pp. 723–729.

Stewart, D. (1993). *Immigration and education: The crises and the opportunities.* Lanham, MD: Lexington Books.

Suárez-Orozco, M., & Suárez-Orozco, C. (1995). *Transformations: immigration, family life, and achievement motivation among Latino adolescents.* Stanford, CA: Stanford University.

Thomas, T. (1992). Psychoeducational adjustment of English-speaking Caribbean and Central American immigrant children in the United States. *The School Psychology Review, 21,* No. 4, pp. 566–576.

Valenzuela, A., & Dornbusch, S. (1994). Familism and social capital in the academic achievements of Mexican-origin and Anglo adolescents." *Social Science Quarterly, 75,* No. 1, pp. 18–36.

Vasquez, J. (1990). Teaching to the distinctive traits of minority students. *The Clearing House, 63,* No. 7, pp. 299–304.

Vaznaugh, A. (1995). *Dropout Intervention and Language Minority Youth.* ERIC Digest No. ED379951: Clearinghouse on Languages and Linguistics.

Wang, J., & Goldschmidt, P. (1999). Opportunity to learn: Language proficiency and immigrant status effects on mathematics achievement. *The Journal of Education Research, 93,* No. 2, pp. 101–111.

Warren, J. R. (1996, April). Educational inequality among white and Mexican-origin adolescents in the American southwest: 1990. *Sociology of Education, 69,* pp. 142–158.

White, M. (1997, April). *Excerpt from executive summary. Chapter 4 from language proficiency, schooling and the achievement of immigrants.* (Report). Washington, DC: U.S. Department of Labor.

White, M., & Kaufman, G. (1997). Language usage, social capital, and school completion among immigrants and native-born ethnic groups. *Social Science Quarterly, 78*, No. 2, pp. 385–416.

Wong, S. L. C. (1987). The language situation of Asian immigrant students in the U.S.: A socio- and psycholinguistic perspective. *NABE Journal, 11*, pp. 203–234.

Yao, E. L. (1987, Dec.). Asian-immigrant students: Unique problems that hamper learning. *NASSP Bulletin, 71*, pp. 82–88.

Zhou, M. (2001). *Immigrant neighborhoods in Los Angeles: Structural constraints and the ethnic resource for the adaptation of immigrant children.* Unpublished Manuscript

Zhou, M., & Bankston, C. (1994). Social capital and the adaptation of the second generation: The case of Vietnamese youth in New Orleans. *International Migration Review, 28*, pp 821–845.

Chapter Nine

# Latino Parents Put Into Words: Immigrant Parents Share Their Beliefs on Education Through an After School Parents, Children, and Computers Project

*Rosita M. A. Ramírez*

## Introduction

School institutions in our increasingly diverse U.S. society continue to grapple with the challenges of educating students who come to school with different life and cultural experiences. The study presented here sheds some light on this issue by describing how Latino parents with elementary school children view education by attempting to understand Latino immigrant parents' beliefs about their involvement in their children's education. This study maintains that the educational attainment of Latinos is neither an issue of deficit nor cultural deprivation; rather the issue is acknowledging and understanding the cultural assets that parents possess which promote the education of their children. In addition, this line of work contributes to existing research that asserts how important it is to develop family and school partnerships in order to strengthen students' academic outcomes (Epstein, 2001). This study extends this line of work to incorporate and explore the strengths found in a Latino community in order to contribute information that may help schools understand the complex nature of Latino families. I examined these issues in the context of an action research project known as the Parents Children and Computers Program (PCCP). Not only was I a researcher at this project site, observing and evaluating outcomes from this program, but I was also the acting coordinator for the particular academic school year under study.

Research has already confirmed that the involvement of parents in their child's education produces positive outcomes in children's academic attainment (Epstein, 1986, 1990, 1992, 1995, 2001). Research concerning the involvement of Latino parents in their child's education illustrates that parents view education as an important asset for their children (Delgado-Gaitan, 1991, 1992; Lopez, 2001; Lopez et al., 2001; Velez-Ibanez & Greenberg, 1992). The work done by Valdés (1996) focuses on the involvement in education of Latino immigrant parents and their attitudes toward school. Her work explores some of the possible misconceptions of why at-risk Latino children perform poorly in school. Lopez (2001) shows that the parenting practices of immigrant Latino parents lay outside traditional school-related models. He further highlighted the distinction between involvement as the enactment of specific scripted school activities and Latino parents' view of involvement as a means of instilling in children the value of education through the medium of hard work.

Understanding parental involvement also entails learning what type of aspirations and expectations parents have for their children and how this affects their child's educational attainment (Goldenberg et al., 2001). This research has focused on how much formal schooling immigrant Latino parents expect for their children to attain and if this influences their children's academic achievement. However, we must make the distinction between parents' aspirations and expectations, and the knowledge that they may actually hold about the U.S. school system. This knowledge, or lack thereof, especially impacts the actual advocacy power that parents may have in their children's education.

Understanding what the U.S. school system requires of parents leaves many Latino parents guessing. Typically, the U.S. school system assumes that parents will take some responsibility for their children's academic success by preparing them for school, teaching their children basic skills, and reinforcing what goes on in the classroom after children reach school age (Epstein, 2001, p. 36). In many cases, low-income Latino immigrant and migrant parents are unfamiliar with this role or may be consumed with more basic survival needs for the family so that this role becomes secondary. In these instances, Latino parents assume that this role belongs primarily to the teachers in the classroom. In some Latin American countries, the role of parents and the role of the school are sharply delineated. A parent's job is to instill respect and proper behavior in their children. It is the school's job to instill knowledge (Nicolau & Ramos, 1990, p. 13). For action researchers, it is important and part of their responsibility to investigate plausible solutions to the unintentional misreading of worldviews that go on between schools and Latino families. One cultural worldview is located within the family and a second cultural worldview is located within the educational system. Having the educational system understand and validate the cultural and familial practices that are occurring in the home of these Latino families is a beginning. Understanding that these families also operate between different worldviews is also necessary. The challenge, I believe, is in trying to find a culturally sensitive way to bridge these disparate outlooks.

How do Latino parents contest and accommodate the array of cultural models held by them, or expected of them, by schools to be able to advocate for their children? Furthermore, how does this affect the way in which Latino families see education and how parents view their role in raising their children? González (1997) offers a borderlands context for the language socialization of children. This borderland is created through the merging of two or more worldviews to create a third border culture. This work suggests that parents both contest and accommodate "worlds" and "worldviews" in their everyday practices to raise their children (p. 55). Hence, children in the borderlands are not the only recipients of a uniform model. Through language socialization Latino parents both challenge and accommodate differing worldviews in order for them to socialize their children and help them to survive in this new host country. In other words, the differing worldviews are inter alia a fusion of work school–, culture–, and familial– related views. The cultural transitions across generations and the constructions of new parental expectations for the socialization of their children laid the groundwork for González's understanding of a processual approach to culture and parents' approach to the education of their children (p. 66).

I argue that the inability of the educational system to validate, assess, and recognize that Latino children are socialized within a context of multiple worldviews becomes detrimental to the academic development of children. In order for these children to succeed, the literacy models that these parents and children possess need to be addressed and implemented into the children's current educational curriculum. Becoming familiar with the beliefs that Latino parents have regarding their involvement in their children's education becomes a stepping stone in making this information accessible to school communities and bridging the gap between schools and families. Many of the underlying ideologies Latino parents have about raising their children in a host country and their views on education are often times manifested in different ways, one of which includes the written word. This present study focuses on the distinct and similar beliefs

Latino parents have about the theme of education and how parents take up an opportunity to utilize the computer resources in an after school program and the assistance of staff members to describe their own beliefs regarding parent involvement and their children's education.


## Contextualizing the Study

Delgado-Gaitan (1992) has attempted to explain the importance that education plays in Mexican families, while focusing on literacy practices. Literacy, according to Delgado-Gaitan, is a sociocultural process dynamically affected by experiences and contexts; therefore it is malleable, ever shifting, and never ending. Furthermore, literacy extends beyond written text. Literacy competency is one's ability to skillfully utilize social power and agency in socially constructed contexts. Consequently, one's ability to participate actively in social contexts permits the expansion and development of one's own cultural knowledge and the use of such knowledge to affect the world (1996, p. 130).

Studying Paulo Freire also contributes in framing this current study. His views are central to understanding the multiple forms of literacies that are used by people to comprehend and conceptualize the world where humans live (Freire & Macedo, 1987). Freire's work illustrates the importance to validate the different forms of literacies that people use and learn in order to live in the world that they have created through their constant negotiation of various cultural and institutional worldviews. Literacy becomes a creative activity where parents can begin to analyze and interpret their own lived experiences, make connections between these experiences and those of others, and, in the process, extend both consciousness and understanding. This dynamic and developmental movement is central to the literacy process. Furthermore, what parents share and what they write about in this study allows for an understanding of their beliefs about education and parent involvement to be illustrated in a more indepth manner.

In addition, using a sociocultural approach (when discussing literacy) explicates the relationship between parental involvement on the one hand, and the cultural, institutional, and historical contexts in which parent's actions occurs on the other (Wertsch, 1998, p. 24). That learning must be socially situated, just as literacy is socially situated, is an aspect of this theory essential to this study (Edwards & Garcia, 1994, p. 243). Sociocultural theories of learning help to demonstrate the way in which learners acquire new skills in order to utilize tools that are available to them in particular contexts to accomplish specific goals (Vygotsky, 1978; Mehan et al., 1996). The aforementioned approaches in this literature review look at the work undertaken on parent involvement, literacy, and sociocultural theory of learning to understand and contextualize parent's beliefs on education and involvement.


## An Overview of the Parent's Children and Computers Project

The study conducted at the Parent's Children and Computers Project promises to be an extension of the work done by other scholars such as Conchas (2001), Delgado-Gaitan (1996), Moll et al. (1992), and Valdés (1996). I begin this discussion by providing an overview of the project, its goals, and the baseline information on the parents who participated in this cycle of activity.

The PCCP is a program that operates through the University of California, Santa Barbara. In one academic school year the PCCP has two cycles of activity and each cycle has approximately 10 sessions. This program was designed to have families participate in an after school program where parents and children came to learn how to use computers in an elementary school's computer lab. Having the families interact with technology serves multiple purposes, the first of which is having the parents learn basic computer skills. Parents learn these basic computer skills through the creation of desktop publications. Another purpose of this program is to have the children participate in enrichment activities such as extra access time to technological resources, playing educational software games, and using the said utilities for homework purposes. A final purpose is exploring the possibility of having parents and children work together to create a joint document for their desktop publication. A fundamental goal of this program is to have a system where the staff attempts to meet the needs of Latino families as a working unit rather than catering to the needs of children or parents independent of one another by creating separate programs.

Data for this study has been taken from the fall 2000 cycle; we had a total of 13 parents and 19 children. Six of those parents were male and seven were female. After administering a background questionnaire we obtained baseline data for the families who participated in this project. The questionnaire focused on family members, residency in the United States, country of origin, language used in the home, employment status, and last level of education completed.

Except for two, all of the parents who participated in this program emigrated from Mexico. The other two parents emigrated from two different countries: one from Guatemala and the other from India—our single non-Latino parent in the cycle under study. The time spent in the United States for the parents ranged from a 1–month residency to 28 years of occupancy. On average, the parents had three children and all of them had at least one child attending this particular elementary school. With the exception of three families, the dominant language spoken at home was Spanish. The other families spoke both English and Spanish. Our sole Indian family spoke Punjabi, English, and Hindi.

The range of employment varied for these participating parents. Most of the parents worked in blue-collar jobs where they were employed in factories, stores, restaurants, and in some instances, parents worked as housecleaners. At the time of our data collection process, five of the parents were unemployed; three women and two males were recent immigrants. When the parents were asked about their educational attainment the breakdown was as follows: two of the parents attended only elementary school; six went on to middle school; three of them finished high school, and one obtained a master's degree in her country of origin. All of these parents were schooled outside the United States except for one parent who attended school in the United States through the 12th grade, but he did not graduate.

## Methodology and Research Questions

The proposed study focused on Latino parents' beliefs on education within a community–based after school computer program so as to answer the following questions: What opportunities did the PCCP offer parents to communicate about their role in their children's education? What do parents' texts reveal about their notion of education?

### Data Gathering Methods

Data from this 10–week cycle of activity was collected in a variety of formats including video recordings of the sessions, data from focus group discussions, and participants' products, such as typed texts produced at the project. Part of doing action research involved purposefully engaging the people in the program in studying their own problems in order to understand the problems one was seeking to solve, in this case, understanding how parents viewed education and parent involvement. Incorporating an inductive process in obtaining this information became imperative.

## Event Mapping

The first level of analysis involved the creation of event maps, developed for each program session, which offered an illustration of what occurred at the PCCP during this cycle of activity. The goal being that the use of event maps would produce a coherent focused analysis of an aspect of life that had been observed and recorded (Emerson, Fretz, & Shaw, 1995, p. 142). These event maps were produced using videotapes of the 11 sessions for this cycle of activity. There were 21 sessions in total.

After each event map was created, this information was then condensed into one table by producing a synopsis of what had occurred in this cycle of activity (see Table 1). This table contains the classifications of the events that were drawn from all 11 event maps. An X was placed in the cell that coincided with the session in which the classification had occurred. This table also indicates how often these classifications occurred throughout the fall cycle of activity. Furthermore, in order to understand when parents had the opportunity to share ideas on education the cell was marked with XX so that the table would illustrate an answer to our first question: What opportunities the PCCP offered parents to communicate about their role in their children's education?

## Content and Ethnographic Analysis

An approach that was drawn upon to analyze how parents discuss education and parental involvement was a content analysis of the two community newsletters that were produced in the fall 2000 cycle of activity. Four parents in this session were used as case studies. They were selected for the following reasons: two of the parents are female (Teodora and Marisol) and two of them are male (Enrique and Juan); two of these parents had participated in the program in a previous cycle of activity (Teodora and Enrique); and two of the parents were participating in this program for their first time (Marisol and Juan). There was diversity in how much exposure the parents have had to the program. As a final note, all of these parents were included as cases because they had attended the program in a more consistent manner than some of the other parents throughout the cycle of activity. Thus, they were able to provide more information within the data collection process regarding their beliefs on education and parent involvement.

Within this content analysis, the typed texts of these four parents (a total of eight documents) were selected to observe how they wrote on the theme of education. The analysis of these texts entailed locating examples within the text that described or mentioned the different ways that parents wrote about parental involvement and education. These texts illustrate that within their writing all four of the parents mentioned parental involvement as important components to the success of their children's education.

## Parents Put Into Words

Selected data sources from this program were explored to learn more about parents' beliefs on education. An account is presented on the different opportunities that parents had in the PCCP to voice their beliefs on education. One objective for this study was to find out how the participating parents' experience in the project, and the content found within their written texts, would foreground different aspects of parent involvement and education.

In order to address the first question an analysis was carried out on the whole cycle of activities (see Table 1) to show how time was spent in the fall cycle of activities. The construction of the event maps made visible the 11 categories of time usage: preparation, presentation, group discussion, parent feedback, announcements, computer or writing time, parent and child activities, closing down, newsletter creation, guest speakers, and research program logistics.

We had a total of 10 sessions including one informational session that introduced and recruited new participants to the program. In the 10 sessions that parents came to the PCCP, eight of those sessions contained presentations for the parents. These presentations consisted of computer skill training necessary for parents to use a computer. Other presentations were on issues of education where parents received or shared information amongst each other about their views on this subject. This program introduced parents to computer skills through the individual assistance provided by staff members to utilize the resources in the school's computer lab. One approach that was utilized to give parents the opportunity to learn and practice these computer skills was to have them create typed texts. The presentations on computer skills provided parents the ability to learn how to use technological resources whereas the group discussions on issues of education provided them with the brainstorming sessions that stimulated parents with ideas for writing texts.

During these group discussions parents often had the opportunity to share ideas they had about education amongst each other. The theme of education was purposefully left as a broad topic so that parents could interpret and write about it in whatever way they felt it pertained to their own lives and their own experiences. Three out of the five group discussions that occurred in the fall cycle of activity dealt with the theme of education. It was during these times, especially, that parents were able to brainstorm on possible ideas for their own documents. Within this cycle of activity the presentations that were offered to parents became opportunities for them to discuss issues of parent involvement in their children's education. These ideas then became available for all parents to utilize in the production of their individual documents. Some of the themes that arose from such discussions were the following: the loss and retention of family culture, traditions, difference in customs between countries of origin and their new host country, language, raising their children, educating their children, parent interactions with schools, and the transmission of beliefs to their children, or lack thereof.

Another component that also made presentations noteworthy was the program's ability to bring in guest speakers to lead such discussions. A guest speaker we had for the PCCP in this cycle of activity was an Early Academic Outreach spokesperson. This presentation revolved around college admission requirements. The purpose of inviting this guest speaker was to inform parents as to what they could do to help their children to obtain a college education. Consequently, the PCCP's attempts to offer parents skills and opportunities for them to think about educational issues prompted parents with the ability for them to write about such issues in their own documents. An analysis of Table 1 also indicates that as parents began their first writing exercise on the computers the staff had already presented education to them as the overarching theme for this particular cycle of activity. Therefore, from the 10 sessions in this fall cycle of activity, eight of those sessions provided the parents an opportunity for them to write on the theme of education. This also became an opportunity for parents to use computer time; here they were able to practice the skills they had acquired during a sessions presentation.

Table 1 shows that out of the eight sessions where parents wrote on the computers, four of those sessions dealt explicitly with the theme of education. As a result of these diverse practices occurring at the PCCP, parents were

*Latino Parents Put Into Words*

**Table 1**
**Synopsis of Event Maps for Fall 2000**

| Categories of Time Usage | Informational Session | Session 1 | Session 2 | Session 3 | Session 4 | Session 5 | Session 6 | Session 7 | Session 8 | Session 9 | Session 10 |
|---|---|---|---|---|---|---|---|---|---|---|---|
| Prep. Time | X | X | X | X | X | X | X | X | X | X | X |
| Presentations | | X | X | X | X | X | | XX | | | X |
| Group Discussions | | XX | XX | | | | | X | X | | |
| Parent Feedback | X | X | X | X | X | | X | X | | | X |
| Announcements | | | XX | | X | X | | | | X | |
| Computer Time to Write | | XX | X | XX | X | X | XX | | X | XX | |
| Parent and Child Activities | | | | | | X | | X | | | |
| Closing Down | | X | X | X | X | X | X | X | X | | |
| Newsletter Creation | | | | | | X | | | | X | |
| Guest Speakers | X | | | | XX | | | | | | |
| Research Program Logistics | | X | | | | | | | | | X |

* Cells marked with XX represent instances where the theme of education was discussed.

afforded a range of opportunities that drew on different knowledge bases. The fact that this setting provided parents with access to physical artifacts (i.e., computers and a range of texts) and sources of information (i.e., presentations and visits) is reflected in the ways that these ideas are expressed as content within physical artifacts such as their typed texts. Similarly, the project set out to provide individual assistance from the staff to parents in order to scaffold parents' learning and use of these new technologies in such a way that enabled parents to write their texts regardless of prior computer knowledge or literacy levels. Furthermore, all of this involved having participants learn new aspects of information which then allowed them to communicate their own lived experiences (Warschauer, 2002, p. 7).

## Case Study Findings

It is not enough, however, to measure only parents' beliefs on education through the opportunities the PCCP offered parents to communicate about their role in their children's education. Research on what parents had to say about their perceived roles and their notion of education must also be taken into account. In order to do this, the study looked at what four parents said and wrote in their texts and how that revealed about their notions about education. Some of the findings from the analysis of these texts show that parents recognized the value in becoming involved in their children's education and explicitly addressed this.

### Parent 1: Enrique

The first parent, Enrique, is a returning parent who during this cycle of activity took on the role of editor for both newsletters. Enrique has lived in the United States for 10 years and he has three children in the school system. He himself had completed "la secundaria" (secondary education) in Mexico. Enrique, who only spoke Spanish, was a welder for a local company during his participation in the program. The documents that Enrique wrote for the newsletters became introductory pieces to the general theme of the newsletter and to the work of the other participating parents. Enrique is a dedicated parent who participates in his children's school activities and who, in this program, has more than once offered positive, as well as critical, feedback in terms of what he envision the goals were for the program in relation to how it would affect other parents including himself. As an editor to the newsletter, Enrique's documents draw on the ideas of the other parents while representing his own views as noted from his first document entitled "Nota de los Editors"/"Note from the Editors." He writes: "A nosotros, los padres latinos, nos hace falta involúcranos un poco en las clases y educación de nuestros hijos."/"We as Latino parents still need to involve ourselves a little more in the classes and education of our children." With his phrase, "We as Latino parents," Enrique, himself, addresses the Latino community and mentions the importance of overall Latino parental involvement needed in their children's education

On a similar note, another excerpt taken from the same document, Enrique engages his potential reading audience, which he assumes/identifies to be Latino parents: "¿Por qué no nosotros como padres también podemos aprovechar de esos conocimientos?"/"Why should we as parents not take the opportunity to learn these concepts?" With this statement, Enrique poses rhetorical questions to the readers and to other parents who may have read this newsletter. By directly addressing the parents reading this newsletter with, "Why should we as parents," not only did Enrique project himself as part of the audience, he also, in a sense, positions himself as part of the community, thereby encouraging other Latino parents to participate in this program through an interpersonal approach as an insider, not an outsider. In his attempt to reach other Latino parents, Enrique utilizes his voice as an editor in this newsletter to share his philosophy with other parents.

In the second editorial, "Del Editor a la Comunidad"/"From the Editor to the Community," Enrique writes about parental involvement in relation to the guiding theme for the newsletter, which is education. This first excerpt taken from the second newsletter revolves around notions of parenting as well:

> Nosotros como padres tenemos el derecho de motivar a los niños y apoyarlos. Desde pequeños es importante que cada niño tenga una idea de lo que es la educación en el hogar.

> We as parents have the right to motivate our children and offer them support. As early as childhood it is important that every child has an idea of what education is in the home.

Here, once again, Enrique stresses the importance of education in the home as he emphasizes that education should be offered to children in their early childhood years. In this next excerpt taken from the second newsletter, Enrique further illustrates the multiple roles that parents could use with their children in order to assist them academically: "Por lo tanto es deber de todo padre explicar, enseñar, y hacerles entender lo que en la escuela no les enseñan." / "Thus, it is every parent's duty to explain, teach, and have them understand what they are not taught in the schools." By acknowledging that parents can also be teachers to their children, Enrique writes about a parent's obligation to teach their children what the school does not and what parents feel is important for their children to know. Through his writing, Enrique lets his readers know that education takes on multiple forms; thereby, teaching can be done not only by teachers, but by parents as well. In addition, Enrique continually seeks parent responses to his statements. By addressing and encouraging the parents who may read this newsletter to take on these multiple roles, he is encouraging parental involvement.

The following excerpt, taken from Enrique's second document, addresses parental issues regarding their Latino identity: "[R]ecordarles sus raíces, tales como su primer lenguaje y sus antepasados que se quedaron en sus país de origen." / "Remind them of their roots such as their first language and their ancestors who have stayed behind in their country of origin." By focusing on the importance of maintaining the primary culture, while living in the host culture, Enrique is also giving attention to the retention of their native language and culture, as well as remembering their cultural ancestors. Enrique's statement signals the diversity that is manifested in this country, where not only Latino families are learning aspects of their new host country, but where the parents retain their primary culture. In this sense, parents and families retain and expand their own worldviews with those of the host country.

The final excerpt also taken from the second newsletter presents the immigrant experiences that parents like Enrique face as they endeavor to raise their children in a foreign (host) country: "Nosotros como padres decimos que venimos a este país a trabajar para darles un mejor porvenir a nuestros hijos."/"We as parents say that we have come to this country to give our children a better future." As the author of this text, Enrique includes himself in this category. When he states that as an immigrant, "parents say that we have come to this country to give our children a better future," Enrique stresses the importance that immigrants place in having their children obtain a better future in this country than they would have in their country of origin. This immigrant experience allows for Enrique to write and express his beliefs as to why parents leave their country of origin and why they see education as a means for their children to obtain a better future.

**Parent 2: Teodora**

Another participant, Teodora, who was a returning parent during this cycle of activity and had also lived in the United States for 10 years, had one daughter who attends the elementary school where the PCCP was operated. Teodora had completed "la primaria" (primary education) in Mexico before coming to the United States where she developed a basic command of English. At the time of the program, Teodora was employed as a housekeeper. Teodora's participation in the PCCP was also used to answer in a descriptive manner the following question: What do parent's texts reveal about their notion of education?

Although her documents tend to be modest in nature, she consistently participated during group discussions that were held in order to facilitate parents with the production of their documents. For example, in one group discussion, she discussed how in her interactions with her daughter's teachers, language and culture had become a concern for her. Teodora spoke about how this particular occasion, visiting with her daughter's teacher, made her feel uncomfortable. Her daughter was being administered a test in English. Because Teodora saw her daughter becoming timid at the beginning of the exam, she attempted to help her. The mother explained to the group, that since both parents spoke predominantly in Spanish to her daughter, she knew that her child spoke primarily in Spanish, too. When the teacher asked Teodora's daughter questions in English, the daughter became hesitant, so Teodora attempted to assist her. It was at this point that the teacher interrupted her and asked her to be quiet.

In the following dialogue, Teodora points out how inadequate she felt because she saw herself invalidated in front of her daughter:

[T]ienen mucho que ver. Tan solo yo ya pasé una experiencia con la niña. No voy a decir con quien estaba verdad. Le estaban haciendo un examen en inglés, si en la casa los dos hablamos puro español, puro español, la niña nos habla más español que en inglés. En el momento que en la maestra le estaba haciendo la pregunta la niña se quedó así y yo le dije, "mi'ja es esto" y ella me dijo por favor usted cállese y no le diga. Yo me sentí tan mal que mejor no digo nombres, pero es que es que tiene que ver mucho la cultura tanto en la clase como fuera de la clase....

[I]t has a lot to do with it. I myself have already gone through an experience with my daughter. I am not going to say whom I was with. They were giving her an exam in English, but in the home we both speak only Spanish, and our daughter speaks to us in

Spanish more so than in English. In the moment that the teacher asked her a question she got like this, so I told her "mi'ja, it's this" and she told me please be quiet and do not tell her anything. I felt so bad that I would rather say no names, but culture matters as much in the classroom as out of the classroom.…

Teodora felt that her role as a parent had been hindered in this particular situation. As a parent she felt she had to assist her daughter. However, she had read the situation in a particular way and the teacher had also read the situation in another. This seemed to be an occasion where a misreading of the situation had occurred by all involved. The mother became unsure as to when the teacher felt it was appropriate for Teodora to assist her child and when to allow the child to do the work unassisted. To Teodora, this encounter with the teacher had become a negative experience.

After Teodora gave her account, parents and staff members discussed some options available to her in dealing with situations of this nature. Having Teodora voice this experience at the PCCP allowed her to have a place where she could reflect on these differences and be able to write about this event in any of her working texts.

The first text Teodora wrote for the program's newsletter was appropriately named, "Aprender a Volar"/"Learning How to Fly." In this text, Teodora, states that her desire to help her daughter with her homework and education overshadowed the difficulty she found in learning how to use computers: "[E]s un poco difícil pero quiero aprender para ayudar a mi hija en sus tareas."/"[I]t is a little difficult but I want to learn to help my daughter with her homework." In hopes of expanding her role to that of a teacher for her daughter's sake, Teodora was willing to develop and expand her role as a parent to that of a learner. Consequently, Teodora's first document illustrated how her involvement in the PCCP derived not only from her wanting to learn how to use computers, but it also revolved around a need that she had to be more involved in her daughter's education. Teodora was placing an emphasis in learning how to use computers due to her need to help her daughter to obtain a better future, one that would be better than hers: "Yo quiero un mejor futuro para mi hija pues, yo no tuve la oportunidad de estudiar lo suficiente. Es por eso que estoy aquí, para aprender y ayudar a mi hija a que tenga un futuro mejor."/"I want a better future for my daughter since I did not have the opportunity to study sufficiently. That is why I am here, to learn and help my daughter have a better future."

In Teodora's second piece, "Aprender en Familia"/"Learning as a Family," she situated her document into two sections. One section describes the difference in customs that children learn in United States from those of the parents' country of origin:

[M]i niña esta aprendiendo diferente aquí en los Estados Unidos. En la escuela la enseñan acerca de calabazas y de pedir dulces. Mientras tanto, en mi cultura nos enseñaban a rezar y llevarles flores al panteón a nuestros muertos.

[M]y little girl is learning differently here in the United States. In school they teach her about pumpkins and asking for candy. On the other hand, in my culture they showed us how to pray and take flowers to our dead in the cemetery.

This particular passage is in reference to how people celebrate holidays here in the United States. Teodora was aware that Halloween in this country meant something completely different than her own experiences in celebrating the Day of the Dead in Mexico. She is also aware that the cultural significance of what this holiday represents is completely different as well. Indeed, this passage illustrates how this parent is very much aware that her children are learning different customs in school, at home, and in contemporary society. Coming to terms with these differences, and learning how to construct her own understanding of what this means, leads Teodora to a new worldview that she was creating for herself and her child.

Moreover, in her document, Teodora also draws attention to the importance of the educational practices that she and her daughter can do together at home as a family: assisting her daughter with her homework and utilizing home objects to teach her daughter how to count and how to write. It is important to note that the educational practices that Teodora mentions in her document are actual recommendations from her daughter's teacher. Thus, although Teodora felt she had had a negative experience in the past with her daughter's teacher, she was still willing to accept the assistance and recommendations that were offered to her in order to support her daughter through her education. Similarly, Teodora, like Enrique, emphasizes in her document that the education that a child receives does not only take place in the school, but that the home is also a learning environment that needs to be acknowledged:

Así que la educación va mas allá de la escuela, empieza con la familia. Yo le apoyo a mi hija de muchas maneras. Ayudándole en la casa con su tarea. Hoy, mi hija y yo fuimos a la escuela porque tuvimos conferencia para saber como esta aprendiendo, y también para saber que y como puede aprender más.

Al igual nos informaron acerca de su comportamiento. La maestra me dijo que Dolores debe de practicar más los sonidos de las letras. Nos recomendó trabajar mucho los nos números y aprender contando los juguetes o su ropa. Es decir, al empezar jugando y así ir contando y luego escribir las cantidades y así sucesivamente. ¡Esto es aprender en familia!

So it is in this way that education goes farther than going to school, it begins with the family. I support my daughter in many ways. Helping her with her homework at home. Today, my daughter and I went to the school because we had a conference to know how she is learning, and to find out what how she can learn more.

In the same way we were informed about her behavior. The teacher told me that Dolores needed to practice more the sounds to the letters. She recommended we work a lot with numbers and learn to count by playing with her toys or her clothes. In other words, in beginning to play and by beginning to count and then writing down the quantities and so on. This is learning as a family!

Teodora's document and the shared experiences illustrates the ways she saw herself while attempting to be involved in her daughter's education. She not only saw her own participation in this program as a way to extend her little girl's knowledge by learning how to use computers, but she also expressed how she felt about her role as a parent and the parenting practices she could involve herself in to help her daughter. This parent also exemplifies the reading and misreading of models (i.e., school and familial/cultural models) that on occasions take place when Latino parents become involved in their children's education. These texts served to illustrate the processual changes that families go through as they constantly read the world of education in order to assist their children in their educational progress.

## Parent 3: Juan

The third parent, Juan, has resided in the United States for 12 years and also had two daughters who attended the elementary school where the PCCP was based. Juan had completed "la preparatoria" (preparatory school) in Mexico and was currently a supervisor at a local company where he had the opportunity to develop his English skills. He was one of our new participating parents and had contributed considerably to the discussions and the written work that was later gathered for the creation of the newsletters. Juan was one parent who took the opportunity afforded to him in the program to share his ideas, beliefs, and concerns with those in the program about the education of his daughter.

For example, the theme of one such parent group discussion dealt with this issue of culture and education: Should their own culture be something that should be a part of their children's education? In this particular group discussion, Juan mentioned one concern for him was his daughter's resistance to speaking his native language, Spanish:

> Una pregunta bien importante ahorita que hablamos de eso de cómo educar a los hijos. Qué es lo que puedo hacer yo pa que mi hija se entusiasme y agarre interés en el idioma español. No le gusta no lo quiere y tiene apenas seis años y medio.

> One question that is very important right now that we are speaking about how we educate children. What can I do so that my daughter becomes excited or get her to become interested in the Spanish language? She does not like it she does not want it and she is only 6, and half years-old.

Interestingly, Juan saw that one of his roles as a parent was the future welfare of his daughter's language maintenance and promoting pride in her cultural language. The issue of parenting practices in the home became important factors in his daughter's education. Incorporating this idea of culture as a part of a child's education developed as a theme for parents to speak and write about. This is what prompted Juan to ask for suggestions from the other parents as to how he could resolve his dilemma—this fear of his daughter losing her Spanish. Juan received feedback not only from the parents, but also from the PCCP staff at this discussion who had had similar experiences. Suggestions included: having him and his wife speak to his daughter in Spanish only; reading to his daughter in Spanish and having his daughter read to them in Spanish; allowing the daughter to watch Spanish cartoons; taking her to Mexico for visits so that she could immerse herself in the language; placing the daughter in a classroom that would require her to speak in Spanish.

Accordingly, in his document, Juan focused on the customs that he hopes his own daughters would carry on as they continued to live in this country. For example, he mentions that the Day of the Dead as a custom that he trusts his daughters would appreciate and maintain as a family. "Nada me gustaría más que mis hijas siguieran la misma tradición y cultura para que ellas continúen con algo tan hermoso como esto."/"I would like nothing better than to have my daughters carry on the same tradition and culture so that they can continue with something as beautiful as this." These aspects clearly show that important educational practices not only take place in the schools, but Juan's discussions show they take place in the home as well.

**Parent 4: Marisol**

In order to address the question: What do parents' texts reveal about their notion of education? this study also relies on passages taken from another parent, Marisol, whose document is entitled "La Participación de los Padres en la Educación"/"The Participation of Parents in Education." Marisol is a mother who had only participated in the PCCP for this one cycle of activity. Of the four parents interviewed for this chapter, she was the individual with the most formal education. She had completed a vocational degree program in Mexico, her country of origin. Marisol, who had resided in the United States for 10 years, was employed with the dining services unit of a local university residence hall. Some of the topics covered in her document were her suggestions to other Latino parents about how they could enhance and supplement the education that their children received in school.

The first excerpt offers implications for how this participating mother read the world of education and how she had a particular view of parental involvement in children's education:

> Sirva de inspiración a sus hijos aumentando sus posibilidades de aprender y estudiar, visite con ellos centros de interés como museos, teatros, etc.

> Serve as an inspiration for your children, augment their possibilities to learn and study by visiting with them centers of interest such as museums, theaters, etc.

By writing about augmenting students' knowledge, Marisol speaks about taking children out to excursions where they would be exposed to cultured environments, like museums and theaters. Marisol's reading of what constitutes educational practices as a worldview is being accommodated to what would be acceptable in her native culture if it were not already a part of her previous worldview.

The second passage selected from Marisol's first document allows for two relevant points to be made:

> Establezca contacto con los maestros de sus hijos…para participar en actividades que podrían ser de mucha ayuda para los maestros…. [T]ambién anímelos y ayúdelos con sus tareas escolares y sus hijos se sentirán más seguros y capaces de hacer trabajos difíciles.

> Establish contacts with the teachers of your children…to participate in the activities that could be of a lot of help to the teachers…. [A]lso encourage and help them with

their homework and your children will feel more secure and capable in doing difficult work.

The two relevant points of this passage are: Having parents make connections to the school community, and pointing to how parents like Marisol are able to write about their own worlds through this newsletter. Marisol's text is one in which she imparts advice to other Latino parents on how parents can involve themselves more in their children's education. This parent urges other Latino parents to make crucial connections with their children's teachers. Similarly, she urges parents to offer their assistance to their children in such school activities as homework. That is why Marisol postulates that if parents learn how to read the different practices that are established in the context of the school, parents will be better able to advocate for their children's education. One such supposition that Marisol makes in her document is that maintaining a working relationship between the school and the home will lead to educational success in children's lives.

A final excerpt selected from Marisol's document entitled "La Participación de los Padres en la Educación"/"The Participation of Parents in Education," discusses an emphasis on the multiple school practices and links that could be made possible between the school and the home:

> Foménteles el amor a la lectura, tomando en cuenta los intereses de cada uno, y ofreciéndoles libertad. Eso ayudará a que amplíen su vocabulario. Solo vigile que el material que leen sus hijos no sea nocivo.

> Encourage a love toward literature, taking into account each child's individual interest and offering them this liberty. This will help and expand their vocabulary. However, keep vigilant that the material that your children read is not harmful.

Interestingly, Marisol selected literature as one of the school subjects that she believes parents could encourage their children to participate in. By doing so, Marisol emphasizes in her writing the importance of language and reading development as components of school practices, that reading at home can be seen as a tool to be developed in order to encourage a love for literature. This is one way in which Marisol believes parents can make an association between reading and vocabulary development that will not occur just in the classroom, but also in the home. Through her writing, Marisol is able to create a constant awareness of the home as a learning environment. For these reasons, Marisol, through her text, is able to suggest to the readers of the newsletter that they as parents can

make a difference in their children's education by monitoring, helping, and of-
fering support to their children in the home as well as at school. She is interpreting the different ways in which parents and children learn together outside
of the classroom, and at the same time complemented the learning that took
place in the classroom. She exemplifies how some parents began to discover the
overlap of their worldviews in order to assist the educational progress of their
children. This clearly shows that Marisol perceives how schooling does not just
occur in the classroom, but also occurs outside of the classroom, such as in the
home or different learning environments.

## Conclusions and Implications

The findings presented in this study illustrate how these four parents draw on
personal resources and experiences to write their documents. Although the parents realized that their children are being educated in the American school system and that this provides their children hope of a better future, they also
realized that if their children are not learning about their own culture in the
school, then it is necessary for them as parents to maintain that part of their
culture in the home. Parents wrote about the importance of education and how
coming to this country afforded their children the possibility of a better future
through the attainment of an education. Similarly, parents wrote about the construction and the maintenance of a Latino identity for the members in their
family in this host country. Furthermore, through their writing, parents showed
an awareness of the different practices that the U.S. educational system recom-
mends that Latino parents use in their homes.

The findings in this study demonstrate how parents are able to take something personal, their own lived experiences, and then present their views to
other parents in the PCCP who they might have not known. This collaborative
sharing of information amid the participating parents becomes a process that
allows them to interact with one another in order to incorporate and dissemi-
nate multiple ideas to create a collective desktop publication. These four parents
show how they are integrating the messages being sent home through the
worldview of the school with the knowledge that their own worldviews provided them. The parents' documents also illustrate how aware they are that their
children learn different customs in school, at home, and in contemporary society. Parents have to come to terms with these differences and learn how to con-

struct their own understanding of what this means in the context of a new country. Moreover, this understanding itself leads to a new worldview that parents are constantly creating for their children in order to have them obtain educational success (González, 1997).

The data presented in this study demonstrates how a social space (i.e., the PCCP) provides participating parents an opportunity to communicate their beliefs regarding their parenting practices and their views on education. Furthermore, this study explores how the beliefs that these parents voice are evidenced in the texts that they produced at the PCCP. This (on–going) after school computer program provided different approaches for family members to voice their ideas about different themes of interest to them. This study further supports literature on parent involvement and it helps to illustrate how the use of technology offers Latino parents a new and unique vehicle for them to publish their beliefs on education and parent involvement in documents they wrote in newsletters that become disseminated to a school community. Furthermore, this study has demonstrated how the parents who participated in this study were in fact not operating under a cultural or deficit model rather they were applying an overlapping and interweaving of worldviews to assist their children through the oftentimes challenging educational pathways.

Parents' documents show that if they learn how to read the different practices that were established in the context of the school, parents would be better able to advocate for their children's education (Freire & Macedo, 1987). This study illustrates how the PCCP presents the potential of having individual development where participating Latino families could be seen as constructing their own sense of community development. This type of program is not one that is commonly seen in areas of community development, and through the findings found in this study, one could infer that the gains of having parents publish their own beliefs on issues that pertain to their own lived experiences is a source of untapped knowledge that could be taken advantage of for the development of the Latino community.

Some possible pedagogical directions that other similar projects might consider given this study's findings are: providing instructions and means of communication in a language that is available to the participants of a program; providing participants with individual assistance to master new skills that they have been introduced to in the program; providing parents with forums to discuss experiences and concerns that may be familiar to them to tap into their own funds of knowledge; having parents write on their own experiences and belief systems, once again attempting to tap into parent's own funds of knowledge; and incorporating teacher participation in parent community–based programs to bridge school and family partnerships.

# Bibliography

Conchas, G.Q. (2001). Structuring failure and success: Understanding the variability in Latino school engagement. *Harvard Educational Review, 71,* 475–504.

Delgado-Gaitan, C. (1996). *Protean literacy: Extending the discourse on empowerment.* Washington, DC: Falmer Press.

Delgado-Gaitan, C. (1992). School matters in the Mexican American home: Socializing children to education. *American Educational Research Journal, 29,* 495–513.

Delgado-Gaitan, C. (1991). Involving parents in the schools: A process of empowerment. *American Journal of Education 100,* 20–46.

Edwards, P.A., & Garcia, G.E. (1994). The implications of Vygotskian theory for the development of home-school programs: A focus on storybook reading. In V.J. Steiner, C.P. Panofsky, and L.W. Smith (Eds.), *Sociocultural approaches to language and literacy: An interactionist perspective,* (pp. 243–264). New York: Cambridge University Press.

Emerson, R.M., Fretz, R. I., & Shaw, L.L. (1995). *Writing ethnographic fieldnotes.* Chicago: University of Chicago Press.

Epstein, J.L. (2001). *School, family, and community partnerships: Preparing educators and improving schools.* Boulder, CO: Westview Press.

Epstein, J.L. (1995). School, family, and community partnerships: Caring for the children we share. *Phi Delta Kappan, 76,* 701–712.

Epstein, J.L. (1992). School and family partnership. In M. Alkin (Ed.), *Encyclopedia of educational research,* 6th ed. (pp. 1139–1151). New York: Macmillan.

Epstein, J.L. (1990). School and family connections: Theory, research, and implications for integrating sociologies of education and family. In D. Unger & M. Sussman (Eds.), *Families in community settings: Interdisciplinary perspectives* (pp. 99–126). Binghamton, NY: Hayworth.

Epstein, J.L. (1986). Parents' reactions to teacher practices of parent involvement. *Elementary School Journal, 86,* 277–294.

Freire, P., & Macedo, D. (1987). *Literacy: Reading the word and the world.* Boston: Bergin and Garvey.

Goldenberg, C., et al. (2001). Cause or effect? A longitudinal study of immigrant Latino parents' 'aspirations and expectations, and their children's school performance. *American Educational Research Journal, 38,* 547–582.

González, N. (1997). Contestation and accommodation in parental narratives. *Education and Urban Society, 29,* 55–70.

Lopez, G.R. (2001). The value of hard work: Lessons on parent involvement from an (im)migrant household. *Harvard Educational Review, 71,* 416–437.

Lopez, G.R., Scribner, J.D., & Mahitivanichcha, K. (2001). Redefining parental involvement: Lessons from high-performing migrant-impacted schools. *American Educational Research Journal, 38,* 253–288.

Mehan, H., et al. (1996). *Constructing school success: The consequences of untracking low-achieving students.* New York: Cambridge University Press.

Moll, L.C., et al. (1992). Funds of knowledge for teaching: Using a qualitative approach to connect homes and classrooms. *Theory and Practice, 31,* 132–141.

Nicolau, S., & Ramos, C.L. (1990). *Together is better: Building strong relationships between schools and Hispanic parents.* New York: Hispanic Policy Development Project.

Soffer, E. (1995). The principal as action researcher: A study of disciplinary practice. In S.E. Noffke & R.B. Stevenson (Eds.), *Educational action research: Becoming practically critical,* (pp. 115–126). New York: Teachers College Press.

Valdés, G. (1996). *Con respeto: Bridging the distances between culturally diverse families and schools. An ethnographic portrait.* New York: Teachers College Press.

Velez-Ibanez, C.G., & Greenberg, J.B. (1992). Formation and transformation of funds of knowledge among U.S.–Mexican households. *Anthropology and Education Quarterly, 23,* 313–335.

Vygotsky, L. . (1978). *Mind in society: The development of higher psychological processes.* Cambridge, MA: Harvard University Press.

Warschauer, M. (2002, June 14). Reconceptualizing the digital divide. *First Monday: Peer-Reviewed Journal on the Internet.* [Online]. Available: <http://www.firstmonday.dk/issues/issue 7_7/warschauer/>.

Wertsch, J. (1998). *Mind as action.* New York: Oxford University Press.

Chapter Ten

# Latina and Latino Education: Rearticulating Discourses, Pedagogies, and Praxis

*Nancy López*

## Re-articulating the Problem

Television and newspaper articles bombard us with plentiful "commonsense" explanations for the low academic attainment of Latinos, as well as other racially stigmatized youth such as blacks: teenage pregnancy, welfare moms, the culture of poverty, drugs, lack of family values, female-headed households, bilingual programs, oppositional cultures, youth who fear being accused of "acting white," etc. While there is much talk about the problems of urban schools and inner-city at-risk youth, there is a deafening silence on social justice along race, class, and gender lines. The reality is that "savage inequalities"[1] exist between low-income and middle-class schools, as well as between schools attended by most students who are racialized as white and those who are racially stigmatized are seldom explored as part of the problem. Although adequate resources and quality educational opportunity programs are rarely available in many of the schools attended by the vast majority of Latinas and Latinos, policy makers, teachers, principals, and other school officials tend to repeat the litany of aforementioned commonsense explanations, which generally frame the low academic achievement among Latino students as simply a matter of their individual shortcomings.

As long as the problems of Latino education are framed in terms of the hegemonic commonsense explanations that blame individual Latino students and their families for their educational plight, the structural problems that plague the Latino community, such as racism, segregation, inequitable distribution of resources, etc., will continue to remain unexamined (see Ibarra, Chapter 6). Antonio Gramsci's *The Prison Notebooks* (1971) posits that dominant groups justify their policies and institutional practices by producing commonsense ideologies, beliefs, values, and practices. Commonsense, then, is the uncritical and largely unconscious way of perceiving and understanding the world. It is through adherence to common sense that members of society give legitimacy to the way in which society is organized and ruled. Hegemony refers to the way in which society is ruled through a combination of coercion and consent. Accordingly, it is important to interrogate the role of the state in creating the very differences it purports to eradicate.

In this light, the task before us is the rearticulation of the problem of Latino and Latina low educational attainment.[2] It is my goal to debunk some of these dominant uncritical explanations for the educational crisis among Latino students, thereby paving a new road for finding radical solutions to the crisis.[3] Toward this end, we attempt to create counter-hegemonic discourses that would lead to alternative solutions for the improvement of the education of Latina and Latino students.

In this concluding chapter, we hope to pose some questions that will aid us in creating real educational opportunities for Latino and Latina students, as well as other racially stigmatized youth in the United States. I include a brief theoretical discussion of our approach. Next, I describe my own journey through in New York City public education system. Finally, I end with a series of questions that can aid us in fashioning a democratic and egalitarian educational system and improvement in the education of Latinas and Latinos. It is my hope that through these contributions we will chart a new era in improving the educational outcomes of Latino and Latina students as well as other racially stigmatized youth.

## Critical Race Theory and Critical Pedagogy

Our theoretical analysis of Latino and Latina education in the United States draws on two bodies of literature: critical race theory and critical pedagogy. Critical race theory is a body of literature that emerges from legal studies as a reaction to the colorblind position in United States politics and law (see Apple, 1999; Agger, 1998; Bonilla-Silva, 2003; Delgado, 1995; Crenshaw et al., 1996; Haney-Lopez, 1996;). The colorblind position assumes that the United States is a racially egalitarian meritocracy.[4] As a challenge to the view that racism is a phenomenon of the past, critical theory brings race to the forefront of the analysis of social policy in the United States. Critical race theory conceptualizes race as a social construction that is historically variable and denotes a relationship of power.[5] While critical theorists acknowledge that there are no biological races, they also maintain that "race is a concept which signifies and symbolizes social conflicts and interests by referring to different types of human bodies…the concept of race continues to play a fundamental role in structuring and representing the social world" (Omi & Winant, 1994, p. 55). In this light, race is understood as constitutive of social structures and social institutions. Another premise of this framework is the notion of institutional racism or racism that occurs through the normal operations of our schools without "prejudice" or ill intent on behalf of civil servants. As Michelle Fine (1991) points out in *Framing Dropouts*, racist policies affect our youth despite the good intentions of teachers and policy makers.

Another fundamental assumption of critical race theory is the notion that social science is not politically neutral (Agger, 1998; Bonilla-Silva, 2003; López, 2003). All research paradigms have inherent political orientations and policy implications, whether or not these are made explicit. Therefore, unlike other frameworks that make claims to objectivity, critical theorists clearly state their political orientations by making a definitive commitment to the elimination of oppression and the promotion of social justice. Last, borrowing from feminist traditions, critical race theorists value experiential knowledge and employ autobiography in their research.

Critical pedagogy emerges out of a critique of traditional authoritarian pedagogical practices. For Freire (1993) a banking education, whereby students are constituted as empty receptacles to be filled with knowledge by an omniscient teacher, is a form of oppression. In contrast, dialogic education, involving the role of a teacher as facilitator rather than omniscient professor, is emancipating for both students and teachers, as shown by Lorna Rivera (Chapter 7). Freire affirms that a language of possibility can emerge from the oppressed when they are able to construct their own voices and validate their contradictory experiences. In *Teaching to Transgress*, bell hooks (1994) offers us a road map for creating classrooms based on dialogic education, which leads to education as the practice of freedom.

## Autobiographical Notes on Latina and Latino Education

While reflecting on my own educational trajectory, I discovered that my experiences could be a window to the challenges faced by most low-income Latinos in the U.S. educational system. I was born in the lower east side of

Manhattan, New York City, during the 1960s. My parents, Spanish-speaking immigrants from the Dominican Republic, had only been able to attend grade school and worked as factory workers in the lower Manhattan garment industry sweatshops. Despite all the factors that would lead most educators to label me as at-risk, I published my first book in 2003: *Hopeful Girls, Troubled Boys: Race and Gender Disparity in Urban Education*. I earned a Ph.D. in Sociology (1999) from the Graduate School and University Center, City University of New York. Since then I have worked as an assistant professor of sociology and a research associate at the Gastón Institute for Latino Community Development and Public Policy at the University of Massachusetts, Boston, and presently, I am an assistant professor of sociology at the University of New Mexico, Albuquerque. Given all the challenges I faced as a low-income Latina who was raised in public housing projects by a mother who had no formal schooling, did not speak English and raised five children by herself, a question remains: How did I beat the odds?

Two narratives can be used to explain my academic achievements: first a hegemonic, commonsense perspective would focus mainly on my individual-level characteristics, such as my parents' family values, my intelligence, my self-esteem, and my willingness to work hard and pick myself up by the bootstraps. However, as a sociologist, I turn to an alternative interpretation, one that examines larger historical social structures and processes. A more convincing explanation of the educational attainment of an entire category of students, such as Latinos, would be one involving not just a sample of one individual student's characteristics and her family structure, but institutions such as the school system itself, or other social structures that are beyond the individual, such as race, gender, and class stratification.

A counter-hegemonic perspective would explain my educational attainment as due in large part to my serendipitous birth during the peak of the civil rights movement, and the women's movement, and the expansion of opportunity programs for low-income and racially stigmatized youth. Had these programs not been in existence I would not have been able to pursue higher education, much less attend graduate school and become a professor.

### Fashioning New Discourses on Latino Education

Critical pedagogy and critical race theory have important roles to play in helping us fashion new emancipatory discourses and practices in the education of

Latino and Latina students, as well as other racially stigmatized youth. Before we begin fashioning new discourse on Latino and Latina education, three hegemonic so–called commonsense ideologies need to be dismantled. These are: the notion that the United States is a meritocracy, the belief that cultural deficits among Latinas and Latinos is the main reason why our communities have low educational attainment, and the belief that since the 1960s civil rights legislation the United States has eradicated discrimination and it has become a colorblind society.

In a meritocracy, students' educational success is viewed as solely a product of their hard work. Accordingly, educators can measure students' merit by using so-called "objective" standardized test. In this light, if students fail, it is not due to the fact that they were not provided with adequate resources and curricula, but it was because they did not work hard enough. As explained by Omi and Winant, "merit is a political construct by which employers, schools, state agencies, etc., legitimate the allocation of benefits to favored (i.e., organized) constituencies and deny the validity of competing claims" (1994, p. 130). To be sure, if GRE scores had been used to determine my admission to graduate school, I surely would not have been admitted.

Another popular explanation for the educational crisis among Latino students stems from the racist notion that Latinos have cultural deficits because their families are immigrants who do not speak English and do not value education. Accordingly, as Ramirez argues (see Chapter 9), it is believed that if Latino students are not doing well in schools, it is directly related to their so-called deficient family backgrounds and lack of family values. Valenzuela, in her book, *Subtractive Schooling* (1999), challenges the assumption that Mexican–origin youth have an oppositional stance toward education. Through a 3–year ethnography of a Houston public high school in the early 1990s, Valenzuela demonstrates that Mexican youth and their families believe in the value of an education; however, the subtractive nature of the schooling processes, which define Latino/Mexican cultural backgrounds and the Spanish language as deficient and problematic, undermine the cultural resources of Mexican youth. Valenzuela finds that it is not the opposition to education, but rather the students reject a system of schooling that consistently devalues their families and communities, and chips away at their social and cultural resources. In the end, Mexican students experience schooling as a subtractive process where their cultural and language backgrounds are defined as problems that need to be stripped in order for them to succeed.

Perhaps the most enlightening contribution of Valenzuela's study is the realization that subtractive schooling is a reversible process. If the goal is to improve the educational attainment of Latino students, schools can become models of democratic practices, which actively build on the cultural assets of their students, their families, and their communities. By pointing to antiracist pedagogical practices among some teachers, Valenzuela shows that schools have the potential to eliminate the subtractive schooling process. To this end, schools can foster honest and open dialogue among students, teachers, and the larger community about their explicit efforts to encourage social justice through their curriculum, pedagogical praxis, and community involvement. As explained by Valenzuela, and supported by Ramirez (Chapter 9) and Gonzalez (Chapter 8), caring needs to be rearticulated so that it connotes concerns over inequitable schooling resources, overcrowded and decaying school buildings, and a lack of sensitivity toward Spanish-speakers, Mexican culture, and things Latina and Latino.

The next step in creating radical social change in the education of Latinas and Latinos is debunking the myth that the United States is now a colorblind society. The colorblind understanding of race assumes that racism exists when you notice color. Therefore, it is argued that the state must be colorblind, even when it is working toward eliminating racial oppression. Bonilla-Silva illustrates how the colorblind racism that characterizes post-Civil Rights racialization in the United States is responsible for the continued racial subjugations of racially stigmatized groups, such as Latinos and blacks (see López, 2003).

In keeping with the view that to notice race is racist, colorblindness has now become the new racism in the United States.[6] The colorblind discourse has been used to justify the dismantling of affirmative action programs that are designed to challenge the status quo in admissions and hiring across the nation. Perhaps the most worrisome trend in the political backlash against the civil rights movement is the dismantling of affirmative action programs in education. The casualties of this political climate are many: the end of open admissions at the City University of New York; the U.S. Court of Appeals ruling against the University of Texas Law School's admissions policy; the state referendum (Prop. 209) banning affirmative action at the University of California campuses; and the decision to end proactive admissions consideration by race at the University of Massachusetts, Amherst. If the simultaneous retrenchment of affirmative action in education and the expansion of the prison industrial complex continue unabated, the United States will be turning back the clock toward a period in our history where a permanent cleavage between the haves and the have-nots, and racially dominant and subordinate groups, will be considered as normal (Davis, 1997; Steinberg, 1995).

In 2003 the U.S. Supreme Court upheld the affirmative action admissions policies at the University of Michigan Law School and allowed a revised affirmative action admissions policy at the undergraduate school to continue. However, the majority opinion argued that they expect these affirmative action programs to be temporary and predict that the will be irrelevant after 25 years. I dream of the day in which racially based educational opportunity programs will no longer be necessary because all students will have access to a quality education, as required by law, and they will not have to compete for a few slots in a select number of quality schools. However, until that day comes, the presence of programs that target students by race, class, gender, and sexual preference is critical for the expansion of educational opportunities for everyone in American society (Bowen et al., 1998). These programs have been providing the missing link for youth who experience inequality and oppression in a variety of domains: health, housing, income, and education.

## The Future of Latina and Latino Education

What will the future of Latino and Latina education look like? Through posing the questions that follow, I attempt to get us on a path of constructing alternative discourses and practices that will lead to significant changes in the ways we approach the issue of low educational attainment among Latina and Latino students in contemporary United States society:

1.  What would schools look like if they were geared toward nurturing Latino students, their families, neighborhoods, and communities?
2.  What would a classroom look like that thrives on collaborative and cooperative learning rather than individualistic rote memorization and individualistic competition?
3.  What if school administrators, policy makers, teachers, and staff considered the Spanish language an asset to be preserved and nurtured?
4.  What if instead of multiple-choice exams, emblematic of banking education, we had portfolio evaluations incorporating community–based research projects?
5.  What if instead of high–stakes testing we had portfolio evaluations?

6.  What if teachers were given the resources to work with students so that each could produce near perfect results?

7.  What if students had the opportunity to incorporate their rich migration histories and issues of their respective neighborhoods where our Latino students and their families reside?

8.  What if students themselves were involved in the day-to-day curriculum and decision-making in their own schools?

9.  What if the curriculum reflected the rich migration histories of Caribbean and Latino immigrants?

10. What if there were programs, beginning in elementary school, linking Latino students with colleges throughout their education trajectories?

11. What if teachers, principals, and administrators paid attention to the formal and informal ways in which oppressive and liberating race(ing) and gender(ing) take place in their classrooms and schools? (See López, Chapter 3.)

12. What if schools were organized to meet the needs of Latina and Latino parents, who are struggling to learn the English language, obtain high school diplomas and pursue higher education?

13. What if parental involvement were reconceptualized from conventional Parent Teacher Association meetings and bake sales to other forms of parental involvement that account for real day-to-day experiences of Latino parents—many of whom work two or more jobs but can contribute by teaching Spanish or contributing their artwork or other talents?[7]

14. What if every student had access to equitable resources, books, and computers?

15. What if schools were not segregated?

Although I do not provide answers to these questions, I believe that these questions will lead us down the right path in creating radical changes in the education of Latinas and Latinos. In constructing an education reform strategy, there must be an overarching examination of social justice issues, such as income inequities and separate and unequal schools. Politicians and policy makers who cling to neo-liberal political perspectives, which seek to turn schools into businesses that are punished and rewarded according to student performance, as well as those who are upset about the amount of money that is being wasted on education without results, need to know that equity does not amount to equal dollars. Rather, it means ensuring that all students, Latinas and Latinos included, have access to first-rate resources, technology, and teachers.[8]

As argued by Superintendent Negroni of Springfield, Massachusetts, the truth is that no one is doing our children a favor by providing fair and equitable funding. It is the legal obligation of the governor and the legislature. Equity and social justice must be placed at the center of the education reform debates.

Perhaps if Latino parents, students, and teachers had been involved in the framing of the problem they would not have been unjustly identified as the cause of an inequitable schooling system. Before we castigate students for possessing "defective intelligence genes" and "dysfunctional cultures," we need to ensure that all students have access to an equitable education. As Fernandez argues (Chapter 4),

> ...while school systems across the country have been placing a stronger emphasis on high–stakes testing, little attention has been paid to the disparities between white students and students of color in various measures of educational success. To the extent that it is addressed, the achievement gap is often dealt with exclusively in the context of student performance on high–stakes tests.

Accountability should not fall solely on the backs of students and their teachers; it should be redefined to include federal, state, and local responsibility for providing opportunities to learn for all students. Accountability should mean that all of our school buildings are in excellent condition, have the latest technology and library resources, and treat and compensate their teachers as professionals. Schools, teachers, policy makers, and communities that want to improve the education of Latinos must make an explicit commitment to the promotion of social justice and the elimination of race, class, gender, and oppression of sexuality. As argued by Michelle Fine (2000), we need standards for inclusion, not exclusion (see Fernandez, Chapter 4).[9]

Another important ingredient in promoting the educational success of Latino students is the respect and affirmation of their cultural differences. Educators and policy makers must play close attention to how our educational policies and programs meet the needs of our students from diverse linguistic and cultural backgrounds. More often than not, both formal and informal school policies discourage the use of Spanish in the classroom and make no attempt to welcome the Latino community within the school setting. Silencing the cultural background of Latinas and Latinos students is a form of academic violence which may lead students to feel that their culture is deficient. In order to foster social justice, schools need to be culturally sensitive, work toward abolishing stereotypes, and provide Latino students with opportunities to learn about their diverse histories.

We are at a critical juncture in the history of the United States. According to the 2000 Census, the Latino population is climbing, and looks as if they will continue to flourish into the millennium, making them the largest so-called minority group in the United States. At the dawn of the twenty-first century, now more than ever, access to education will determine the social mobility and life chances of generations to come. For this reason we need to construct alternative theories and discourses that address the urgent need of closing the achievement gap between Latinas and Latinos and other racially stigmatized groups. If we believe in a democratic society, we all have an important role to play in reversing the trends of low student achievement among Latinas and Latinos and other racially stigmatized students. We can support and expand programs that provide real educational opportunities to all students. Alternatively, we can stand by and witness the increasing educational neglect and scapegoating of an entire generation of young people, as well as the dismantling of educational opportunity programs.

Our goal, though, is to create an alternative discourse and new pedagogies that thrive on valuing Latina and Latino students, as well as their families for the brilliance and vitality that they possess as we nurture the next generation of leaders of our nation—Latino youth.

# Bibliography

Agger, B. (1998). *Critical social theories: An introduction.* New York: Westview.

Apple, M. (1999). The absent presence of race in educational reform. *Race, Ethnicity and Education, 2,* No. 1, pp. 9-16

Bonilla-Silva, E. (2003). *Racism without racists: Color-blind: Racism and the persistence of racial inequality in the United States.* Oxford: Rowman & Littlefield.

Bonilla-Silva, E. (2001). *White supremacy and racism.* Boulder, CO: Lynne Rienner.

Bowen, W., Bok, D. C., & Schulman, J. J. (1998). *The shape of the river: Long-term consequences of considering race in college and university admissions.* Princeton, NJ: Princeton University Press.

Crenshaw, K, et al. (1996). *Critical race theory: The key writings that formed the movement.* New York: New Press.

Davis, A. (1997). Race and criminalization: Black Americans and the punishment industry. In W. Lubiano (Ed.), *The house that race built* (pp.264-279). New York: Vintage.

Delgado, R., et al. (1995). *Critical race theory: The cutting edge.* Philadelphia: Temple University Press.

Delgado-Gaitan, C. (2001). *The power of community: Mobilizing for family and schooling.* New York: Rowman & Littlefield.

Fine, M. (2000, March 31). *Panel Presentation at Teacher's College, Columbia University.* (Oral Presentation.) New York: Conference on High Stakes Testing.

Fine, M. (1991). *Framing dropouts: Notes on the politics of an urban public high school* Albany: SUNY Press.

Freire, P. (1993). *Pedagogy of the oppressed,* 20th ed. New York: Continuum.

Gramsci, A. (1971). *Selections from the prison notebooks.* Q. Hore & G. N. Smith (Eds.). New York: International.

Haney-Lopez, I. (1996). *White by law: The legal construction of race.* New York: New York University Press.

hooks, bell. (1994). *Teaching to transgress: Education as the practice of freedom.* New York: Routledge.

Kozol, J. (1991). *Savage inequalities: Children in American schools.* New York: Crown.

López, N. (2003). *Hopeful girls, troubled boys: Race and gender disparity in education.* New York: Routledge.

Oakes, J. (1985). *Keeping track: How schools structure inequality.* New Haven, CT: Yale University Press.

Omi, M., & Winant, H. (1994). *Racial formation in the United States: From 1960s to 1990s.* New York: Routledge.

Steinberg, S. (1995). *Turning back: The retreat from racial justice in American thought and policy.* Boston: Beacon.

Valenzuela, A. (1999). *Subtractive schooling: The politics of schooling in a U.S. Mexican high school.* Albany: SUNY Press.

# Notes

## Chapter 2

1. The alternative presented emphasizes valuing the students' own cultural capital, their "cultural integrity," by emphasizing "school-based programs and teaching strategies that engage students' racial ethnic backgrounds in a positive manner toward the development of more relevant pedagogies and learning activities" (Tierney, 1999, p. 84).

2. Moreover, a comparison, utilizing the more detailed year-by-year statistics of the parent table, of non-Hispanic whites with non-Hispanic blacks and those of Hispanic origin, reveals a steady increase for non-Hispanic whites and fluctuating rates for non-Hispanic blacks and Hispanics. Hispanics exhibit the largest mean yearly percentage decreases on both dimensions of enrollment as a percentage of 18–24 year-olds (0.55 vs. 1.33), and enrollment as a percentage of high school graduates (0.81 vs. 1.98).

## Chapter 3

1. Please note this article was previously published by *Teachers College Record*, Volume 104, Number 6, September 2002, pp. 1187–1203. Permission was granted to republish in March 2003.

2. I draw on the insights of critical theory and critical race theory, which seek to unveil and dismantle processes of domination, oppression, and resistance (Crenshaw, Gotunda, Peller, & Thomas., 1996; Delgado, 1995; Fine, 1991; Gramsci, 1971, Hill-Collins, 1990; Hurtado, 1996; Omi & Winant, 1994).

3. Omi and Winant (1994, p. 56) define a racial project as "simultaneously an interpretation, representation, or explanation of racial dynamics and an effort to reorganize and redistribute resources along particular racial lines. Racial projects connect what race means in a particular discursive practice and the ways in which both social structures and everyday experiences are racially organized, based upon that meaning."

## Chapter 4

1.  A paraprofessional is a nonteaching member of a school who assists classroom teachers with instruction.

## Chapter 5

1.  See Ybarra, Raul. (1977). *Latino students and Anglo-mainstream instruction: An ethnographic study of classroom communication.* Ph.D. dissertation. Chicago: University of Illinois, Chicago.

2.  All the names of the students and instructor have been changed.

## Chapter 6

1.  Portions of the analysis and study group data profiles in this chapter are taken directly from the CGS monograph, *Latino Experiences in Graduate Education: Implications for Change,* Ibarra, 1996, pp. 6–9.

2.  Specific verbal quantifiers will be used in this study to denote relative size of a group of respondents who expressed particular perspectives or described similar experiences. These quantifiers are:

| | |
|---|---|
| a few = up to 10% | a majority = 50% to 75% |
| some = 10% to 25% | most = 75% to 90% |
| many = 25% to 50% | virtually all = 90%+ |

This format is fashioned after a similar model used by the LEAD (Learning through Evaluation, Adaptation and Dissemination) Center at the University of Wisconsin, Madison.

## Chapter 7

1.  See: <http://usatoday.com/news/nation/census/2002–10–10–census–Hispanicdropouts_x.–outs_x.htm.>

2. Freire's work has been criticized by feminists and poststructuralists for not recognizing race and gender differences or the subjectivity of learners. See Martin (2001), Schugurensky (1998), Weiler (1994).

3. Freire developed a three-step model for understanding the development of a critical consciousness. See Shor (1992) for an overview.

4. According to Beder (1996) popular education programs in the United States are more likely to be offered in community-based organizations (CBO) rather than in organizations funded by federal or state governments. Government and for-profit organizations are more likely to reflect the interests of those in power and operate in a "top-down" manner. Whereas the work of a CBO is compatible with the popular education philosophy: "education that serves the interests of the popular classes (exploited sectors of society), that involves them in critically analyzing their social situation and organizing to act collectively to change the oppressive conditions of their lives" (Beder, 1996, p. 74).

5. This research was funded by the Society for the Study of Social Problems and the Spencer Foundation.

6. The AELS encompasses a variety of programs such as Family Literacy, English for Speakers of Other Languages (ESOL), Adult Basic Education (for adults with 0–8 years of education), and Adult Secondary Education (for adults with 9–11 years of education).

7. In 2003, all Massachusetts 10th graders must pass the MCAS tests in order to graduate from high school. Latinos have the highest failure rates in all subject areas and across all grade levels. See: <http://www.gaston.umb.edu/mcas/edreport_mp.html>

## Chapter 8

‡This research was supported in part by a grant from the American Educational Research Association which receives funds for its "AERA Grants Program" from the National Center for Education Statistics and the Office of Educational Research and Improvement (U.S. Department of Education) and

the National Science Foundation under NSF Grant #RED–9452861 while the author was in the Department of Sociology at Harvard University. Opinions reflect those of the author and do not necessarily reflect those of the granting agencies. The author would like to thank Christopher Jencks, Christopher Winship, and Orlando Patterson for their comments.

1. Accounting for clustering is necessary for "honest" estimates of standard errors, valid p-values, and confidence intervals whose true coverage is close to 95%. If we use estimators that assume independence, the standard errors will be too small—the difference can be as much as a factor of 2 or more. Weights are equal to (or proportional to) the inverse of the probability of being sampled. Including sampling weights in the analysis gives estimators that are approximately unbiased for whatever we are attempting to estimate in the full population.

2. For more information about NELS data collection and sampling, see Hafner et al. (1990) and Haggerty et al. (1996).

3. Although attrition is often a problem in any survey design of the magnitude of NELS, my final sample does not differ dramatically in racial and ethnic proportions, or in social status of parents, from the original 1988 sample constructed by NELS administrators. I am thus quite confident that my final sample, with weights, is similar to national measures of our population.

4. Ordered logistic regression is maximum likelihood estimation where an underlying score is estimated as a linear function of the independent variables and a set of "cut points." The probability of observing outcome $i$ corresponds to the probability that the estimated linear function, plus random error, is within the range of cut points estimated for the outcome.

5. This question is from the student questionnaire, so although there might be reliability problems in a child determining exact numbers of their friends' parents their own parents know, the question's responses are broad enough to allow for some error on the child's part.

## Chapter 10

1.  See Kozol (1991).

2.  The Civil Rights Movement's efforts to desegregate schools in the 1950s were made possible because the leaders of the movement rearticulated the "separate but equal" clause as immoral and antithetical to the principles of democracy in American society. In a similar way, the United Farm Workers Movement led by César Chávez gave new meaning to La Virgen de Guadalupe, such that a religious icon now became the symbol of the poor people and resistance to oppression. See Omi and Winant (1994, p. 64).

3.  Part of the reason why the colorblind position has achieved such hegemony in contemporary United States politics is that it appears to be consistent with the goals of the original leaders of the Civil Rights Movement, such as Rev. Dr. Martin Luther King, Jr. who sought an end to race-thinking and to assure equality to each individual (Omi & Winant, 1994).

4.  The social constructionist approach of race differs in fundamental ways from the essentialist approach, which assumes that race is a biological essence (Omi & Winant, 1994).

5.  In *Racial Formation in the United States: From the 1960s to the 1990s,* Omi and Winant (1994) define rearticulation as the process by which political interests and identities are redefined by giving new meaning to "commonsense" values and ideologies.

6.  See Eduardo Bonilla-Silva. (2001). *White Supremacy and Racism.* Boulder, CO: Lynne Rienner, 2001.

7.  Delgado-Gaitan, Concha. 2001. *The Power of Community: Mobilizing for Family and Schooling.* New York: Rowman & Littlefield.

8.  Tracking is an insidious practice that needs to be abolished. All too often, low–income and working–class students, especially those who are defined as racial minorities, are funneled into low-curriculum tracks that provide little challenge. See Oakes (1985).

9.  While no one would argue with the expansion of high–quality curriculum for all students, especially those who have historically been denied access to it, it is problematic to frame students as the cause of having inferior curricula and resources. The reality is that there are not even any mechanisms in place to assure that the instruction leading to positive outcomes is actually taking place in the classroom for all students.

# Contributors

**Steve Fernandez** is a physics teacher at the John D. O'Bryant School of Mathematics and Science in Boston, Massachusetts. Prior to joining the staff at the O'Bryant School, Mr. Fernandez taught at the Boston Latin School, Boston, Massachusetts, for 14 years. Mr. Fernandez received a Bachelor's in Physics from the Massachusetts Institute of Technology and a Master's in Energy Engineering from the University of Massachusetts, Lowell.

**Gabriella C. Gonzalez**, Ph.D., is an Associate Social Scientist at RAND in Santa Monica, California.

**Ramona Hernández**, Ph.D., is at The City College, of the City University of New York where she holds the positions of Director of the CUNY Dominican Studies Institute and Associate Professor in the Sociology Department.

**Roberto A. Ibarra**, Ph.D., is a Special Assistant for Diversity Initiatives in the Office of the President and Associate Professor of Sociology at the University of New Mexico, Albuquerque.

**Glenn Jacobs**, Ph.D., is an Associate Professor of Sociology at the University of Massachusetts, Boston.

**Nancy López**, Ph.D., is an Assistant Professor of Sociology at the University of New Mexico, Albuquerque.

**Lorna Rivera**, Ph.D., is an Assistant Professor of Sociology in the College of Public and Community Service at the University of Massachusetts, Boston.

**Rosita Ramírez** is a doctoral candidate at the University of California, Santa Barbara, in the Gevirtz Graduate School of Education completing a Ph.D. in Cultural Perspectives and Comparative Education.

**Raul E. Ybarra**, Ph.D., is an Associate Professor of English at the College of Public and Community Service at the University of Massachusetts, Boston.

# Index

1996 Personal Responsibility and Work
Reconciliation Act, 148

**-A-**

achievement gap, 46
achievement motivation, 126
Ada, A. F., 147
adult literacy education, 5
Adult Education and Family Literacy Act, 135
Adult Education and Literacy System, 148
*Adult Literacy in the United States*, 135
Adult Secondary Education, 148
Advanced Work Class (AWC), 54, 55
Agger, B., 222, 223
Alexander-Kasparik, R., 165
Alfonso, 124
Alves, M., 55
American Federation of Teachers, 46
Anyon, J., 29
Apple, M., 222
Aronowitz, S., 38, 41, 136
Auerbach, E., 138
Ayvazian, A., 41

**-B-**

Bain & Company, 75
banking education, 223
Bankston, C., 163
Bartholomae, D., 2, 100, 101, 107
Battacharya, G., 187
Beder, H., 133, 135, 136, 141, 146
Benmayor, R., 1, 138, 139
Bennici, F. J., 165
Berryman, P., 137, 138
Betts, J, 159
Bhattacharya, G., 166
bicognition, 125, 127
Binder, A., 33
Bingham, M. B., 146

Bizzell, P., 104
Black, C., 184
Blau, P., 159
Bonilla-Silva, E., 222, 223, 226
Borjas, G., 163, 164, 169, 170
Bornstead-Bruns, M., 162, 168
Boston Latin School, 52
Boston Private Industry Council, 47
Boston public school
    achievement gap in, 57–61
    demographics of, 47–48, 56
    desegregation in, 45–48
    disparities in educational outcomes, 76–78
    dropout rates in, 78, 80–81
    dual-track education system in, 83–84
    "educational reform" in, 49–51
    elimination of affirmative action/desegregation programs in, 51
    high stakes testing in, 49–51
    honors and advanced placement classes in, 78–80
    supervision of, 48–49
    standardized testing in, 61–75
        statistics on, 61
        support of students taking, 74–75
    success of transition programs in, 75
Boston Redevelopment Authority, 47
Boston's Children First, 51
Bowen, W., 227
Breton, R., 163
Broad Foundation, 47
Brodkey, L., 135
Broeder, P., 165
Brooks-Gunn, J., 183
Brown, B. B., 185
*Brown v. Board of Education*, 45
Buettner, R., 31
Bulger, W., 19
Buriel, Raymond, 166, 187
Bush, G. W., 46

**-C-**

Calderone, J., 31

Calderone, M., 138

Caldwell, K., 74, 75

California State University, Fresno, 89

Caplan, N., 184, 185, 186

Cardoza, Desdemona, 166, 187

Carspecken, P. F., 140

Casteñeda, A., 125, 126

Cazden, C., 101

Center for Popular Education and Participatory Research, 136

Cervero, R., 142

charter schools, 46

Chaves, L., 165

Cheng, L. R. L., 183

Choy, N., 184, 185, 186

circular migration, 181

City University of New York, 226

cognitive codes, 183

Cohen, R. A., 125, 126, 128

Coleman, J., 162

Comings, J., 148

Conchas, G. Q., 199

Cooperative Extension Service, 136

Council for the Advancement of Adult Literacy, 134

Council of Chief State School Officers, 165

Council of Graduate Schools, 114

Crenshaw, K., 222

critical pedagogy, 222–23

critical race theory, 222–23

Crosby, D. A., 146

Cuello, J., 119

Cummins, J., 41

**-D-**

D'Amico, D., 134, 149

Daniels, H., 90, 97, 99, 104, 106

Darder, A., 138

DeBlassie, R., 184

Degener, S. C., 136, 137

Delgado, C., 39, 222

Delgado-Gaitan, C., 147, 183, 184, 186, 196, 198

Del Piñal, J., 165

Department of Social Services, 142

Department of Transitional Assistance, 142

De Paul University, 90

dialogic education, 223

Dillingham, W. B., 99, 100

Dodson, L., 142

Dornbush, R., 182

Dornbusch, S., 185

Dorsey-Gaines, C., 146

Downs, N., 90

Drennon, C., 146

Driscoll, A., 165

Duncan, O. D., 159

Duncan socioeconomic index (SEI), 167

Dunn, J., 27

Dunn, K., 184

Dunn, R., 184

Durkheim, E., 9

**-E-**

Early Academic Outreach, 203

Ebert, O., 146

Edmonston, B., 157

Education Trust, 47

Edwards, P. A., 198

Effective Practice Schools, 59

El Barrio Popular Education Program, 139

Elementary and Secondary Education Act, 46

Emerson, R. M., 201

Epstein, J. L., 195, 196

Erickson, F., 105

ESL (English as a Second Language), 170

ESOL (English for Speakers of Other Languages), 1

essayist literacy, 97

ethnic capital, 163, 164, 169, 180

**-F-**

Family Reunification Act (1965), 5

Family Shelter, 137, 139, 140, 143, 145, 146, 149
Farkas, G., 183
Farr, M., 90, 97, 99, 104, 106
Featherman, D., 167
Ferriera, E. C., 137
Ferriera, J. C., 137
Fernandez, R., 165
Fernandez, S., 1, 2, 3, 229
Fine, M., 33, 34, 35, 38, 142, 143, 223, 229
Fingeret, H. A., 138, 146
Fiorina, M., 163
Fitzpatrick, T., 142
Flores-Gonzales, N., 138
Flower, L., 103
Flynn, R., 50, 55
Focus on Children, 57
Fogg, N., 27
Fraher, R., 98
*Framing Dropouts* (Fine), 223
Freire, P., 38, 41, 83, 105, 133, 137, 150, 198, 216, 223
Frensch, P. A., 127, 128
Fretz, R. I., 201
Friedman, M., 45
Fuligni, A., 183
functional literacy, 135

-G-
Gadotti, M., 137
Gándara, P., 116, 117, 121, 124, 126
Ganzenboom, H., 167
Garcia, E., 138, 165
Garcia, G. E., 198
Garcia, J., 165
Garrity, W. A., 45, 51, 52, 55
Gastón Institute for Latino Public Policy, 17, 47
GED (General Education Diploma), 133
generative themes, 133
Gennep, V., 9, 10
Giarelli, J. M., 138
Gibson, M., 182

Giroux, H., 2, 38, 41, 104, 136, 137
Giuliani, R., 33
Goldenberg, C., 196
Goldschmidt, P., 183
Gonzalez, G. C., 5, 226
González, N., 197, 216
Gordon, M., 180
graduate schools, 4
Gramsci, A., 137, 221
Granovetter, M., 163
Grebler, L., 126
Greenberg, J. B., 196
Griggs, S., 184
Gumperz, J. J., 101
Gutierrez, H., 138
Guzmán, R. C., 126

-H-
Hale-Benson, J. E., 125, 126
Hall, E. T., 124, 125
Haney-Lopez, I., 222
Hao, L., 162, 168
Harmon, D., 135
Harrison & Goldberg, 75
Hartocollis, A., 38
Harvard University, 55, 75
Hausafus, C., 184
Hauser, R., 167
Hayes, E., 148, 183
Heaney, T., 135
Heath, S. B., 97
hegemony, 222
Hernández, R., 2
Hickey, M. G., 184, 185
High context cultures, 124, 129, 130
high-stakes testing, 148
Hirano-Naknishi, N., 165
Hodgkinson, H. L., 117, 157
Holman, L. J., 165
hooks, b., 2, 38
*Hopeful Girls, Troubled Boys* (López), 224
Horton, M., 149
Huber-White standard errors, 166

Hugh, 165
Human Capital Theory, 136, 164
Hunter, C., 135
Hurtado, A., 116, 165
Hymes, D., 97

-I-
Ibarra, R. A., 4, 114, 120, 121, 125, 127, 221
Independent Secondary Entrance
   Examination, 53, 76–77
integration and assimilation model, 9

-J-
Jacobs, G., 2
Jalali, 184
Jencks, C., 183
Jones, F., 167
Jurmo, P., 138

-K-
Kao, G., 162, 168, 184
Kaufman, G., 170, 183
Kaufman, P., 165
Kleinfeld, J., 27
Knowles, T., 58, 74
Kroshko, J., 27
Kutz, E., 96

-L-
language capital, 170
Lankshear, C., 136
Laosa, L. M., 126
Lapham, S., 157
Latino/a adult learners, 139–40
   dropouts and, 142–43
   motivation for going back to school,
      141–43
   theoretical framework of study of, 134–
      39
   popular education and, 133–34

   obstacles for, 143–48
   origins of, 137
   statistics about, 134
Latino/a families, 172–83, 183–86
   academic success and, 113, 114–15, 115–
      20
         graduate school attendance, 119–20
   afterschool programs and, 195–98, 202–
      205, 205–15, 215–17
   circular migration and, 181
   cultural context of, 120–21, 123–27
   language and, 116
   school support, 127–30
   statistics on, 116, 118, 173
   status attainment process and, 158–66
   values and, 121–23, 123–27, 127–30
Latino/a students, 157–58, 167–68, 172–83,
      183–86
   adult literacy education, 5
   choice of language in school, 31
   future for, 227–30
   graduate school attendance, 4, 119–20
   graduation rates among, 27
   high-stakes testing and, 3
   parental involvement in education, 196–
      97, 202–205
   race-gender gap among, 2, 27–29, 32–34,
      34–38, 38–40
   retention and persistence among, 2, 4, 9–
      11, 11–12, 12–18, 18–21
         enrollment rates, 23, 24
   status attainment process and, 158–66
   writing process and, 89–90, 90–92, 92–
      97, 97–104, 108–109
         academic discourse cultural model,
            104–105
Latino Leadership Opportunity Program, 17
Lauren, D., 165
Lee, Y., 185, 186
Lewin, T., 27
literacy
   meaning of, 133
   social change and, 134–38
Lockwood, A. T., 142

Lofland, J., 140
Lofland, L., 140
Lofstrom, M., 159
Lollock, L., 157
Lopez, G. R., 196
López, N., 6, 27, 39, 223, 226
Low context cultures, 124, 129, 130
Loyola University, 91

**-M-**
Macedo, D., 135, 198, 216
Mace-Matluck, B., 165
MacLeod, D., 162, 166, 187
Malloy, C. E., 184
Malloy, W., 184
Marin, B. V. O., 92
Marin, G., 92
Massachusetts Comprehensive Assessment
  System, 148
Massachusetts Department of Education, 47
Matute-Bianchi, M. E., 180
Mau, W. C., 166, 187
Mayer, S., 183
MCAS tests, 62–70
McCormick, J., 33
McLaren, P., 136, 137, 138
McLaughlin, J., 52
Mehan, H., 103, 104, 199
Meier, D., 38
Menino, T., 50
Mills, D., 74
Moll, L. C., 105, 199
Moore, J., 113, 115, 120, 126
Morris, N., 181
Mujeres Unidas en Accion, 138
multicontextualism, 125, 127

**-N-**
National Education Longitudinal Study, 158,
  166
National Institute for Literacy, 135

Newman, J., 27
New York Immigration Coalition, 29
Nieto, S., 39, 138, 147
No Child Left Behind Act, 46
Northeastern University, 47, 75

**-O-**
Ogbu, J., 106, 183
Okagaki, L., 127, 128, 129
Olivas, M. A., 10, 138
Omi, M., 28, 33, 223, 225
Ortiz, V., 115
Outtz, J. H., 117

**-P-**
Pachon, H., 113, 115, 120
Padilla, M., 1, 138, 139
Palma, S., 27
Parents Children and Computers Program,
  195
  overview of, 199–200
Park, R., 180
Pascarella, E. T., 101
Pastor, J., 33
Paulsen, R., 165
Payzant, T., 50
Paz, H., 184
pedagogy of inclusion, 107
*Pedagogy of the Oppressed* (Freire), 105, 137
Perez, S. M., 10
Pierce, G., 75
Polakow, V., 149
Poonwassie, D., 184
Portes, A., 161, 162, 163, 166, 182, 184, 187
Portz, J., 75
Powell, L., 38
Price, G., 184
*Prison Notebooks* (Gramsci), 221
Private Industry Council, 81
Purcell-Gates, V., 146
Putnam, R., 163

**-Q-**

Queen, R. M., 165
Quigley, B. A., 142

**-R-**

racial project, 33
Ramirez, G. M., 17, 225
Ramírez, M. III, 125, 126
Ramírez, R., 1, 6, 226
Randell, D. R., 106
Ray, D., 184
Reder, S., 138, 142
Rigual, A., 10
Ripke, M. N., 146
rites of passage, concept of, 10
Rivera-Batiz, F., 181
Rivera, L., 1, 5, 89, 138, 139, 144, 146, 147, 223
Robinson, J., 96, 97, 101
Rosa-Salazar, D. de la, 10
Rosenbaum, J., 33
Roskelly, H., 96
Rumbaut, R., 161

**-S-**

Santiago, C., 181
Santos, Jr., A de los, 10
Schneider, B., 185, 186
Scollon, R., 97, 104, 107
Scollon, S. B., 97, 104, 107
Secada, W., 157, 165
segmented assimilation, theory of, 161, 162, 168
Shaw, L. L., 201
Shor, I., 137
Simons, H., 183
Slavin, R. E., 138
Smith, M., 146, 184
social capital, 162, 163, 164, 180, 182
social control, 163
Solis, J., 116
Sommerville, J., 38

Spanos, G., 138
Sparks, B., 138, 149
standardized testing, 46, 61–75
standards for inclusion, 229
Stanford 9 tests, 62–70
Stanic, G., 184
Stanton-Salazar, R., 34, 39, 138, 182
Steinberg, L., 185
Steppingstone Foundation, 47
Sternberg, R. J., 129
Sticht, T., 133
Stock, P., 96, 97, 101
Strang, W. E., 165
Strawn, C., 142
Strickon, A., 127
Suárez-Orozco, C., 162
Suárez-Orozco, M., 162
subtractive schooling, 225, 226
*Subtractive Schooling* (Valenzuela), 225
successful intelligence, 129
Sum, A., 27, 148

**-T-**

Tauro, Judge, 52
Taylor, D., 146
*Teaching to Transgress* (hooks), 223
Tienda, M., 162, 168
Tierney, W. G., 10
Tinto, V., 9, 101
Torres, C. A., 138
Torres, R., 138
Toro-Morn, M. I., 115
Treiman, D., 167
Trueba, H. T., 147, 183, 184, 186

**-U-**

University of California, Santa Barbara, 199
University of Illinois, Chicago, 90, 95
University of Massachusetts, Boston, 2, 10, 13, 14, 15, 18, 47, 224
University of Massachusetts, Amherst, 13, 226
University of Michigan Law School, 227

University of Texas Law School, 226
Urban High School, 28, 29–32
   security measures in, 33
U. S. Adult Education Act, 134
Uvin, J., 148

**-V-**

Valdés, G., 1
Valdés, G., 199
Valdes, G., 146, 147
Valentine, T., 141
Valenzuela, A., 2, 40, 106, 182, 225, 226
Valverde, S. A., 101
Van Gelder, L., 33
Vasquez, J., 184
Vaznaugh, A., 165
Vega, W. A., 115
Velez-Ibanez, C. G., 196
vouchers, 46
Vygotsky, L., 199

**-W-**

Wallerstein, N., 138
Wang, J., 183
Warren, J. R., 166, 187
Warschauer, M., 205
Washington, V., 27
Watkins, F. C., 99
Way, N., 143
Weis, L., 38
Wertsch, J., 198
Wessman, S., 52
*Wessman v. Boston School Committee*, 56
white flight, 45
White, M., 170, 183
Whitmore, J. K., 184, 185, 186
Wikelund, K., 141
Williams, L., 133, 138
Willie, C., 55
Wilton, J., 10
Winant, H., 28, 33, 223, 225
Wong, S. I. C., 184

writing process. *See* Latino/a students, writing
   process
Workforce Investment Act, 135

**-Y-**

Yao, E. I., 184
Ybarra, R., 3, 39, 105, 106, 107
Young, E., 1, 138, 139

**-Z-**

Zane, N., 142
Zhao, M., 160, 161, 162, 163
Zubizarreta, R., 147

# Studies in the Postmodern Theory of Education

*General Editors*
*Joe L. Kincheloe & Shirley R. Steinberg*

Counterpoints publishes the most compelling and imaginative books being written in education today. Grounded on the theoretical advances in criticalism, feminism, and postmodernism in the last two decades of the twentieth century, Counterpoints engages the meaning of these innovations in various forms of educational expression. Committed to the proposition that theoretical literature should be accessible to a variety of audiences, the series insists that its authors avoid esoteric and jargonistic languages that transform educational scholarship into an elite discourse for the initiated. Scholarly work matters only to the degree it affects consciousness and practice at multiple sites. Counterpoints' editorial policy is based on these principles and the ability of scholars to break new ground, to open new conversations, to go where educators have never gone before.

For additional information about this series or for the submission of manuscripts, please contact:

> Joe L. Kincheloe & Shirley R. Steinberg
> c/o Peter Lang Publishing, Inc.
> 275 Seventh Avenue, 28th floor
> New York, New York 10001

To order other books in this series, please contact our Customer Service Department:

> (800) 770-LANG (within the U.S.)
> (212) 647-7706 (outside the U.S.)
> (212) 647-7707 FAX

Or browse online by series:

> www.peterlangusa.com